Praise for
Sallie Mae How to Pay for College

"A 'must read' for every parent of a college student. The book is easy to read, accurate and contains all the information a family needs to assist them in getting thousands of dollars in financial assistance for college. This is one book that you cannot afford to skip."

—*Courtney McAnuff, Vice President for Enrollment Services, Eastern Michigan University*

"An extremely comprehensive guide…more than you will ever want to know about financial aid and how to pay for college. It is every parent and student's 'dream' about being knowledgeable about financial aid and college costs."

—*Peggy Loewy-Wellisch, Associate Vice President for Student Financial Services, Nova Southeastern University*

"The words 'practical guide' say it all. Parents can learn all they need in as much detail as they want expressed in common, easy to understand language. The 'Straight Talk' sections cut through the jargon and give real word answers to real world questions."

—*Dr. Lawrence Burt, Associate VP for Student Affairs & Director of Student Financial Services, University of Texas at Austin*

"Financial aid is all about creating the possible."

—*Jim Belvin, Director of Financial Aid, Duke University*

"A wonderful tool for students and parents that provides answers to frequently asked questions as well as helpful hints in planning."

—*Veronica J. Leech, Director of Financial Aid, Central State University*

SallieMae®

How to Pay for College

A Practical Guide for Families

By Gen and Kelly Tanabe

Sallie Mae How to Pay for College: A Practical Guide for Families
By Gen and Kelly Tanabe

Published by SuperCollege, LLC
3286 Oak Court
Belmont, CA 94002

Credits: Cover design by TLC Graphics. Cover concept and photo by MRA. Edited by Bob Drews and Tamara Orr.

Trademarks: All brand names, product names and services used in this book are trademarks, registered trademarks or tradenames of their respective holders.

Disclaimers: The authors and publisher have used their best efforts in preparing this book. It is intended to provide helpful and informative material on the subject matter. Some narratives and names have been modified for illustrative purposes. SuperCollege, Sallie Mae and the authors make no representations or warranties with respect to the accuracy or completeness of the contents of the book and specifically disclaim any implied warranties or merchantability or fitness for a particular purpose. There are no warranties which extend beyond the descriptions contained in this paragraph. The accuracy and completeness of the information provided herein and the opinions stated herein are not guaranteed or warranted to produce any particular results. SuperCollege, Sallie Mae and the authors specifically disclaim any responsibility for any liability, loss or risk, personal or otherwise, which is incurred as a consequence, directly or indirectly, of the use and application of any of the contents of this book.

ISBN: 9781932662313

Manufactured in the United States of America
10 9 8 7 6 5 4 3 2 1

Cataloging-in-Publication Data
Gen S. Tanabe, Kelly Y. Tanabe
     Sallie Mae How to Pay for College: A practical guide for families / by Gen S. Tanabe and Kelly Y. Tanabe. —2nd ed.
        p.   cm.
        Includes appendices and index.
        ISBN 9781932662313
        1. College Guides I. Title
        2. Reference   3. Personal Finance

*This book is dedicated to parents, as they help their children
open the gates to opportunity.*

Acknowledgements from the Authors

Contrary to the image of a lone writer tapping away at a keyboard in a quiet, out-of-the way studio, it takes the full effort of an entire team to develop a book such as this. To the members of our team, we owe a debt of gratitude.

As you look through these pages, you'll see the valuable contributions that financial aid professionals have made. Their insights and "Straight Talk" cut through the jargon and provide readers with a virtual visit to a college financial aid office. We extend thanks to James Bauer of the University of Miami, Jim Belvin of Duke University, Lawrence Burt of the University of Texas, Jevita de Freitas of George Mason University, Veronica Leech of Central State University, Peggy Loewy-Wellisch of Nova Southeastern University, Courtney McAnuff of Eastern Michigan University and Dawnia Smith of Cincinnati State Technical and Community College.

Beyond that, there are many people whose names do not appear within these pages and to whom we also are grateful. Thanks go to the members of the Sallie Mae team, who, in addition to their regular "day jobs," pitched in to oversee all stages of development. Among them are Mark Overend, Kathleen deLaski, Tom Joyce, Nancy Deck, Keith D'Ambra, Barb Goffman, Cathy Eckerman, Mark Merithew, Christy Marble, JoAnn Ross, Katherine Bontrager, Desire Cilmi-Vitali, Mary Doyle, Laura Archuleta, Kathy McGlinn and Heather Rowse. We are also indebted to our fine public relations team, comprised of Martha Holler, Erin Korsvall and Rick Castellano.

And finally, we owe special thanks to Sallie Mae employees Deborah Finkel and Barbara O'Brien, whose knowledge of education financing, editorial talents and many hours of hard work helped make this book possible.

—Gen and Kelly Tanabe

Table of Contents

Straight Talk from Financial Aid Administrators

Throughout this book you will meet financial aid administrators who will share with you their insights, tips and strategies for making college affordable.

Introduction

In the United States, the ticket to success is often a 9" x 12" document, framed and mounted on the wall in the spare bedroom or hidden away somewhere in the attic.

It is a college diploma.

Higher education is the passport to the American Dream, and one of the best investments you and your child can make. According to studies, college graduates earn, on average and over the course of a lifetime, $1 million more than their high school counterparts. There are also non-monetary benefits: greater workplace productivity and flexibility, increased personal and professional mobility, better physical health, better quality of life for offspring, even a longer life expectancy.

Clearly, the cost of a college education is money well spent.

However, it is money just the same, and headlines proclaiming tuition increases have many parents naturally concerned. Surprisingly, though, the *real* price of admission is not necessarily as high as one might think. With the availability of financial assistance—either from the federal government, from individual states, from the colleges themselves, or from a nearly limitless number of scholarships—the actual "out of pocket" cost to the average American family is far less than you might believe, and, in many cases, is identical to that of a decade ago.

Sadly, millions of students and their parents fail to take advantage of financial aid opportunities available to them. Many of these families are under the impression that their income level makes them ineligible for government programs, while the simple reality is that everyone is at a minimum entitled to low-cost student loans sponsored by the federal government. Many others qualify for additional aid, including grants and subsidized loan programs.

Financial aid is, of course, only one part of the funding picture. There are an abundance of savings plans, tax benefits, private scholarships, and other opportunities to help you and your child turn what could easily be an expensive dream into an affordable reality. We hope this book is a helpful guide to help you navigate your course through the financial aid journey.

This book would not have been possible without the contributions of financial aid professionals—those unsung champions who work directly with students on college campuses throughout the country. They gave generously of their time to make certain that college-bound students and their parents would have the "Straight

Talk" they deserve. Thanks go to James Bauer of the University of Miami, Jim Belvin of Duke University, Larry Burt of the University of Texas, Jevita de Freitas of George Mason University, Veronica Leech of Central State University, Peggy Loewy-Wellisch of Nova Southeastern University, Courtney McAnuff of Eastern Michigan University, and Dawnia Smith of Cincinnati State Technical and Community College.

With real-life examples, behind-the-scenes advice from these financial aid professionals, and a comprehensive description of the many options available, we hope this book will start you on the financial path toward a college education for your child. It will help you through the labyrinth of the financial aid process, explain borrowing opportunities, educate you about financial award packages, alert you to state programs, inform you of the many scholarship programs available, enlighten you about the benefits (and drawbacks) of college savings plans, and even warn you about some common financial aid scams. Most of all, we hope this book illustrates that with a little planning and preparation, a higher education is within the reach of every high school graduate.

Let the journey begin.

Thomas J. Fitzpatrick
Vice Chairman & Chief Executive Officer
Sallie Mae, Inc.

The Sallie Mae Fund

Sallie Mae will donate the net proceeds of all sales from *How to Pay for College* to The Sallie Mae Fund's Unmet Need Scholarship Program to help the neediest families in the country access higher education.

The Sallie Mae Fund, a charitable organization sponsored by Sallie Mae®, supports programs and initiatives that help open doors to higher education, prepare families for their college investment and bridge the gap when no one else can. In addition, The Sallie Mae Fund encourages employee volunteerism and community service in the more than a dozen communities where Sallie Mae employees live and work.

Sallie Mae established a donor-advised fund in 1992, with an initial grant of $2 million, to institutionalize its history of educational programs, scholarships, employee volunteerism and community service. The Sallie Mae Fund builds on this foundation and today directs annual giving programs that exceed $12 million.

CHAPTER 1

How Are We Going to Pay for College?

What you'll learn:

- How this book will help you pay for college
- Why you're not alone when it comes to funding a college education
- What college financial aid administrators say they can do to help

College.

The very word probably conjures up a mix of emotions for you. On one hand, you are thrilled. Your child stands at the doorstep to adulthood, the exciting world of higher education at his or her feet. The courses will be challenging. The professors will be thought-provoking. The possibilities will be infinite.

On the other hand, somebody's got to pay for it.

As a parent, you will realize that most of the financial decisions and some if not most of the financial responsibility for your child's college expenses will fall on you. And on one level, you welcome that challenge. You realize that the costs of higher education are returned many times over in terms of greater earning power, improved career options and, in numerous ways, a better quality of life. Still, you can't help but wonder how you'll foot the bill.

Will you have to mortgage the house (again)? Insist your child attend only the cheapest college possible? Subsist on rice and beans for the foreseeable future?

Fortunately, the answer is none of the above.

Sending your child to college shouldn't mean burdening yourself with unreasonable debt or limiting your child's choices. There are many resources available to help you pay for college, all of which can combine to give your son or daughter access to the best education possible.

But first, it's time for YOUR education...a "review course" into the world of college funding.

The Myth About Paying for College

You've undoubtedly seen the headlines about the latest double-digit increases in tuition, but you probably haven't heard much about the tremendous amount of help that's available. Few families pay the full sticker price for their child's college education. In the 2006-2007 school year, American families received more than $97 *billion* in financial aid to pay for college.

And you're entitled to some of this aid, too. All you have to do is ask, and this book will show you how…and why…and when.

How Is This Book Different from Others?

You have a lot of choices when it comes to books on financial aid, but this book has the following unique features:

You Are the Focus

Your child may be the one attending college, but you are likely the one who will pay for (at least some of) it. That responsibility includes saving, researching financial aid options and encouraging your child to apply for scholarships. And so this book is directed squarely at you.

Collaborative Approach

Some books on financial aid view the college as an adversary, an approach that is not productive and can actually reduce your chances of getting aid. Instead, our method encourages you to work with the college financial aid office, where you'll find that financial aid administrators have tremendous resources and can provide a great deal of help.

TIME SAVER . . . .

This is the only financial aid book that doesn't require a pencil. Hardly anyone enjoys filling out complex financial worksheets. Don't worry: Sallie Mae has developed a website (www.salliemae.com) that features online calculators to do the hard work for you. Throughout this book, you will find references to tools that will permanently free you from that No. 2 pencil. (Of course, if you like filling out worksheets, you'll find more than enough in this book.)

Straight Talk

Financial aid has its own language, acronyms and formulas. This book presents information in an easy-to-understand format. You won't need an advanced degree to understand how financial aid works or where to find scholarships. We promise you a jargon-free zone.

Straight Talk with a Financial Aid Administrator ▶ **Is applying for financial aid worse than pulling teeth?**

Financial aid has a bad reputation for being bureaucratic. There are forms to complete and many rules and regulations. Unfortunately, this turns off some families who assume applying is just not worth the effort. In fact, some people think applying for financial aid is worse than pulling teeth. The reality is that for the vast majority who go through the process, it is not that difficult and certainly a lot less painful. The FAFSA (financial aid application) is only 102 questions—it's not as bad as parents assume.

By completing the FAFSA, besides getting your share of financial aid one other big reason to apply is that life happens. If your circumstances change in the future, the college will have your application on file and can respond quicker. The FAFSA is like an insurance policy against negative change in your financial situation.

Remember, too, that if at any time during the process you run into trouble, there are a lot of places to get help. You can always speak to anyone in a financial aid office to get answers to questions. We will gladly help you complete the FAFSA. While we have to adhere to the federal and state regulations, we strive not to make applying for financial aid more trouble than it's worth. We have aid counselors available to students and their families to assist through the financial aid process and can offer options on how to finance their college education.

Jevita R. de Freitas, Director, Office of Student Financial Aid, George Mason University

The application process includes some formulas and worksheets, but we explain each number and line and provide plenty of examples that show how each concept works in the real world.

We walk you through the applications step by step. In fact, you won't even need a calculator, because we'll direct you to a time-saving website that does the number crunching for you. Just plug in your numbers and let the computer do the work.

Tips from Financial Aid Administrators

Among your strongest allies are the people who work in the college financial aid office—they are there to help you. In writing this book, we assembled an all-star cast of financial aid administrators from a variety of colleges and universities. Together,

Straight Talk with a Financial Aid Administrator ▶ Cooperation between parents and college is critical

While some parents assume the financial aid process is adversarial, most are eager to work with us to figure out how to create a plan for paying for college. Of course, we occasionally get a parent who views this as a poker game and wants to wring out of Duke as much money as they can. But the vast majority of parents are honest and grateful for the financial aid they receive.

At the core, the financial aid process is based on cooperation between the family and financial aid office. After all, our decision is based on the information parents give us. In most cases, the information families provide is reasonably straightforward. When there are exceptions we are responsible for looking into them. For example, we recently had a family that showed no income on their application. But how many families can survive without any financial resources? We looked at their lifestyle; where they lived, how many cars they owned and their household size. We know what the minimum amount of income would be for a family to support this lifestyle. Therefore, we were able to go back and ask them to show us how they could survive without any income whatsoever. In out-of-the-ordinary cases like this, there may very well be a good explanation, but we need for the family to help us understand.

As a financial aid administrator I want to be as supportive of each family as possible, but it is equally important that we deal fairly and equitably with every applicant. We want families to complete the process with the sense that they understand the process and the knowledge that they have been treated fairly. I think the majority of parents understand this and want to make it easy for us to help them.

Jim Belvin, Director of Financial Aid, Duke University

these professionals have seen and dealt with every situation imaginable. They share their insights on how you can get all the financial aid you deserve and how you can avoid common mistakes.

More Than Financial Aid

Financial aid is an important part of paying for college, but it's not the only help available to you. This book tells you how you and your child can find and win scholarships, take advantage of money-saving tax incentives, save for college and make college less expensive. Paying for college means accumulating money in a variety of ways.

Practical Advice

It's one thing to know how the financial aid system works; it's another thing entirely to know how to get the most from the system. This book focuses on how you can apply the knowledge you gain to improve your individual situation. You'll understand not only how the process works but also what to do to get the best results.

Finally...Who Is Sallie Mae?

Never heard of Sallie Mae? Well, she's not a real person. Sallie Mae is the nation's leading provider of student loans. Founded in 1972, the organization owns or manages student loans for more than 8 million borrowers. In addition to student loans, Sallie Mae provides a tremendous amount of resources to students and parents to guide them through the financial aid process. This book draws on Sallie Mae's expertise in helping families make college affordable.

Throughout the book, we refer to tools on the Sallie Mae website (www.salliemae.com). Here you'll find pointers on the entire "going-to-college" process, from saving to getting loans. Sallie Mae has interactive tools that enable you to analyze the affordability of schools, compare financial aid award letters and search for scholarships. And you can register for the $1,000 college scholarship that is awarded each month.

BRIGHT IDEA . . . . . .

This book helps fund educational scholarships. As part of its mission to help families make college affordable, Sallie Mae will donate the net proceeds from this book to The Sallie Mae Fund, a charitable organization sponsored by Sallie Mae. Donations will be directed to The Fund's Unmet Need Scholarship Program to help low-income students overcome financial barriers and meet the cost of college.

You Are Not Alone

You're not alone in facing the daunting prospect of paying for college. Whether your child is in preschool or high school, whether you have a five- or seven-figure income, whether you've saved forever or never...there is help for even the most expensive education. The key is to know where and how to ask for this assistance. And that's what this book is all about.

CHAPTER 2

How Much Does College Really Cost?

What you'll learn:

- Why college may not cost as much as you think
- How most families avoid paying the full "sticker price" for tuition
- How to quickly determine the total cost of any college

Do you remember when a restaurant hamburger cost less than a couple of dollars and a new car was less than $8,000? The year was 1980, and one year of tuition at an elite private college like Harvard was just $5,300, while a year at a public university cost a mere $1,200.

A lot has changed in almost 30 years. You have to go to a fast-food place to find a cheap hamburger, and cars cost what houses used to. But it's the sticker shock on a college education that has many parents feeling that they're headed for the poorhouse: The average cost for tuition and room and board at a private college is $32,307 a year, while the cost at a public university has risen to $13,589 a year.[1]

With increases like these, it's no wonder some parents wish they had a time machine so they could push a few buttons and roll back prices.

Fortunately, there is a bright spot. In 1980, the total amount of financial aid awarded to students was about $25 billion. For the 2006-07 academic year, that number is $97 billion. With the availability of so much more financial aid, many students pay less out of pocket now than students did 30 years ago.

---

1. The College Board, *Trends in Student Aid 2007*, October 22, 2007.

What the Headlines Don't Tell You

Each fall, the media report the ever-increasing cost of a college education. What these headlines don't mention is that, although the cost has increased, so, too, has the amount of financial aid. The real issue is not how much college will cost, but rather how much you will have to pay out of your own pocket.

> *College A charges $10,000 a year for tuition and room and board.*
> *College B charges $20,000 a year.*
> *Which college will cost you more?*

The answer seems obvious, but what if College A offers zero financial aid while College B offers $15,000? Even though College B is more expensive, you would pay less out of pocket.

To accurately assess the cost of a college, you need to know two things: (1) the sticker price, and (2) how much financial aid you will receive. When you add in the value of financial aid and scholarships, the equation changes.

The New Reality: Few Families Pay Full Sticker Price

According to the College Board, in the 2006-07 academic year, a record $97 billion[2] in financial aid was distributed to students. More than half of all college students received financial aid; the average amount was $10,472.[3] Because of this aid, the amount families pay has increased only modestly for nearly all income brackets. The following chart shows what families in each income bracket paid for college at the beginning and end of the 1990s.

Public Universities[4]

Income	1992-93	1999-2000
Lowest 25%	$7,500	$7,500
Middle 50%	$9,200	$9,800
Highest 25%	$10,100	$10,800

Private Universities[4]

Income	1992-93	1999-2000
Lowest 25%	$11,300	$11,500
Middle 50%	$13,800	$15,600
Highest 25%	$18,800	$19,500

2. The College Board, *Trends in Student Aid 2007*, October 22, 2007.
3. US Dept. of Ed., Nat'l Center for Education Statistics, *Student Financing of Undergraduate Education: 1999-2000*.
4. US Dept. of Ed., Nat'l Center for Education Statistics, *What Students Pay for College: Changes in the Net Price of College Between 1992–93 and 1999–2000.*

So, although college costs have risen, the cost to families has been softened by the steady increase in financial aid. In fact, the costs for low-income families whose children attend public universities did not increase at all during this period. Moderate increases can be small consolation when you are facing a five-figure bottom line—but the situation is not as daunting as you may think.

Sticker Price Tunnel Vision

Mary Beth Valdez was a high school senior who faced some difficult choices about which colleges to apply to. She knew that her parents didn't have a lot of money, so she limited her choices to schools she knew they would be able to afford. But when she showed the list to her counselor, he asked why she was applying only to budget-priced schools. Mary Beth told him that other schools cost too much and she did not want to put pressure on her parents.

The counselor insisted she apply to at least one of her dream colleges. In the spring, Mary Beth received acceptance letters from every college she had applied to. She was amazed when the financial aid letters arrived—the seemingly unaffordable dream school offered the largest financial aid package, making it less expensive than any of the others. If not for her counselor, she would have paid more to go to a college that was not her top choice.

Straight Talk with a Financial Aid Administrator ▶	**College costs may not be as high as you've been led to believe**

In some ways the cost of a college education can be compared to that of an automobile. Depending on the make and model you choose, costs vary widely. For example, if a student attends a local community college and lives at home, the out-of-pocket costs for the entire academic year may only be a few thousand dollars or less. In addition to community colleges there are state-supported public universities that range in academic mission and cost. It is very likely a public university can meet most students' academic goals and have a total cost typically from $15,000 to $20,000 a year. Of course, you hear a lot about Ivy League colleges costing $30,000 or $40,000 a year. If a student's educational goals include attending Ivy League institutions, the same as purchasing a better automobile, one can expect that $30,000 to $40,000 price tag. But it's important to note that nearly 70 percent of students in this country spend less than $9,000 a year for college tuition.

Dr. Lawrence Burt, Associate VP for Student Affairs & Director of Student Financial Services, University of Texas at Austin

Straight Talk with a Financial Aid Administrator ▶ **Running a college is not cheap**

The costs of operating a college today are astronomical. There are many expenses besides the obvious costs of paying the professors. Day-to-day expenses from salaries for the support staff to the electric bills keep increasing just like the cost of living. Also, a public institution depends heavily on the economic health of the state, which provides the bulk of its funding. When Virginia went through a budget crisis, the university suddenly didn't receive the funding it expected, which affected tuition rates. One thing parents may not realize is that universities are constantly looking for ways to become more efficient and cut costs. Some have privatized housing or meal programs, even departments within the school. When this happens every part of the university is required to cut a certain percentage of its expenses. It's a very difficult job, and when cuts have to be made we always make sure they have the smallest impact possible on the quality of our students' education.

Jevita R. de Freitas, Director, Office of Student Financial Aid, George Mason University

Too many families make the same mistake: prematurely ruling out colleges because of high costs. Students should apply to colleges that offer the best academic programs and campus environments, regardless of the cost. Don't assume that a college is out of reach financially; you may be pleasantly surprised.

So, What Does It Cost to Go to College?

Now that you know not to judge a school by its sticker price, we will examine what goes into that price tag. There are both direct costs and hidden costs of attending a college.

The official term for the price of a college is the cost of attendance (COA). This is the total amount it will cost to go to a school—usually expressed as a yearly figure. Each school determines its annual average COA using a formula established by Congress. (Remember, though, your actual expenses will vary based on your child's lifestyle.)

Some expenses depend on your child's choices: public or private school; in-state versus out-of-state school; living on campus, off campus or at home. Some expenses, such as the cost of textbooks, are similar regardless of which school your child attends. The following are the major components of the COA at a typical college.

Direct Costs

This category includes expenses paid directly to the college: tuition, fees and room and board.

Tuition: If your child has selected a state school, the tuition (cost of classes) will depend on his or her residency status. The difference between in-state and out-of-state tuition can be thousands of dollars a year. Some schools base tuition on the number of credit hours taken in an academic period. Others rely on enrollment status (full time versus part time). These details are easy to obtain from the financial aid or admissions office or school brochures.

Fees: Most schools charge set fees for services, activities or facilities. Fees usually appear on the tuition bill and are not charged on a per-use basis.

On-campus room and board: Your child may choose to live on campus and eat in dining facilities. Meal plans can vary significantly.

Indirect Costs

These expenses are not paid directly to the school but are associated with attending. You have some control over them.

Books and supplies: Textbook costs are similar from school to school but they vary greatly depending on the courses taken. Students can save by buying used books, buying online or sharing with classmates. Some classes require more supplies than others, such as printing, copying and computer costs.

Computers: Many schools require each student to have a personal computer. Check the admissions requirements to determine whether a basic PC will do or a more expensive laptop is required. Don't forget software, a printer and—if your child lives off campus—connection to the school network and the Internet.

Off-campus room and board: This category includes rent, furnishings, utilities and meals. If you haven't taught your child how to cook, now

TIME SAVER . . . .

Abracadabra! Instantly know the cost of any college! It's not quite magic, but you can find the cost of nearly any school by using the School Search Tool on the Sallie Mae website (www.salliemae.com). Just select the college and press the button. In an instant, you'll know the cost of tuition, required fees, room and board and even books.

is the time! Even if your child lives at home, there will be expenses related to food and commuting.

Transportation: If the student is commuting, factor in the cost of public transportation or gas, car insurance, maintenance and parking fees. Some schools provide free parking, while others require a paid permit. If the school is far away, don't forget the cost of air travel to get home on breaks and holidays. Your child can lower these costs by carpooling and by shopping around for student rates on airfare.

HEAD START . . . .

Look beyond tuition to get the true cost of a college. When you're projecting how much college will cost, don't forget to add all the expenses beyond tuition, such as room and board, books, personal expenses and travel to and from the school. Often these costs can be just as expensive as tuition.

Personal expenses: Students have countless personal expenses, and lifestyle has a huge impact in this category. Consider clothing, laundry, haircuts, phone (land and cell) and entertainment. A written budget is critical, as these expenses can easily spiral out of control.

Other costs: Count on some extra expenses such as special lab fees for science courses, fees for course changes and expenses for participating in athletics or joining a sorority or fraternity. Try to keep a little extra money in the budget to cover emergencies.

Where to Find Your College's Price Tag

To find the COA of a college, visit the school's website or look at its brochure. For example, these are the annual costs for an in-state resident at one public institution:

Tuition:	$3,508
Estimate for books:	$823
Estimate for transportation:	$394
Room and board:	$6,453
Estimate for personal expenses:	$2,479
Total cost of attendance:	$13,657

Here's another example—this time for a private institution:

Tuition:	$29,500
Additional required fees:	$1,140
Estimate for books/supplies:	$810

Estimate for transportation:	$330
Room and board allowance:	$8,435
Estimate for personal expenses:	$1,010
Total cost of attendance:	$41,225

If you're researching several colleges, you can get a quick estimate of the costs of attendance by using the School Search Tool at www.salliemae.com, which provides a breakdown of college costs and includes useful information such as the average amount of financial aid each school awards.

Knowing the COA is only the first half of figuring out college costs. What really counts is how much you'll pay out of pocket.

Long-Term Planning

If your child is heading to college in the next year or two, you may already have a good idea of what it will cost. But what if college is five or 10 years away? It is useful to have a rough projection of what it will cost, especially if you are starting a savings plan (see Chapter 10 on how to do this) and want to set some goals.

The best way to estimate future costs is to use the College Cost Calculator at www.salliemae.com. Enter the current cost of college (the College Board reports a private college costs $32,307 a year and a public university $13,589) and the number of years until your child will attend. You'll also need to select the annual cost increase. Tuition and fees continue to outpace inflation, and most experts predict this trend will continue, so you can safely enter 7 percent. Enter the number of years your child will be in college (usually four). The calculator will quickly tell you how much money you will need.

For example, if your child will attend college in 10 years, the calculator states that a private college will cost $282,171 for four years and a public university will cost $118,687.

Determining this cost will help you set annual goals for saving. At the very least, knowing the cost should motivate you to start saving, if you haven't done so already.

CURRENT TRENDS .

The future is bright for college graduates. Without a doubt, it pays to get a college education. College graduates earn more, have lower rates of unemployment and have better career opportunities. But a college education offers more than monetary benefits. From lower levels of smoking to higher levels of civic participation, volunteerism and voting rates, college has a profound positive influence. It's no exaggeration to say that college is an investment with benefits that last a lifetime.

Source: College Board, *Education Pays*, 2007.

College Education as an Investment

Some parents and students question whether college is worth the financial struggle. The answer is "Absolutely!"

Going to college is one of the best investments a person can make. Studies show that workers with a bachelor's degree earn an average of 62 percent more a year than those with only a high school education. Over a lifetime, this translates to over $1 million more in earnings.[5]

And the gap between those with college degrees and those without is growing. According to a recent study, more than a million new jobs for college graduates were added in one year, while two million non-degree jobs were eliminated.[6] Clearly, job opportunities are growing for those with college degrees and shrinking for those without degrees.

Going to college is about much more than future earning potential. It is a chance to grow as an individual, to develop critical thinking and reasoning skills and to pre-

---

Straight Talk with a Financial Aid Administrator ▶ **Believe it or not, colleges raise tuition only as a last resort**

Parents should understand colleges do not attempt to raise tuition unless it is absolutely necessary. Many colleges and universities may lose students by raising tuition and make every effort to curb the increase to assure students are able to afford the tuition. College costs are driven by such factors as high health care expenses, wages, utilities, technology, building and upkeep of facilities and capital improvements. These costs rise through the years, and colleges must cover them. Without grants and other funding from the federal and state governments, colleges have no choice but to cover the cost in other ways, such as increasing tuition. Parents should definitely question and read about the institutions their children will attend to understand why the tuition is high. But parents should also keep in mind that education is an investment for the future. Without a good education, their child will not, in most cases, be able to get better-paying jobs, and their salaries will be lower than individuals who receive a college degree.

Peggy Loewy-Wellisch, Associate Vice President for Student Financial Services, Nova Southeastern University

---

5. The College Board, *Trends in Student Aid 2004*, October 19, 2004.
6. The College Board, *Trends in Student Aid 2002*, October 21, 2002.

pare for a satisfying career. Most parents find that the child they send off to college returns as an adult.

And if these reasons are not motivation enough, consider some of the nonacademic benefits of going to college. A recent survey by the College Board showed that college graduates are less likely to smoke cigarettes and more likely to describe themselves in excellent or very good health.[7]

Going to college is an investment in the future. Like anything worthwhile, it requires dedication and effort, but the returns are priceless.

KEY CONCEPT . . . .

Never rule out a college based on sticker price. Some families prematurely eliminate a college because of its price tag, but the sticker price of a college is not necessarily what you would pay. Once you factor in financial aid, it is entirely possible that a college with a higher sticker price may cost less than one with a lower price.

7. The College Board, *Trends in Student Aid 2007*, October 22, 2007.

**Straight Talk
with a Financial Aid
Administrator**

Why college is so expensive

There is no question college is expensive. Unfortunately, public universities are faced with declining state support in most parts of the country and thus students are often charged with making up for the loss with higher tuition and fees. A typical public university today has many fixed costs over which it can exercise minimal control. These include:

- Faculty and staff medical benefits, which have annual increases of 10 to 25 percent.

- Constantly increasing costs for utilities and for maintenance of the facilities that are projected to add significantly to the universities' bottom line for operations.

- Technology cost is escalating rapidly. Computers must be replaced at least every three years to keep instruction current. New equipment for labs and classrooms continues to increase at a level beyond most universities' capacities.

- The cost of student financial aid. Universities must budget a greater portion of their resources each year to assist needy students.

- Research is very expensive. Professors often get federal and private grants to do the research, but the universities also must pay a significant share. Plus, faculty members doing research do not teach as many students.

- Athletics and campus life are expensive. Students want to experience a vibrant campus life with programs such as concerts, plays and sporting events. While some universities generate sufficient revenue to maintain athletic programs, with the implementation of Title IX (gender equity) most programs require additional support.

- Wage increases are required to keep talented faculty and staff.

Universities are essentially maintaining "mini cities." They must take care of roads, parking, construction projects, food services, snow removal and public safety. All these elements add to the cost of higher education.

Courtney McAnuff, Vice President for Enrollment Services,
Eastern Michigan University

CHAPTER 3

How Much Financial Aid Will We Get?

What you'll learn:

- Why everyone qualifies for financial aid
- What factors affect the amount of financial aid you'll receive
- How the government calculates how much you can afford
- How financial aid officers supply the human element
- What strategies can maximize your financial aid package

Picture it. You're sitting at the dining table on a fall evening, high school senior to your left, stack of bank statements to your right, stomach-grinding anxiety front and center. With college looming, it's time for some serious number-crunching to meet the anticipated expense.

If you're like many parents, you underestimate federal financial aid—or fail to consider it at all. You assume that government assistance is only for the needy. You believe there's nothing in Uncle Sam's wallet for you and your child. If this is what you think, it could cost you a bundle.

Even the 'Millionaire Next Door' Qualifies for Financial Aid

No matter how much income you earn, no matter how substantial your assets, you qualify for some form of financial assistance. You could have more money than Donald Trump and *still* receive some of the $97 billion[1] in financial aid awarded annually.

The idea that financial aid is available only to low-income families is a common misconception. In reality, certain programs, such as the unsubsidized federal Staf-

1. The College Board, *Trends in Student Aid 2007*, October 22, 2007.

ford Loan (see Chapter 6), offer below-market rates and deferred payments to everyone who applies. All you have to do is ask.

But as with any government program, asking means paperwork. Is it time-consuming to apply? Of course. Is it worth it? Definitely! Although financial aid applications seem intimidating at first glance, they're no more difficult than doing your taxes. In fact, if you've already done your taxes, you're halfway there.

This chapter explains the financial aid process from start to finish. You'll learn how the government analyzes your personal finances and how the college financial aid office makes decisions. You don't need to be an accountant, tax attorney or rocket scientist to understand financial aid. If you can balance a checkbook, you can learn how to apply for financial aid.

The Financial Aid Cornucopia

The term *financial aid* can be confusing. Although sometimes referred to as all money that doesn't come from your own pocket, financial aid specifically is money either from the government or from the college. Regardless of the source, financial aid can be divided into three major categories:

Grants and scholarships: Money with no strings attached. Neither you nor your child needs to pay it back. These are the financial aid jackpots.

DEADLINE . . . .

Financial aid is awarded on a first-come, first-served basis. Most colleges award their financial aid dollars in the order in which they receive applications. Does this mean you need to be the first in line? No. But it does mean that your child's application should arrive before the college's "priority deadline." Many are in February or March, but some are earlier. This is the date after which the college may not be able to fully fund a student's financial need. To guarantee that your child will receive as much aid as possible, heed the deadline.

Loans: Money you or your child borrows that must be repaid. There are two types of loans. With a *subsidized* student loan, the government pays the interest while your child is in college. With an *unsubsidized* loan, the interest accrues while your child is in college and is later added to the loan balance.

Don't discount a student loan just because it's borrowed money; it may be exactly what you need to make up for any shortfall in your ability to pay for college. Student loans offer below-market interest rates, protection against rising rates and flexible repayment programs.

Work-Study: Money your child earns by working. But work-study is not the typical part-time job. Here the government subsi-

Straight Talk
with a Financial Aid
Administrator

Don't wait until your child is accepted to apply for financial aid

Some parents think they should wait until their son or daughter is admitted to a college before asking for financial assistance. This is unnecessary and can cause a significant delay, which costs the student access to grant money. By design, the application process allows students to apply for financial assistance for several schools at the same time—even before they know whether or not they have been accepted. Applicants who apply on time often receive multiple financial aid offers and can then compare these to the desirability of the academic institution and how closely the institution matches their academic goals. It also ensures students will get the most gift aid (i.e. grants) they deserve.

Dr. Lawrence Burt, Associate VP for Student Affairs & Director of Student Financial Services, University of Texas at Austin

dizes part of the wages so your child qualifies for choice on-campus employment, with good pay and flexible hours that accommodate a student's busy schedule.

Of course, to get any of the above types of financial aid you must ask for it. Exactly what kind and how much you receive are determined by the financial aid process carried out by the federal government and the college financial aid office.

The Financial Aid Process Demystified

Each year thousands of parents apply for financial aid with no idea of what happens to their applications; smart applicants know this is not the way to obtain the best financial aid package. Investing a little time to learn how the process works can yield huge dividends. Learn about the process *before* submitting your application, so you'll know how much aid you qualify for. Also, you'll want to know about a few simple things you can do to significantly increase the amount of money you receive.

The FAFSA

The first word you will learn in the language of financial aid is FAFSA (FAF-suh), the U.S. Department of Education's Free Application for Federal Student Aid. All colleges participating in the Department of Education's financial aid programs require the FAFSA. In Chapter 4 we describe how to fill out the FAFSA line by line.

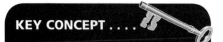

KEY CONCEPT . . . .

Every family is expected to pay something for college.
A college education is not an entitlement. The government and the school are willing to help, but they will not pay for everything. Every family (both student and parents) is expected to contribute some money. This expectation underlies the entire financial aid process.

Many private colleges also require the College Scholarship Service (CSS) PROFILE from the College Board. This application includes information nearly identical to that on the FAFSA. The difference is how the College Board uses the information to calculate eligibility.

Both the FAFSA and the CSS/PROFILE paint a detailed picture of a family's finances, including all sources of income and assets.

Hitching a Ride on the FAFSA

You may think your work is done when you drop the FAFSA into the mailbox or click your mouse to send it over the Internet. But that's only the beginning. To see the entire process, let's hitch a ride with your application from the day you send it off to the day you receive the financial aid award letter.

Step 1: You submit the FAFSA. Most people complete the FAFSA online, although a paper version is available. There is a Spanish version as well.

Step 2: The Department of Education calculates the Expected Family Contribution. All FAFSA information is run through a series of financial aid formulas. The end result is known as the Expected Family Contribution (EFC): the amount your family is expected to pay for one year of college. The EFC can range from zero to more than $50,000.

Step 3: You review the Student Aid Report. About four weeks after you submit the FAFSA, you'll receive the Student Aid Report (SAR). The SAR reiterates the information you provided and tells you what your EFC is. Review the SAR carefully and make sure it contains no errors.

Step 4: The college financial aid office assembles an aid package. Each college your child applies to will receive your results. Financial aid administrators at each school consider your EFC and put together a financial aid package that may be composed of federal, state and the school's own aid programs. The financial aid administrator reviews any special circumstances and may use his or her professional judgment to adjust the aid package.

Step 5: You compare financial aid packages. Your child's financial aid package will be spelled out in an award letter from each college and may contain a mixture of grants, loans and work-study. You may choose which parts of the aid package you want to accept. It is important to compare offers from different schools (see Chapter 5 for details).

The process is similar for the CSS/PROFILE, except that the form is sent to the College Board, which uses a slightly different financial aid calculation than that used by the Department of Education. The results are provided directly to the colleges. Unless there is a problem with the application, you won't hear anything until you receive the financial aid award letters from the colleges.

Confusion over the Financial Aid Formula

The leading cause of confusion about financial aid is the second step, in which the government determines how much money your family can afford to pay for college. Not surprisingly, your idea of what you can afford may differ from Uncle Sam's.

Many parents figure out what they can afford by looking at what's left in the bank account after they meet the family's living expenses. The government, however, seeking an equitable process for all families, relies on a series of calculations that it applies to everyone. To understand the government's approach, consider the following scenario:

> *Imagine two families. They live in identical towns and have identical children who attend identical schools and receive identical grades. The families earn an identical amount of money. The only difference is that one family saves for college, while the other spends money on extravagant vacations and luxury automobiles. Should the responsible family be penalized by receiving no financial aid, while the spendthrift family is rewarded with a fat grant?*

The answer is no (although the government doesn't reward the family that saves, either). Under the federal financial aid system, both families would be evaluated by the exact same financial aid calculation—which does not take into account a family's discretionary spending. The result is usually that the family that spends beyond its means thinks the government has an unreasonable expectation of what it can afford for college, while the family with more modest spending habits feels the expectation of what it should pay is fair. In addition, the family that saves for college may not have to borrow any money (or at

KEY CONCEPT . . . .

Needs analysis. This is the process of evaluating a financial aid application (FAFSA and/or CSS/PROFILE) to determine the amount of financial aid the student is eligible to receive. Using various formulas and computations, the government and the college will determine your Expected Family Contribution, which is the foundation for determining how much financial aid your child receives.

least will borrow far less) than the family that didn't save.

The Person Behind the Process

Of course, families don't always have a choice about how much to spend and how much to save. Some families face prolonged unemployment or debilitating medical expenses. Fortunately, while the government relies on calculations, colleges use human beings—financial aid administrators—to evaluate applications.

These professionals have years of experience helping families pay for their children's education and can use judgment to take individual situations into account. A financial aid administrator knows that between two families with the same income, one may deserve more financial aid than the other. The financial aid administrator can be your biggest ally in helping meet college costs. While computers start the financial aid process, it's nice to know that human beings finish it.

USEFUL TERM . . . . .

EFC. The Expected Family Contribution is the amount of money your family—including both student and parents—is expected to pay toward the cost of one year of education. Typically, the lower your EFC, the more financial aid your child will receive. Factors such as family size, number of children in college, savings and income—all of which are included on the FAFSA—are used to calculate your EFC.

The Power of the EFC

But regardless of the human component, the government's determination of your EFC is crucial. The following sections explain how the EFC formula works. In addition, you can use the EFC Calculator on the Sallie Mae website (www.salliemae. com). Although the calculator makes the number-crunching easy, you'll still want to understand how the formula works. So let's look at what the government considers when determining your EFC.

Parent Income: The Largest Factor

Your income will typically have the largest impact on the EFC. Income can come from

- Employment
- Sale of stocks or mutual funds
- Interest from bank accounts
- Rental property
- Other sources of cash

The financial aid formula uses the adjusted gross income (AGI) reported on your tax return (line 37 on Form 1040, line 21 on 1040A or line 4 on 1040EZ).

The Automatic Zero EFC

If you and your spouse's combined adjusted gross income (AGI) is $15,000 or less, and you, your spouse and your dependent child are all eligible to file an IRS 1040A or 1040EZ, your EFC is automatically zero. There is no need to do further calculations. An EFC of zero means that your child may receive a financial aid package that covers up to 100 percent of college costs.

Understanding Your Adjusted Gross Income

In addition to your salary here are some other items factored into your AGI:

- Money from Social Security not included in AGI
- Veteran non-education benefits
- Child support
- Earned income credit
- Child tax credit

Straight Talk with a Financial Aid Administrator ▶ **Responsibility for paying for college primarily rests with the family**

One of the foundations of need-based financial aid is that it's primarily the family's responsibility to help a student finance an education. Even when a student is "emancipated," it still does not free the family from this responsibility. In fact, there are strict rules for when a student is considered to be independent from a parent for the purposes of financial aid. In my experience, it is not unusual to meet parents who claim that as taxpayers they are entitled to all the money they need. I even had a parent whose son was on a scholarship that covered the full costs of tuition, room and board, books and supplies and even provided a living stipend. Yet this parent was adamant he was entitled to more money from financial aid than it actually cost to go to school for that year. Unfortunately, there are some families who simply do not believe it's their responsibility to pay for college—that society owes it to them to pay for their child. The reality is need-based financial aid programs are designed to help fill the gap left after the family has reasonably used their resources.

James M. Bauer, Assistant Dean of Enrollment Management and Director of Financial Assistance Services, University of Miami

---

- Payments to tax-deferred pension or savings plans
- Deductions and payments to SEP, SIMPLE and Keogh retirement plans
- Untaxed IRA and pension distributions
- Foreign income exclusion
- Worker's compensation
- Housing and food allowances paid to members of the military and clergy
- Credit for federal tax on special fuels
- Welfare

Once all these benefits and income are added up, the government does a little subtraction. It deducts from your AGI the Hope and Lifetime Learning tax credits, federal work-study and fellowships and scholarships reported as income.

The result of these calculations is your total income for purposes of the EFC.

Deducting Taxes

The government then subtracts from your total income all federal and state income taxes you have paid, as well as Social Security taxes, which vary according to your income.

Straight Talk with a Financial Aid Administrator ▶ **People make the system work**

At Duke University every application is reviewed and massaged by an actual human being. We don't make any mechanical aid awards. Never. In our office we assign students based on their last names to a specific financial aid counselor. If your last name is "Baker," you will be assigned to Kelly Kay, and she will work with you and your family for the entire four years you are at Duke. In fact, she will get to know you and your family very well. If you need help at any time during school, even with establishing a budget or controlling spending, she will be there to work with you.

Jim Belvin, Director of Financial Aid, Duke University

Income Protection

This allowance is a provision for the basic living expenses of a family. You are allowed two types of income protection. The first is a simple income protection allowance based on household size and the number of students currently in college. For instance, if your household has four people (including the child for whom you are seeking aid) and your household has one college student (again including the child for whom you are seeking aid) your income protection allowance would be $23,660.

TABLE

Income Protection

Number of people in household including student	Number of college students in household				
	1	2	3	4	5
2	$15,380	$12,750			
3	$19,150	$16,540	$13,900		
4	$23,660	$21,020	$18,410	$15,770	
5	$27,910	$25,280	$22,660	$20,030	$17,410
6	$32,650	$30,010	$27,400	$24,770	$22,150

For each additional family member, add $3,680.

For each additional college student (except parents), subtract $2,620.

The second income protection is an employment expense allowance, which is determined as follows:

TABLE

Employment Expense Allowance

Two working parents: 35% of the lesser of the earned incomes or $3,300, whichever is less

One-parent families: 35% of the earned income or $3,300, whichever is less

Two-parent families, one working parent: zero

Calculating Your Available Income

Let's summarize. To calculate your available income, you started with adjusted gross income, added untaxed income, then subtracted the value of certain education benefits, taxes and income protections. Here is a breakdown of this calculation.

WORKSHEET

Adjusted gross income	$
Untaxed income and benefits +	$
Education benefits, work-study, scholarships counted as income –	$
Federal taxes –	$
State taxes –	$
Social Security taxes –	$
Income protection –	$
Employment expense allowance –	$
Available income =	$

Meet the Lee Family

The Lees are a typical family of four; one child is in elementary school and the other will start college in the fall. Both parents work; together, they make $60,000 a year. In filing their taxes, the Lees also reported $200 in interest from their savings account and $800 in capital gains from the sale of stock. Their total income for tax purposes is $61,000. The Lees contributed $3,000 to their retirement accounts, so they are allowed to subtract this, which means that their total adjusted gross income (line 37 of Form 1040) is $58,000.

Straight Talk with a Financial Aid Administrator

Fairness is the name of the game

The basic tenet of financial aid is horizontal and vertical equity. Horizontal equity means we treat families with similar financial circumstances in a similar way. But vertical equity means we also treat families with different circumstances in a proportionally different way. Let's say we have two families with incomes on paper of $50,000. But on closer examination we see one family had rental property and was able to write off $40,000 to bring their income down to the $50,000 that is reported. So this family with rental income actually has more financial resources even though on paper they appear the same as the other family. Although these two families have the same income, they are not the same. By looking at the financial situation within the context of the family's circumstances, we are able to make decisions that are both fair and appropriate.

Jim Belvin, Director of Financial Aid, Duke University

Beginning with the Lees' AGI, the federal financial aid formula first adds any untaxed benefits, such as their $3,000 tax-deferred contribution to retirement accounts. The Lees also received a $1,000 child tax credit. From the perspective of the financial aid formula, the Lees have a total income of $62,000.

	$58,000 adjusted gross income from tax return
+	*$3,000 untaxed benefits from retirement contributions*
+	*$1,000 untaxed benefits from tax credits*
=	*$62,000 total income*

Next, the financial aid formula subtracts the Lees' federal, state and Social Security taxes. The Lees paid approximately $8,100 in federal income tax and $4,300 in state income tax. Using the Social Security tax table as a guide, the Lees' income bracket is 7.65% of their earned income, or about $4,600 ($60,000 x 7.65% = $4,590). Subtracting these taxes, the Lees now show a total income of $45,000.

	$62,000 total income
−	*$8,100 federal income taxes*
−	*$4,300 state income taxes*
−	*$4,600 Social Security taxes*
=	*$45,000 new total income*

The Lees are also allowed to take two types of income protection. The first is based on the size of their household and the number of children who are or will be in college. The Lees, as a family of four with one child in college, will receive an income protection amount of $23,660. Because both parents work, they also may take an employment expense amount. Each parent earns about $30,000, so the maximum they may take is $3,300. Altogether, the Lees have an income protection of $26,960.

>   *$23,660 income protection*
> *+ $3,300 employment expense*
> *= $26,960 total income protection*

The financial aid formula calculates the Lees' available income by taking their total income of $45,000 and subtracting the income protection of $26,960. The Lees' available income is $18,040.

>   *$45,000 total income*
> *− $26,960 income protection*
> *= $18,040 available income*

This is the income figure that enters into the calculation the government makes when determining your EFC.

Straight Talk with a Financial Aid Administrator ▶ ## Answers to the brazen questions parents have asked

At one financial aid presentation I did at a high school, a parent asked, "Where should I hide my savings?" I've also had parents probe to find out if it would be a good tactic to get divorced just to get more aid! I have to remind these parents that when submitting their FAFSA, they are also affirming the information is true and accurate. There are stiff penalties including major fines and jail time if a parent or student intentionally provides false information. I also remind parents that contrary to popular belief, given the type of information the FAFSA requires there is actually very little room to maneuver unless you outright lie. Plus, if you are selected for verification, those half-truths will be discovered. Very few things can't be verified, and this certainly helps to safeguard the system and dissuade parents from trying.

Jevita R. de Freitas, Director, Office of Student Financial Aid, George Mason University

Parents' Assets

The second part of the formula for determining the EFC is the parents' assets. Over the years, most families accumulate assets, such as a house, savings and stocks. Assets include the present value of everything in your bank account and stock portfolio. If you own a business or farm (but not a family farm that you live on), your assets include the net worth of those holdings. The good news is that the federal financial aid formula does not consider the value of your home or any retirement accounts as assets that can be used to pay for college. Nor does the formula include non-liquid assets, such as the value of your car or furniture. The bad news is that everything else—your savings, checking account, stocks, bonds and mutual funds—is fair game.

Asset Shelters

Some parents miss out on a simple asset shelter because they file the wrong tax form. If your adjusted gross income is less than $50,000 and you file a 1040EZ or 1040A, your assets are excluded from the financial aid calculation. However, if your AGI is less than $50,000 and you file any other tax form—such as the regular 1040—you may jeopardize this shelter. If you are near this income limit, speak to your tax preparer to find out if you can use the 1040EZ or 1040A to file your taxes.

If you own a business or farm that is not a family farm where you live, you'll need to determine its net worth since a percentage of this figure will be considered part of your assets under the financial aid formula.

TABLE
Business or Farm Net Worth Adjustment

If the net worth of a business or farm is—	Then the adjusted net worth is—
Less than $1	$0
$1 to $110,000	40% of net worth of business/farm
$110,001 to $330,000	$44,000 + 50% of excess over $110,000
$330,001 to $550,000	$154,000 + 60% of excess over $330,000
$550,001 or more	$286,000 + 100% of excess over $550,000

The financial aid formula also shields a portion of your assets on the basis of your age or that of your spouse, whoever is older. Use the following table to determine the amount of assets you may protect.

TABLE

Education Savings and Asset Protection Allowances

Age of older parent	Allowance if there are two parents	Allowance if there is only one parent
25 or less	0	0
26	2,600	1,100
27	5,100	2,100
28	7,700	3,200
29	10,200	4,300
30	12,800	5,300
31	15,400	6,400
32	17,900	7,500
33	20,500	8,500
34	23,000	9,600
35	25,600	10,700
36	28,200	11,700
37	30,700	12,800
38	33,300	13,900
39	35,800	14,900
40	38,400	16,000
41	39,300	16,400
42	40,300	16,700
43	41,300	17,100
44	42,300	17,600
45	43,400	17,900
46	44,500	18,300
47	45,600	18,800
48	46,700	19,200
49	47,900	19,700
50	49,000	20,100
51	50,500	20,500
52	51,800	21,000
53	53,300	21,500
54	54,600	22,100
55	56,300	22,600
56	57,600	23,200
57	59,300	23,700
58	61,100	24,400
59	62,900	25,000
60	64,700	25,700
61	66,600	26,300
62	68,500	27,000
63	70,800	27,800
64	72,800	28,500
65 or over	75,200	29,300

Total Assets

To calculate your assets, begin with the total amount of your assets (not including the value of your home or retirement accounts) and make the following adjustments:

WORKSHEET

Savings and checking accounts	$
Value of stocks, bonds, mutual funds +	$
Net worth of business or farm +	$
Education savings and asset protection allowance –	$
Total assets (discretionary net worth) =	$
Asset conversion rate x .12*	
Contribution from assets =	$

---

*You'll notice that once you total up your assets and subtract the protection allowance, you multiply the result by 12 percent (.12). This is known as the *asset conversion rate.*

Back to the Lee Family

On the asset side, the Lees own their home, which is valued at $250,000, and they have $40,000 in IRAs. The good news is that none of this money is considered available to pay for college. The family also has $18,000 in a savings account and a stock portfolio worth $30,000; the financial aid formula will include this $48,000 as assets. If the Lees owned a business or a farm, they would have to include a percentage of its net worth.

To shield part of their assets, the Lees use the education savings and asset protection allowance based on the age of the older parent. Mr. Lee, the older parent, is 45 years old, which means an allowance of $43,400. Subtracting $43,400 from $48,000 yields $4,600. Multiply this by the asset conversion rate of 12 percent (.12) and the Lees are left with just $552 in assets.

	$18,000 savings and checking accounts
+	$30,000 present value of non-retirement investments
−	$43,400 asset protection allowance based on parent age
=	$4,600 total assets
x	.12 (asset conversion rate)
=	$552 contribution from assets

Parent Income + Assets = Parent EFC

Once you've figured out your available income and your contribution from assets, you can determine your portion of the Expected Family Contribution. Add the income and asset totals to get your adjusted available income (AAI), and locate your part of the EFC in the following table. If you have more than one child in college, divide your contribution by the number of students.

TABLE

Parents' Contribution from Adjusted Available Income

If parents' AAI is—	Parents' contribution is—
Less than −$3,409	−$750
−$3,409 to $13,700	22% of AAI
$13,701 to $17,300	$3,014 + 25% of AAI over $13,700
$17,301 to $20,800	$3,914 + 29% of AAI over $17,300
$20,801 to $24,300	$4,929 + 34% of AAI over $20,800
$24,301 to $27,800	$6,119 + 40% of AAI over $24,300
$27,801 or more	$7,519 + 47% of AAI over $27,800

(Divide contribution by number of students in college.)

This is your contribution to one year of your child's college expenses, but you're not finished yet. You must calculate the second half of the EFC—the part that comes from your child.

The Lee parents ended up with $18,040 from available income and $552 in contributions from assets, resulting in a total adjusted available income of $18,592. Consulting the Parents' Contribution from the Adjusted Available Income table, the parents' contribution is $3,914 plus 29 percent over $17,300 ($3,914 + $375), which equals $4,289. Dividing this amount by the number of students in college (in this case, one) the parents' contribution is $4,289.

Your Child's Contribution

Before your pride and joy rushes out to spend that graduation gift money, remind him or her that the government's financial aid formula expects students to contribute significantly to their own education. In fact, the government expects a child to be able to spend more of his or her income and assets (50% and 20%, respectively) than it expects of his or her parents.

Student income is figured in the same way as parent income. Start with the adjusted gross income and subtract federal, state and Social Security taxes. Add back any untaxed benefits and subtract any educational benefits counted as income. Students have a standard income protection allowance of $3,080. Finally, multiply this number by 50 percent to get your child's contribution.

The Lees' son does not have much income, as he works only during the summer and earns minimum wage. This past summer, his total wages were $3,640. After subtracting allowances for taxes and the standard income protection allowance of $3,080, the Lees' son has only $560 in available income. Multiply that by 50 percent, and he is expected to use $280 of his income to pay for college.

Your child may have assets as well. Add any money that is in your child's name, such as bank accounts (including custodial accounts), stocks, bonds and trust funds, and multiply the total by 20 percent. That's it—for students there is no asset protection.

CURRENT TRENDS .

Seventy percent of all students receive financial aid. Your child's odds of receiving help paying for college are extremely high—as long as you apply. While need-based aid depends on your personal financial situation, the majority of students today receive some form of financial aid, whether it is a grant, loan or work-study. It's definitely worth the time and effort to apply.

The Lees' son has been working every summer since he was a freshman in high school. Over the years, he has received various gifts from relatives. Currently, he has $17,500 in his name in a savings account. There is no asset protection allowance for students. The full $17,500 is considered available and assessed at the 20 percent rate, which yields $3,500 available for college.

Your Total EFC

Now that you know the amount from parent and student contributions, you can add it all together and have the EFC. Here's how it looks:

EFC = parent contribution (from income and assets) + student contribution (from income and assets)

To get the Lees' EFC, take the parent contribution ($4,289) and add in the son's income contribution ($280) and asset contribution ($3,500). This yields a total Expected Family Contribution of $8,069. This number is passed from the Department of Education to every college where the Lees' son is

| Straight Talk with a Financial Aid Administrator | **Our job description is to help** |

Parents should understand financial aid administrators are here to help. In fact, we are eager to help—that's our job. At Duke we have a "need blind" admissions policy, which means applying for aid has no bearing on whether or not a student gets admitted. We actually want students to apply for financial aid. There·is no question some families would have qualified for aid but for some reason just didn't apply. That is unfortunate.

As the head of the financial aid office, my job is to manage the process and our resources, both institutional and federal, as well as our staff of counselors. Although our frontline points of contact are our counselors who work closely with parents and students, I still speak with parents and students and get involved in special cases. We have structured our program so we can provide an on-going hands-on relationship with parents and students. Of course, there are some families whom we don't hear from for some time and some we hear from every day.

Jim Belvin, Director of Financial Aid, Duke University

applying for financial aid. Each college will use this number to determine his financial need.

Financial Need—A Moving Target

Figuring out the EFC is the hardest part of the financial aid process. Once you know the EFC, it's a simple matter to calculate financial need. Take the cost of attending one year at a college (including tuition, room and board, books and transportation) and subtract your EFC. If the remaining number is positive, that's your financial need.

TIME SAVER . . . .

Get a sneak peek at your Estimated Family Contribution. You don't have to wait until you submit the FAFSA to know your EFC. Go to the EFC calculator on the Sallie Mae website (www.salliemae. com), plug in your numbers and instantly get an estimate of your EFC. Remember, the accuracy of this estimate is only as good as the numbers you provide.

Cost of Attendance – EFC = Financial Need

Financial need is the gap between the cost of going to a certain college (known as the cost of attendance) and what your family is expected to pay. The more expensive the college, the more likely you will have financial need—and, as a result, the greater your financial aid award will likely be. That means that you and your child should not ***automatically*** eliminate the possibility of a higher-priced school since your actual out-of-pocket expense for a college that costs $10,000 could be the same as for a college that costs $40,000. Moreover, even if your financial aid award does not cover the total cost of attendance at a higher-priced college, you could take out private loans to cover the total cost of attendance. The cost of doing so may be worth it in the long run. Let's take one last look at the Lees.

> *The Lees have an EFC of $8,069. If the cost of attendance at College A is $30,000, the Lees would qualify for $21,931 in financial aid, the difference between what it costs and what they can afford. If the cost of attendance at College B is $8,000, the Lees do not qualify for any financial aid, as their EFC is higher than the cost of attendance.*

FAFSA or CSS/PROFILE?

Where your child applies to college determines which financial aid forms you will need to complete. All colleges participating in the Department of Education's financial aid system rely on the FAFSA and abide by the federal financial aid formula, known as the *federal methodology,* to determine EFC. However, some colleges also require you to complete the CSS/PROFILE. On the surface, the FAFSA and CSS/PROFILE look the same, but there are some differences.

Through the CSS/PROFILE, colleges use a slightly different formula, known as the *institutional methodology,* for calculating EFC. One big difference is that the institutional methodology may consider a portion of your home equity as an asset. On the other hand, the institutional methodology has more realistic income protection amounts based on current consumer surveys.

The Financial Aid Administrator: The Human Behind the Process

The initial stages of the financial aid process are very mechanical. Don't spend hours composing a long and detailed letter to include with the FAFSA explaining why your family needs financial aid. The Department of Education's computers can't read your letter, and it will be discarded. The government is concerned only with the calculations based on the aid formula. It is only *after* the results are sent to the colleges that the human element takes over.

The FAA as Ally

At each college, a financial aid administrator (FAA) reviews your EFC and calculates your financial need. For certain federal programs—such as Pell Grants and subsidized Stafford Loans—the FAA must abide by federal guidelines. If your EFC and financial need meet these guidelines, you are automatically awarded the funds.

But colleges have other resources, and the FAA may apply other standards to determine whether you deserve more support.

The FAA may also review special circumstances not accounted for in the federal financial aid formula. For example, suppose a family has sold its house but has not yet found a new one. To the computers, the proceeds from the sale show up as income, yet clearly this is not disposable income, since they intend to purchase another home. While the government process is black and white, the financial aid administrator can see all the shades of gray. If the FAA knows about special circumstances,

KEY CONCEPT . . . .

Remember at a minimum all families qualify for some form of financial aid. Too many families don't apply for financial aid because they think they won't get any. A recent study found that more than 850,000 students could have received federal grants (that's free money!) but didn't, simply because they failed to apply.

Source: American Council on Education, *Missed Opportunities: Students Who Do Not Apply for Financial Aid,* 2004.

Straight Talk with a Financial Aid Administrator

How we keep the system honest

If you were a millionaire but for some reason were able to legally show negative income on your tax return, you could qualify for a Pell grant from the federal government. I would have no ability to change this since you did nothing illegal and by law I must award this grant to you. However, would I give you additional money from the college? No, that would be inappropriate.

In financial aid we must follow the laws and rules that govern how we award money, but at the same time we also use our own judgment to safeguard the system. In addition to the expertise of the financial aid administrator, there are many built-in mechanisms that protect the system. Like the IRS does with tax returns, some financial aid applications are randomly selected for verification. We also have a computerized system that checks and flags any unusual applications. If we suspect something is wrong, we can flag an application, which means the applicant will have to provide additional documentation. But the bottom line is our experience and training usually allow us to spot dubious applications.

Dr. Lawrence Burt, Associate VP for Student Affairs & Director of Student Financial Services, University of Texas at Austin

he or she can adjust your EFC at the college level, which will help you qualify for more aid.

Many books on financial aid portray the FAA as an ogre who wants to squeeze as much money from you as possible; in reality, the FAA can be your biggest ally. This person's job is to help you find the money you need to attend college. No FAA wants to see a student turn down an offer of admission because he or she cannot afford the tuition.

Helping the FAA Help You

Financial aid administrators wear many hats. At times they are *advisers* who can help you figure out where to find more money. Some days they are *instructors* who can walk you through a difficult section of the FAFSA. And every so often they are compassionate *listeners* who understand your concerns and fears about the future. But when it comes down to business, FAAs are *accountants*, people who use numbers to understand a family's situation. Problems are expressed in numbers and so are the solutions.

USEFUL TERM . . . . .

Verification. Ever wonder what keeps the financial aid process honest? It's done through verification. As with tax audits, a certain number of FAFSA applications are randomly selected and those applicants are asked to provide additional documentation. Colleges also run automated checks on applications, and FAAs are trained to spot discrepancies and flag the application for verification.

When you speak to an FAA, use numbers to support your statements. Don't say, "My family needs to take care of my elderly father." Say instead, "My family supports my elderly father, and this costs us an additional $8,000 a year in food and medical expenses that are not covered by Medicare or Social Security."

As much as possible when dealing with the FAA, substantiate your claims with numbers—even if they are only estimates. The more quantitative information you provide, the easier you make it for the FAA to give you money.

Some families are embarrassed to reveal their financial information, especially their misfortunes, to a total stranger, but this kind of pride can cost you money.

One FAA said he knew about a husband's impending job loss before the wife did. The husband was still figuring out how to break the news to his family, but he informed the college immediately. Because the FAA could see that this family was about to take a major income hit, he was able to secure additional grant money for the student. Had the husband delayed informing the college, the FAA might not have had resources available to help. So the bottom line is simple: FAAs can save you money only if you let them.

A Peek Inside a Financial Aid Office

Every college has its own approach to doling out financial aid. While the specific procedures vary, the goal is the same: Give as many students as possible the money they need to make college affordable.

The financial aid administrator's job begins when he or she receives your child's information electronically from the FAFSA or CSS/PROFILE. A large university may receive as many as 20,000 applications within a two- or three-month period. That's a huge amount of data to process. Large institutions may rely on computer systems to identify applications that need individual attention; at small schools, each application may be reviewed by a financial aid administrator.

Whether the checking is done by computer or human, if an inconsistency in the data is found, you may be contacted to provide additional information. If you have indicated special circumstances, a financial aid administrator will definitely review your application. (For details about when and how to present special circumstances, see Chapter 5.) A certain number of applications are randomly selected for verification; if yours is chosen, you may have to provide additional documentation. This is one of the many built-in checks that protect the system from fraud.

Once the financial aid office has reviewed your data, it's time to package your aid. Every school has its own policies for awarding aid. Typically, a college decides what grants a student is eligible for and, after factoring these grants into the student's financial need, decides what federal loans and work-study a student is eligible for to try to cover his or her remaining financial need.

All schools that receive money from the government follow the federal guidelines for awarding this aid. For example, Pell grants are an entitlement program and are awarded on the basis of a sliding scale of the Expected Family Contribution (EFC), so most students with a certain EFC will receive a specific amount of Pell grant money. More details about the Pell grant are provided in Chapter 5. While the college is doling out federal money, it also considers a student's eligibility for state-based aid programs. Each state has its own rules for these programs.

In addition to federal and state aid the financial aid administrator will consider each student for institutional money, such as grants and scholarships from the college or even specific academic departments.

Throughout this process, the financial aid administrator attempts to achieve two primary goals:

1. Provide a reasonable financial aid package to every student who qualifies, so that the student can attend the college.

2. Ensure that the financial aid budget is used to cover the largest number of students while still achieving the first goal.

Achieving both goals requires the financial aid administrator to keep one eye on the individual student and the other focused on the big picture. This delicate balancing act is made more difficult by the fact that the financial aid administrator does not know for sure which students will actually attend the college or how much of each package a student will accept. Often the financial aid

KEY CONCEPT . . . .

Professional judgment. The federal government relies on calculations to analyze a family's financial strength, but the law allows financial aid administrators to use their "professional judgment" to make adjustments that take special circumstances into consideration. For example, the FAA may use professional judgment if your family has secondary school tuition expenses, unusual medical expenses, child care costs or recent unemployment. This ensures that families are not penalized by the financial aid formula if they have unique situations that are not covered by the formula.

Straight Talk with a Financial Aid Administrator ▶ **Keep us in tune with changes**

Very often our only indication something has changed in a family's finances is when the parents call to tell us. The FAFSA is driven by a tax return that could be more than eight months old. A lot can happen in eight months. But since tax information is verifiable, we rely on it as a good "base" for our calculations. That means we assume a family's situation will usually not get worse between years—in fact, the assumption is a family's finances get better each year. Of course, reality can be different. For a family whose circumstances do get worse, this can have an impact on the financial aid results. In this situation, the process known as "professional judgment" comes in play. This allows the financial aid administrator to make adjustments to a student's aid package if there are special circumstances. But the only way we will know if a family has suffered a negative change is if they tell us.

James M. Bauer, Assistant Dean of Enrollment Management and Director of Financial Assistance Services, University of Miami

administrator's job involves as much art as science to ensure that decisions are fair and that the budget covers the college's commitments.

When students receive the financial aid package, they may find errors in the calculation or they may have new special circumstances that require a reassessment of the award. Often the busiest time in the financial aid office is after the awards have been packaged, as parents and students call with questions or provide new information that must be considered.

Even at the largest universities (which process tens of thousands of applications), a tremendous amount of one-on-one decision making occurs, as financial aid administrators spend large amounts of time becoming familiar with each family's situation and making adjustments to the aid package. In the final phase of the process, it is the financial aid administrator's expertise, professionalism and compassion that carry the day.

Can You Lower Your EFC?

Countless trees have been sacrificed to publish books that purport to show you how to "game" the system to get more financial aid. In each case, the strategy boils down to the same thing: Try to appear to have fewer financial resources than you do to receive more aid. Before getting into the legal and practical issues related to this strategy, we should mention the ethical issue.

Financial aid works only if each family provides an accurate picture of its financial resources (its income and assets). This allows the financial aid calculation to be applied uniformly to each family. If a family manipulates the system to appear less financially healthy than it actually is, it might receive more money than a family that didn't manipulate the system. Because financial aid funds are limited, this family may take money directly from another family that truly needs it. When this happens, the financial aid process ceases to be equitable.

To reduce the temptation to game the system, strict rules exist that disallow deceptive practices. Outright lying on a financial aid form is a federal offense, punishable by stiff fines and jail time. Every student and parent must sign the FAFSA. Your signature carries the same weight and penalties as it does on your tax return. If you try to cheat the system, you may end up paying a fine or, worse, spending some time in jail.

In addition to the ethical and legal aspects of shifting assets and income, the practice is not recommended for practical reasons. Almost anything you do to affect your EFC will have an impact on your personal income, assets and taxes. For example, if you decide to spend all your personal savings on a luxury car, this would affect your EFC, as it would completely deplete your assets. But would spending $40,000 on a car mean your child would get $40,000 more in financial aid? No. Only a maximum of 5.64 percent of your assets are counted in the financial aid formula. This would be like trading $40,000 for (at most) $2,260 in additional financial aid (some of which will be loans). Not only would you be exchanging real dollars for pennies in aid, but when you actually needed the money, you wouldn't have it. You'd have to borrow the funds and pay them back with interest.

The bottom line is that most strategies that claim to increase your financial aid do so at a cost. Sometimes the cost is having fewer personal assets or paying more taxes. Either way, the additional financial aid may end up costing more of your own money.

Commonsense Rules

But—keeping the above caveats in mind— as with any system, you can take certain

USEFUL TERM . . . . .

U.S. Department of Education. This federal agency is responsible for administering federal financial aid programs. The Department of Education runs the Federal Student Aid Information Center (1-800-4-FED-AID/1-800-433-3243), which can help answer questions about aid programs or the FAFSA. The department also maintains a website (www.studentaid.ed.gov) that is a good source of information on applying for federal financial aid.

actions to get the most out of the financial aid system. The following are not strategies but rather commonsense principles that will affect how financial aid works for your family. Following these principles should keep you from having a higher EFC than you should.

Don't overpay your share. Some parents believe that they are 100 percent responsible for financing their child's education; they pay for everything, even if the child has savings. This is not the view of the federal government or college financial aid offices. They believe that the responsibility rests with the student first, parent second and college, including financial aid, last. The financial aid formula assumes that students will contribute a large percentage of their income and assets to pay for each year of college. If parents pay for everything and let their children keep their savings accounts untouched, they will be penalized, because the formula will keep assessing the same high percentage against the child's assets every year. If you're in

Straight Talk with a Financial Aid Administrator ▶ **A behind-the-scenes look at the financial aid office**

Once the family's information from the FAFSA is downloaded into our system, we check if the application needs to be verified. If the application is selected for verification, a letter is sent to request additional information. If an application was rejected, we will contact the family to correct the information and resubmit the FAFSA. Assuming the information we receive is complete and there are not errors, a "packaging report" is run. This report is provided to the financial aid counselors to review the student's information with regard to programs and budgets. The counselor then awards the students specific financial aid packages.

Since at any time during this process the student or parent may have a question, we have created a University Call Center to act as a one-stop shop. Whether a family calls or e-mails, each inquiry is tracked to make sure a response is given quickly. Before we established the call center six years ago, we sometimes had parents waiting on line for two hours to get a question answered. Now, the average time to answer a call is 15 seconds and our response time for additional financial aid documents is under 24 hours. The University Call Center has dramatically increased our efficiency and has helped to ease the stress parents face by making sure they get the right answers in a timely manner. Plus, there's no more waiting on line!

Peggy Loewy-Wellisch, Associate Vice President for Student Financial Services, Nova Southeastern University

this situation, have a serious discussion with your child about how the family will pay for college. Make it clear that everyone is expected to contribute. An added bonus is that when students contribute, they are more highly motivated to do well in school because they understand the cost of an education.

Build your 401(k) and IRA accounts. Under both the federal and institutional methodologies, your retirement accounts are not considered assets that can be used to pay for college. Plus, under current tax laws you may withdraw money from these accounts and use it to pay tuition without paying a penalty. For most families, it's important not to neglect retirement accounts even as you save for college.

Check your pride at the door. Some parents are embarrassed to reveal financial information—especially financial misadventures—to a total stranger, but this kind of pride could cost you. Financial aid administrators are there to help. While financial aid calculations can seem very mechanical, it is the financial aid administrator who brings that all-important professional judgment to the process. If you have suffered a setback—especially one that is not reflected in your past year's taxes—inform the financial aid office. They have the power to modify the results of the financial aid calculations. The bottom line is quite simple: Financial aid administrators can save you money only if you let them.

Best Advice for a Low EFC

Don't waste time with strategies that may result in tiny increases in financial aid (which may be offset by higher taxes or lower asset levels) and that, at worst, could result in fines or jail time. Instead, focus on getting your taxes done early and correctly. Learn how to fill out the financial aid forms (see Chapter 4), and turn in the applications on time. In short, instead of looking for ways to game the system, focus on providing the most accurate and complete information possible to enable the financial aid administrator to help you get all the aid you deserve.

**Straight Talk
with a Financial Aid
Administrator**

A day in the life of a financial aid administrator

Varied and hectic are two words that come to mind for a financial aid administrator's workday.

One of the first things we do each morning is check on the spending availability of funds. We are managers, primarily of others' money. We are responsible for millions of dollars and must plan our spending accordingly. How many students are we able to help before funds are exhausted?

Our days are often spent dealing with students and their parents who have difficulties either registering or remaining in school. Families often don't understand that aid administrators must comply with the law. We can't disburse aid simply because we like you or you seem like a great person. Aid administrators also must deal with faculty and administrators from all over the university as well as run complex staff operations.

Amid these responsibilities, it's important for parents to know financial aid administrators are on their side. We always try to put students first. We all want your child to enroll in our college. To that end we will do whatever is legally in our power to assist you.

The best thing you can do is to let us know your personal situation. Sometimes the financial aid application doesn't adequately reflect a family's true financial situation. There may be circumstances that impact the needs analysis calculation. With proper proof, we can and will make adjustments to help make college affordable for you.

Courtney McAnuff, Vice President for Enrollment Services,
Eastern Michigan University

CHAPTER 4

How Do We Apply for Federal Financial Aid?

What you'll learn:

- How to complete the FAFSA, line by line
- Information you'll need to complete the aid application
- How to ensure a quick and painless filing
- What to do if you are selected for verification
- Tips for completing the CSS/PROFILE

When Nathan Rogers brought home a catalog for Washington University in St. Louis and enthusiastically described how "cool" the college was, his mother knew she could wait no longer. In eight months, Nathan would head off to college, which meant that Charity Rogers was running out of time to find the money to pay for it.

Charity knew that the first step was to sit down and help Nathan fill out the Free Application for Federal Student Aid (FAFSA), so she blocked out an entire weekend. To her surprise, they were finished in just over an hour. "I couldn't believe how straightforward it was!" she said.

If you're dreading the FAFSA, take a deep breath and relax. It takes time, but it's not as difficult as you may think. With some simple planning you can finish it in as little as an hour or two.

Filling Out the FAFSA

Asking for free money from the government is no more difficult than filling out the Free Application for Federal Student Aid (FAFSA). If your child is applying to a private college, you may also need to complete the CSS/PROFILE. The two forms require similar information.

HEAD START . . . .

Do your taxes. The best way to quickly and accurately complete the FAFSA is to do your taxes before you fill out the form. For most families, this means completing taxes in early January. You don't have to actually submit your taxes to the IRS—you can still wait until April—but having a completed tax return to lift numbers from will save a tremendous amount of time in calculations and will ensure that you don't have to amend the FAFSA later.

This chapter focuses on the FAFSA, as it is the form that all families must complete to be eligible for federal financial aid. Many state aid programs and private scholarships also rely on information from the FAFSA. At the end of the chapter are tips for completing the CSS/PROFILE.

The amount of time it will take you to complete the FAFSA depends on two factors: (1) how long it takes to gather the required information, and (2) the complexity of your family's finances. The best way to address both issues and ensure a painless FAFSA experience is to do your taxes early.

Do Your Taxes Early

If you are one of the millions of families who wait until April to start figuring out your taxes, it's time to change your ways—at least while your child is in college. The reason is simple: You'll need some of the numbers from your tax return to fill out the FAFSA. If your taxes aren't done, you'll spend more time doing calculations and will have to use estimates and update them later. If your taxes are done, you'll have the numbers you need.

Track Down Your Deadlines

When should you turn in the FAFSA or CSS/PROFILE? The earliest you may submit the FAFSA is January 1 of your child's senior year in high school, because the FAFSA requires tax information from the previous year. You may submit the CSS/PROFILE as soon as you receive it, which may be in October or November.

Every college sets its own deadline for the FAFSA and CSS/PROFILE, and the key is to find the earliest deadlines for the schools your child is applying to. Colleges often list their deadlines in the application forms. If your child's application arrives after the deadline, there may not be any funding left, even if your family deserves it.

The W-2 Catch-22

As a diligent parent who plans to do taxes early and submit the FAFSA as soon as possible after January 1, you might find yourself in a slight dilemma: You can't do taxes until you receive your W-2s, and some employers do not send them out until weeks after the end of the year. Tell your employer that you need a copy of your W-2 as soon as possible to file for financial aid. Or use your final paycheck stub for the previous year—it probably lists your cumulative earnings for the year, along with taxes paid. Don't be delayed by a late W-2.

Basic Eligibility Requirements

Before you fill out the FAFSA, make sure your child is eligible to receive federal financial aid. To receive aid, your child must meet the following requirements:

- Have a high school diploma or General Education Development (GED) certificate or pass an approved "ability to benefit" test
- Be a U.S. citizen or an eligible noncitizen
- Have a valid Social Security number (unless you are from the Republic of the Marshall Islands, the Federated States of Micronesia or the Republic of Palau)
- Enroll in an eligible associate's, bachelor's or graduate degree program
- Comply with the Selective Service registration, if required
- Not owe a refund on a federal grant or be in default on a federal education loan
- Have no drug convictions

If you have any questions about these requirements, contact the college financial aid office.

Is Your Child Dependent or Independent?

Financial aid is typically based on both the parents' and student's income and assets. Most students entering college directly from high school are considered dependent students, which means that the parent is expected to contribute to the child's educational expenses.

You may have heard that if your child declares independence, only his or her income and assets will be considered, resulting in a larger financial aid package. This is true, but specific rules govern when a student is considered independent for the purposes of financial aid.

A student is considered independent only if one of the following applies. He or she:

- Is at least 24 years old by December 31 of the award year
- Is married as of the date the FAFSA is completed

- Will be enrolled in a master's or doctoral program (beyond a bachelor's degree) during the award year
- Has at least one child who receives more than half of his or her support from the student
- Has a dependent (other than a child or a spouse) who lives with the student and receives more than half his or her support from the student
- Is a student for whom a financial aid administrator makes a documented determination of independence by reason of other unusual circumstances

As a parent, you may not simply say that you will not support your child through college and have him or her classified as an independent student. If this were possible, there would be many more independent students!

Rules for Divorced Parents

If the parents are divorced, the FAFSA should be completed with information from the parent with whom the child lived for the majority of time during the past 12 months. (It does not matter which parent claims the child as a dependent for tax purposes.) If the child did not live with either parent or lived equally with the two parents, the parental information on the FAFSA must be provided for the parent from whom the child received the most financial support during the preceding 12 months or the parent from whom the child received the most support in the last 12-month period during which support was given. If the parent providing the information has remarried, the stepparent's information is also required. A stepparent is considered a part of the student's family and therefore is expected to contribute to the student's educational expenses.

Hard Copy or E-Application?

You may submit the FAFSA through the Internet, using FAFSA on the Web, or you may complete a paper application. Regardless of which method you use, there is no charge for submitting the application.

FAFSA on the Web. To access the FAFSA on the Web, log on to the U.S. Department of Education's website at www.fafsa.ed.gov. Filing the FAFSA electronically has several advantages:

- Online help for each question
- Built-in checking that identifies potential errors before the application is processed
- Faster filing that brings results within one to five days

- Automatic calculations
- Software encryption that protects your personal information

If you use FAFSA on the Web, you will need to decide if you want to sign the application electronically. To sign electronically, request a personal identification number (PIN) at the PIN site (you will find the link at www.fafsa.ed.gov). Both the student and parent must have a PIN to sign electronically. Dependent students will also need to have one parent sign the application. Parents may use the same PIN to sign applications for multiple children.

If you would rather sign by paper, print out the signature page and mail it in. You will receive a PIN when your application is processed. This PIN can be used to access and sign a renewal FAFSA application for the next school year.

Paper FAFSA. If you prefer to fill out the paper application, you can download a copy (English or Spanish version) from www.salliemae.com or get a copy by contacting the Federal Student Aid Information Center (FSAIC) at

FSAIC
P.O. Box 84
Washington, DC 20044
1-800-4-FED-AID (1-800-433-3243)
TTY 1-800-730-8913

Straight Talk with a Financial Aid Administrator ▶ **Everyone should file the FAFSA online**

If at all possible I recommend that students file the FAFSA online. One of the benefits is internal checks within the online form that don't exist on the paper application. Making careless errors or forgetting to answer a question on the paper application can lead to delays that may result in missing the college's deadline or taking weeks to get the FAFSA to the point that a school can determine a student's aid eligibility. The online application won't let you continue if you forget to answer a question. It also does all the calculations for you. It's unfortunate, but even small mistakes can hold up the process. By filing online you avoid many of these pitfalls.

Jevita R. de Freitas, Director, Office of Student Financial Aid,
George Mason University

When you return the FAFSA by mail, include the return postcard so you'll know that the application got there. Also, make a copy of the entire application, in case it gets lost.

Save Time by Getting Your Papers in Order

It will take one to two hours to complete the FAFSA if you have all the necessary information, including your tax return, on hand. You will need the following key information and documents:

TIME SAVER . . . .

Get a PIN to sign the FAFSA electronically. If you are submitting the FAFSA over the Internet, a PIN allows you to sign it electronically without having to mail the signature page. Request a PIN from the Department of Education at www.pin.ed.gov. Both the student and the parent must have a PIN to sign the FAFSA electronically.

Student information:

- ❏ Social Security number
- ❏ Driver's license number
- ❏ Citizenship and state residency
- ❏ Alien registration card (if not a U.S. citizen)
- ❏ Prior year's W-2 forms and other records of money earned
- ❏ Prior year's federal income tax return—IRS Form 1040, 1040A, 1040EZ, 1040 Telefile, foreign tax return or tax return for Puerto Rico, Guam, American Samoa, the U.S. Virgin Islands, the Marshall Islands or the Federated States of Micronesia
- ❏ Asset information, including bank accounts, stocks, bonds, trust funds, etc.
- ❏ Education history
- ❏ Major course of study
- ❏ Marital status
- ❏ Spouse's income
- ❏ Dependency status
- ❏ Interest in student loans and work-study
- ❏ List of schools the student is interested in attending

Parent information:

- ❏ Federal income tax return. If you haven't completed your tax return by the time you fill out the FAFSA, use W-2 forms and other supporting documents. You may use estimates and correct them later.
- ❏ Past year's untaxed-income records—Social Security, Temporary Assistance to Needy Families, welfare or veterans benefit records

- ❑ Current bank statement
- ❑ Current business and investment mortgage information
- ❑ Business and farm asset and balance sheet records
- ❑ Asset information, including bank accounts, stocks, bonds, mutual funds, etc.
- ❑ Marital status
- ❑ Level of education
- ❑ State residency
- ❑ Age

If You File Online, Get the FAFSA on the Web Worksheet

If you complete the FAFSA online, download the FAFSA on the Web Worksheet, which is available in PDF format from www.fafsa.ed.gov/before001.htm. This worksheet contains the questions in the order they appear online. It is very helpful to complete this form before starting the online FAFSA application.

Who Completes the FAFSA—You or Your Child?

The FAFSA is designed to be completed by the student, although the parent may end up doing it. It is important to remember this, as any references in the application or instructions to "you" or "your" mean the student. When the parent's information is required, it will say "your parent." Don't get confused by this terminology.

The FAFSA, Line by Line

The FAFSA has 102 questions; in the following section, we cover each one. The online version asks for exactly the same information, although in a slightly different order. In bold are common mistakes to avoid.

Important note: *The FAFSA and tax form line numbers in this chapter are from the 2008-09 FAFSA and 2007 IRS forms, the most current available at the time of publication. Make sure these line numbers have not changed when you complete the FAFSA. In the following discussion, warnings about common mistakes are set in bold type.*

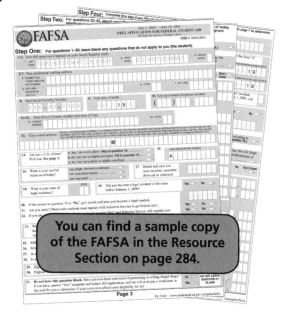

You can find a sample copy of the FAFSA in the Resource Section on page 284.

Straight Talk with a Financial Aid Administrator ▶ **Rule No. 1: Apply on time**

While the FAFSA takes time to complete, the questions are not rocket science level. Many are straightforward such as your name, address and Social Security number. While it's recommended to have your tax return complete before filing the FAFSA, it's certainly not required. You can always use estimates. Check with each college to make sure you are filing before the earliest priority deadline. No other rule will have more impact on how much aid you receive than to apply on time. Do whatever it takes to meet the deadline.

Dr. Lawrence Burt, Associate VP for Student Affairs & Director of Student Financial Services, University of Texas at Austin

Questions 1–31: Basic Student Information

1-3. Student's name. Make sure the student uses his or her legal name, the name on the Social Security card. The name and Social Security number will be compared with government records; using a nickname could delay processing of the FAFSA.

4-7. Student's permanent mailing address. The student should give his or her permanent home address. Don't use a school, dorm or office address.

8. Student's Social Security number. Unless the student is from the Republic of the Marshall Islands, the Federated States of Micronesia or the Republic of Palau, he or she must have a Social Security number to apply for financial aid. To get a Social Security number or a replacement Social Security card, contact the Social Security office at www.ssa.gov or call 1-800-772-1213. **Remember, this is the student's Social Security number; the parent's number is required later.**

9. Student's date of birth. Enter the date the student was born.

10. Student's phone number. Enter the student's permanent phone number.

11-12. Student's driver's license number and state. If the student has a driver's license, he or she must provide the license number and the state in which it was issued.

13. Student's e-mail address. If the student is filing the paper application, he or she should enter an e-mail address to receive confirmation that the FAFSA was received, as well as links to access the Student Aid Report online.

14. Student's citizenship status. To receive federal financial aid, a student must be a U.S. citizen or an eligible noncitizen. For financial aid purposes, an eligible noncitizen is one of the following:

- A permanent U.S. resident who has an alien registration receipt card (I-551 or I-151)
- A conditional permanent resident (I-551C)
- A noncitizen with a departure record (I-94) from U.S. Citizenship and Immigration Services (formerly the U.S. Immigration and Naturalization Service) showing any one of the following designations: "Refugee," "Asylum Granted," "Cuban-Haitian Entrant, Status Pending" or "Conditional Entrant" (valid only if issued before April 1, 1980)

A student is **not eligible** for federal student aid if he or she is in the United States on one of the following:

- An F-1, F-2 or M-1 student visa
- A J-1 or J-2 exchange visitor visa
- A B-1 or B-2 visitor visa
- A G series visa (pertaining to international organizations)
- An H series or L series visa (allowing temporary employment in the United States)
- A "Notice of Approval to Apply for Permanent Residence" (I-171 or I-464)
- An I-94 stamped "Temporary Protected Status"

Note! *If the student is not eligible for federal financial aid, he or she may still be eligible for state or institutional aid and should therefore complete the FAFSA.*

15. Student's Alien Registration Number (A-number). If the student is an eligible noncitizen, the student should enter his or her eight- or nine-digit A-number. Leave the first space blank if entering an eight-digit A-number.

16. Student's marital status. Marital status is reported as of the date the application is completed.

17. Date of marital status. The student should enter the date he or she was married, divorced, separated or widowed, if applicable.

BRIGHT IDEA . . . . . .

Avoid these common FAFSA pitfalls. The four most common mistakes in filling out the FAFSA are (1) not applying early enough, (2) not following the instructions, (3) not fully completing the application and (4) not using the correct Social Security number. Any of these mistakes can cause delays in processing your application, which may cause you to miss the college's deadline.

18. Student's state of legal residence. This information is used to determine the appropriate allowance for state and other taxes paid. It also indicates which state agency should receive a copy of the FAFSA information to determine eligibility for state-based financial aid.

If the student is "dependent," the state of legal residence is usually the state in which the parent lives. If the student moved to a different state for the sole purpose of attending a college, **do not** count that state as the student's legal residence.

19. Legal resident before specified year. States have varying criteria for determining whether a student is a resident for the purpose of state financial aid. However, if the student established a true, fixed and permanent home in any state more than four years ago, he or she will meet its residency criteria. The student should select "Yes" if he or she became a resident of the state before January 1 of the year specified, and "No" if he or she became a resident of the state on or after January 1 of the year specified.

20. Date of legal residence. If the student answered "No" to question 19, he or she needs to provide the month and year he or she became a legal resident of the state. The state will use this date to determine whether the student meets its residency criteria to receive state aid.

21. Are you male? To receive federal student financial aid, male students who are at least 18 years old and born after December 31, 1959, must be registered with the Selective Service.

22. Selective Service registration. If the student is male, is over 18 and has not registered with the Selective Service, he can do so by answering "Yes" to this question. The student can also register at www.sss.gov. **Female students should leave this question blank.**

23. Degree or certificate. The student should enter the one-digit code to indicate the type of degree. If none of the following options fits or the student is undecided, he or she should enter "9."

1   First bachelor's degree
2   Second bachelor's degree

(Select #2 only if the student has received a previous bachelor's degree from a college.)
3 Associate degree (occupational or technical program)
4 Associate degree (general education or transfer program)
5 Certificate or diploma for completing an occupational, technical or educational program of less than two years
6 Certificate or diploma for completing an occupational, technical or educational program of at least two years
7 Teaching credential program (nondegree program)
8 Graduate or professional degree
9 Other/undecided

24. Grade level during the award year. This question helps establish how much money the student can borrow under federal loan limits. Use the following one-digit codes to indicate grade level of the student for the award year.

0 Never attended college and first-year undergraduate
(High school seniors and first-time students should choose #0)
1 Attended college before/first-year undergraduate
2 Second-year undergraduate/sophomore
3 Third-year undergraduate/junior
4 Fourth-year undergraduate/senior
5 Fifth-year/other undergraduate
6 First-year graduate/professional
7 Continuing graduate/professional or beyond

25. Enrollment status. Identify what the student's enrollment status will be for the school year.

1 Full-time
2 Three-quarter-time
3 Half-time
4 Less than half-time
5 Don't know

26. Types of student aid. This question is used to identify which type of financial aid the student is interested in. Grants are not listed because the government assumes (correctly) that all students are interested in grants, which do not need to be repaid. It's recommended that you mark "3" for both work-study and student loans. If you are offered both, you may decide at a later time not to take them.

1 Work-study (student aid that you earn through work)
2 Student loans (which you must pay back)

3 Both work-study and student loans

4 Neither

5 Don't know

27. High school diploma/GED. If the student will receive a high school diploma or earn a General Educational Development (GED) certificate, he or she should select one of the following:

1 High school diploma

2 GED

3 Home schooled

4 Other

28. First bachelor's degree. This question has a direct bearing on eligibility for Federal Pell Grants and Federal Supplemental Educational Opportunity Grants, which are restricted to students who have not yet received a bachelor's degree. The only exception is for certain students taking courses for teacher certification, who may receive a Pell Grant. If the student will not receive a bachelor's degree before July 1, he or she should answer "No" to this question. **If the student incorrectly answers "Yes" to this question, he or she will be ineligible for Federal Pell and FSEOG Grants.**

29-30. Father's/mother's highest school level. These questions do not affect a student's eligibility for federal student aid. Some state and institutional programs offer aid to first-generation college students. "Father" and "mother" in these questions refer to the student's birth parents or adoptive parents, but not stepparents or foster parents. **The definition of "parents" as only birth or adoptive parents is unique to this question. In other parts of the FAFSA, "parents" may include stepparents and/or foster parents.**

31. Illegal drug offenses. This question asks whether the student has been convicted of possessing or selling illegal drugs. If the student has been convicted, he or she is not necessarily ineligible for aid. The student should still complete the FAFSA and will receive a worksheet that will determine whether the conviction affects his or her eligibility for federal student aid. Students who are ineligible for federal student aid may still be eligible for state or institutional aid. **Do not leave this question blank. Doing so will make the student ineligible to receive aid from federal student aid programs.**

DEADLINES . . . . . .

FAFSA. Submit the Free Application for Federal Student Aid (FAFSA) as soon as you can after January 1 of your child's senior year in high school. The earlier the better, since you don't want to miss a college's deadline.

CSS/PROFILE. You may submit the CSS/PROFILE as soon as you receive the form or sign up online. Check the deadlines established by the colleges that require the CSS/PROFILE to make sure you file it before the earliest deadline.

Questions 32–47: Student Income and Assets

This section collects information about the student's (and spouse's, if applicable) income and assets. The information is only about the student. Information about parent income and assets is collected later.

While this section may seem overly complex, it is designed to accommodate students who have complicated finances—such as those who own a business, are married or have worked overseas. For the typical college-bound high school student, this section should be relatively easy to complete.

It is highly recommended that the student (and spouse) complete their income tax return(s) before filling out this section. However, if the student has not completed his or her income tax return, he or she should estimate the adjusted gross income (AGI) and taxes paid. Any differences between the estimated and actual numbers can be corrected later. Even if the student is not required to file an income tax return, he or she will still need to calculate earnings for the year. Use W-2 forms and other records (such as 1099s) to answer the questions in this section.

Note: The tax form line numbers and exemption amounts in this section are from 2007 IRS tax rules. The 2008 rules were not established at the time of publication—be sure to confirm this information when completing the FAFSA.

Base year. For the 2008-09 academic year, the base year for completing income tax questions is 2007. For the 2009-10 academic year, the base year is 2008.

Income earned in a foreign country. Income earned in a foreign country is treated the same as income earned in the United States. Convert all figures to dollars, using the exchange rate in effect on the day the FAFSA is completed. Include the value of any taxes paid to the foreign government in the "U.S. income tax paid" line item. If income earned in the foreign country was not taxed by the central government of that country, the income should be reported as untaxed income on Student Worksheet B (see page 80).

32. Filing return. The student should indicate whether he or she has already completed, is going to complete or will not file a tax return. If the student is not going to file a tax return, he or she may skip to question 38.

33. Type of return filed. Indicate which tax form the student filed or will file.

34. Eligible to file a 1040A or 1040EZ. Indicate whether the student is eligible to file a 1040A or 1040EZ, even if the student filed a Form 1040. **Tax preparers often file a Form 1040 on behalf of tax filers, even though their income would allow them to file a 1040A or 1040EZ. Check with your tax preparer to confirm whether the student is eligible to file a 1040A or 1040EZ.**

While the type of tax form used may not seem like an important distinction, it can make a big difference in financial aid. If both you and your child are eligible to file a 1040A or 1040EZ and you together earn less than $50,000 in income, you may qualify for the "simplified needs test," which ignores the value of all assets. In other words, none of your family's assets will be considered when calculating financial aid, which can have a dramatic impact on how much your child receives.

In general, you are eligible to file a 1040A or 1040EZ if you make less than $100,000, do not itemize deductions, do not receive income from your own business or farm and do not receive alimony. You are not eligible to file a 1040A or

---

Straight Talk with a Financial Aid Administrator ▶ **Applying for financial aid is not the same as doing your taxes**

Some families approach applying for financial aid with the same mentality as filing their taxes. It's easy to see why, since on the surface the process looks similar. But this can lead to problems.

For taxes you try to look for loopholes and do whatever you can to minimize the amount of taxes you pay. Some parents may wonder, why shouldn't I also do this for financial aid? The reason is the underlying philosophies are different. The government uses the tax code to encourage people to make certain decisions. Putting more money toward retirement or buying a house are goals the government encourages through providing tax breaks.

The financial aid process is much different. Our goal is to distribute limited resources to help the most students afford a college education. If everyone fills out the form as they are supposed to, that gives me a good indication of a family's financial strength relative to others. I have to depend on families with resources to do the "morally correct" thing. If you have resources to help your child with their education and you don't tap into those resources, you may be contributing toward denying someone else who is deserving. I know this flies in the face of our capitalistic economy and way of thinking. But we are trying to equalize opportunity for education. Therefore, unlike trying to pay the least amount of taxes possible, when it comes to financial aid, parents need to be as accurate about their financial resources as possible.

James M. Bauer, Assistant Dean of Enrollment Management and Director of Financial Assistance Services, University of Miami

1040EZ if you itemize deductions, receive self-employment income or alimony or are required to file Schedule D for capital gains. **If you filed a 1040 only to claim Hope or Lifetime Learning credits and would otherwise have been eligible to file a 1040A or 1040EZ, answer "Yes" to this question.**

35. Adjusted gross income. The student needs to provide his or her AGI, as well as that of the spouse, if applicable. AGI is found on IRS Form 1040, line 37; 1040A, line 21 or 1040EZ, line 4. If the student has not completed a tax form, he or she should calculate AGI using the instructions for Form 1040.

36. Income tax. Enter the amount of income tax the student (and his or her spouse) paid from IRS Form 1040, line 57; 1040A, line 35 or 1040EZ, line 10. If the student did not pay any income tax, enter zero.

37. Exemptions. If the student has exemptions, he or she should enter them here. Exemptions can be found on IRS Form 1040, line 6d, or 1040A, line 6d. If the student answered "Yes" on 1040EZ, line 5, use EZ worksheet line F to determine the number of exemptions ($3,400 equals one exemption). If the student answered "No" on line 5, enter "01" if single and "02" if married. If the student is divorced, separated or widowed but has filed or will file a joint tax return, he or she should list only his or her portion of the exemptions.

38. Student's income earned. Students are allowed certain protections on income earned from work. The student should enter the total amount of earned income before deductions and taxes. This information is found on W-2 forms and on IRS Form 1040, (total of lines 7 + 12 + 18 + box 14 of IRS Schedule K-1); 1040A, line 7; or 1040EZ, line 1.

39. Spouse's income earned. If the student is married, the spouse's income must be included.

Student Worksheets A, B and C

Worksheets A, B and C help the student compute the answers for Questions 40–42. You can get these worksheets at www.fafsa.ed.gov by clicking on "FAFSA on the Web Worksheet" under "Before Beginning a FAFSA." The worksheets are also printed in the application booklet of the paper FAFSA.

The following income and benefits should not be reported on Worksheets A and B.

Combat pay for non-tax filers. If the student (or spouse) did not file a tax return, he or she must report any combat pay received as income earned from work in Question 38 or 39. None of it should be reported on Worksheet B. This prevents a double counting of funds.

Student financial aid. Past or current student aid is already taken into account when a school determines new aid. Work-study earnings are reported as taxed income in the income questions (32–47) and then excluded on Worksheet C.

Food stamps and other programs. Benefits received from the following federal, state or local government programs are not counted: Food Stamp Program; Special Supplemental Nutrition Program for Women, Infants and Children (WIC); Food Distribution Program; Commodity Supplemental Food Program; National School Lunch and School Breakfast Programs; Summer Food Service Program; and Special Milk Program for Children.

Dependent assistance. The student may be eligible to exclude a limited amount of benefits received for dependent care assistance if certain requirements are met. Generally, up to $5,000 of benefits may be excluded from an employee's gross income, or $2,500 for a married employee who files a separate return from his or her spouse. This exclusion may not exceed the employee's (or the spouse's) earned income. (Note: Some states provide reimbursement for child care expenses incurred by welfare recipients through Temporary Assistance for Needy Families, or TANF. The student must report this on the application, because the student bills the state for child care costs incurred while he or she is on welfare and is reimbursed on that basis.)

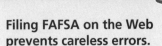

TIME SAVER . . . .

Filing FAFSA on the Web prevents careless errors.
Besides getting faster results, if you submit the FAFSA over the Internet you can dramatically decrease your chances of making careless mistakes that could delay the application. This is because the electronic FAFSA has internal checks that not only perform all calculations but also prevent you from submitting the form if you forget to answer a question.

Per capita payments to Native Americans. The student should not report individual per capita payments received from the Per Capita Act or the Distribution of Judgment Funds Act unless any individual payment exceeds $2,000. Thus, if an individual payment were $1,500, the student would not report it; however, if a payment were $2,500, the student would report the amount that exceeds $2,000, or $500.

Heating/fuel assistance. Exclude from consideration as income or resources any payments or allowances received under the Low-Income Home Energy Assistance Act

(LIHEA). Payments under LIHEA are made through state programs that may have different names.

Student Worksheet A

Student/Spouse	Worksheet A Report Annual Amounts	Parents
For question 40		For question 84
$	Earned income credit from IRS Form 1040—line 66a; 1040A—line 40a; or 1040EZ—line 8a.	$
$	Additional child tax credit from IRS Form 1040—line 68 or 1040A—line 41.	$
$	Welfare benefits, including Temporary Assistance for Needy Families (TANF). Don't include food stamps or subsidized housing.	$
$	Social Security benefits received, that were not taxed (such as SSI), for all household members reported in question 90 (or 66 for your parents). Report benefits paid to parents in the Parents column, and benefits paid directly to student (or spouse) in the Student/Spouse column.	$
$	—Enter in question 40. Enter in question 84. —	$

This worksheet helps the student determine how much in untaxed benefits he or she received. This income will be added to the student's adjusted gross income. You will need the following information to complete Worksheet A.

Earned income credit. Enter the earned income credit from IRS Form 1040, line 66a; 1040A, line 40a or 1040EZ, line 8a.

Additional child tax credit. Report the amount from IRS Form 1040, line 66, or 1040A, line 41.

Welfare benefits. Enter the total amount of welfare benefits the student (and spouse) received, including TANF. Report the amount the student received for the year, not monthly amounts. **Do not include the annual value of food stamps or subsidized housing.**

Untaxed Social Security benefits for all household members for students who are classified as independent. If Social Security benefits were paid to the student's parents because the student was under 18 years old, these are reported as parent income, not student income. But if the student, as head of household, received benefits on behalf of persons included in his or her household, these benefits must be reported as student income. If a member of the student's household, such as an uncle or grandmother, received benefits in his or her own name, the student does not report those benefits as part of student income.

40. Enter the result of Worksheet A.

Student Worksheet B

Worksheet B
Report Annual Amounts

For question 41		For question 85
$	Payments to tax-deferred pension and savings plans (paid directly or withheld from earnings), including, but not limited to, amounts reported on the W-2 Form in Boxes 12a through 12d, codes D, E, F, G, H and S.	$
$	IRA deductions and payments to self-employed SEP, SIMPLE, and Keogh and other qualified plans from IRS Form 1040—line 28 + line 32 or 1040A—line 17.	$
$	Child support received for all children. Don't include foster care or adoption payments.	$
$	Tax exempt interest income from IRS Form 1040—line 8b or 1040A—line 8b.	$
$	Foreign income exclusion from IRS Form 2555—line 45 or 2555EZ—line 18.	$
$	Untaxed portions of IRA distributions from IRS Form 1040—lines (15a minus 15b) or 1040A—lines (11a minus 11b). Exclude rollovers. If negative, enter a zero here.	$
$	Untaxed portions of pensions from IRS Form 1040—lines (16a minus 16b) or 1040A—lines (12a minus 12b). Exclude rollovers. If negative, enter a zero here.	$
$	Credit for federal tax on special fuels from IRS Form 4136—line 17 (nonfarmers only).	$
$	Housing, food and other living allowances paid to members of the military, clergy and others (including cash payments and cash value of benefits).	$
$	Veterans noneducation benefits such as Disability, Death Pension, or Dependency & Indemnity Compensation (DIC) and/or VA Educational Work-Study allowances.	$
$	Other untaxed income not reported elsewhere on Worksheets A and B, such as workers' compensation, untaxed portions of railroad retirement benefits, Black Lung Benefits, disability, etc. Tax filers only: report combat pay not included in AGI (FAFSA questions 35 and 79). Don't include student aid, Workforce Investment Act educational benefits, combat pay if you are not a tax filer, or benefits from flexible spending arrangements (e.g., cafeteria plans).	$
$	Money received, or paid on your behalf (e.g., bills), not reported elsewhere on this form.	XXXXXXXX
$ —Enter in question 41.		Enter in question 85. —$

This worksheet helps the student determine how much untaxed income he or she received. This amount will be added to the student's AGI. You will need the following information to complete Worksheet B.

Payments to tax-deferred pension and savings plans. The student must report money paid into tax-sheltered or deferred annuities (whether paid directly or withheld from earnings), including, but not limited to, amounts reported on the W-2 form in boxes 12a–12d, codes D, E, F, G, H and S. The student must include untaxed portions of 401(k) and 403(b) plans. **Do not report employer contributions to tax-deferred pension and savings plans as untaxed benefits.**

IRAs and other plans. Enter the amount of IRA deductions and payments to self-employed SEP, SIMPLE and Keogh and other qualified plans. These plan payments can be found on IRS 1040, total of lines 28 + 32, or 1040A, line 17.

Child support. Report child support the student received for all children. Do not include foster care or adoption payments.

Tax-exempt interest income. Enter the total amount of tax-exempt interest income the student (and spouse) earned, as reported on Form 1040 or 1040A, line 8b.

Foreign income exclusion. The IRS allows eligible U.S. citizens and residents living in foreign countries to exclude a limited amount of income earned abroad. Although deducted for tax purposes, this amount is considered untaxed income for federal student aid purposes. Give the amount of the foreign income exclusion the student (and spouse) reported on Form 2555, line 45, or 2555EZ, line 18.

Untaxed portions of IRA distributions. This amount can be calculated from IRS Form 1040 (line 15a minus 15b) or 1040A (line 11a minus 11b). If the result is a negative number, enter a zero here.

Untaxed portions of pensions. This amount can be calculated from IRS Form 1040 (line 16a minus 16b) or 1040A (line 12a minus 12b). If the result is a negative number, enter a zero here.

The student does not have to report IRA or pension distributions as income if these distributions were rolled over to another IRA or retirement plan within 60 days of the day on which the student received the distribution from the initial IRA or retirement plan.

Special fuels credit. Enter the total amount of credit for federal tax on special fuels that the student (and spouse) reported on IRS Form 4136, line 18 (nonfarmers only).

Housing, food and other living allowances. Allowances provided to the student (and spouse) that are reported on a W-2 form must be entered here. These may be part of a compensation package that some people (such as clergy and military personnel) receive for their jobs. Include cash payments and cash value of benefits. If the student received free room and board for a job that was not awarded as student financial aid, he or she must report the value of the room and board as untaxed income. (Rent subsidies for low-income housing are not included.)

Veterans noneducation benefits. Enter the total amount of veterans noneducation benefits the student received. Include disability, death pension, dependency and indemnity compensation (DIC) and/or VA educational work-study allowances.

Other untaxed income and benefits. Include untaxed income or benefits not reported elsewhere on Worksheets A and B, such as worker's compensation, untaxed portion of railroad retirement benefits, untaxed portion of capital gains, Black Lung Benefits, Refugee Assistance, disability, foreign income that wasn't taxed by any government and so on. Do not include benefits from flexible spending arrangements (e.g., cafeteria plans), student aid or Workforce Investment Act (WIA, formerly JTPA) educational benefits.

Money received. Report any cash support the student received from a friend or relative (other than parents, if the student is a dependent). Cash support includes payments made on the student's behalf. For example, if an aunt pays the student's rent or utility bill, the student must report those payments on Worksheet B.

41. Enter the result of Worksheet B.

Student Worksheet C

Worksheet C

For question 42	Report Annual Amounts	For question 86
$	Education credits (Hope and Lifetime Learning tax credits) from IRS Form 1040—line 49 or 1040A—line 31.	$
$	Child support paid because of divorce or separation or as a result of a legal requirement. Don't include support for children in your (or your parents') household, as reported in question 90 (or question 66 for your parents).	$
$	Taxable earnings from need-based employment programs, such as Federal Work-Study and need-based employment portions of fellowships and assistantships.	$
$	Student grant and scholarship aid reported to the IRS in your (or your parents') adjusted gross income. Includes AmeriCorps benefits (awards, living allowances and interest accrual payments), as well as grant or scholarship portions of fellowships and assistantships.	$
$ —Enter in question 42.	Enter in question 86. — $	

This worksheet helps the student determine what may be excluded from income for the purposes of financial aid. This amount will be subtracted from the student's adjusted gross income. Because the items listed in this worksheet will be excluded from income, the student should not subtract them from responses to the previous income questions. You will need the following information to complete Worksheet C.

Education credits. The Hope and Lifetime Learning tax credits benefit students or parents who pay tuition and related expenses for attendance at least half time in a degree-granting program. These tax credits are subtracted directly from the total federal tax on a tax return. Enter the total amount of Hope and Lifetime Learning credits the student received from Form 1040, line 49, or 1040A, line 31.

Child support payments. Report any child support payments made by the student (or spouse) because of divorce or separation, or as a result of a legal requirement. Do not include support for children in the student's household.

Taxable earnings from need-based employment programs. These are earnings from any need-based work programs, including Federal Work-Study and need-based employment portions of fellowships and assistantships.

Student grants and other awards. Report any student grant and scholarship aid that was reported to the IRS as income. This category includes AmeriCorps benefits (awards, living allowances and interest accrual payments) as well as grant and scholarship portions of fellowships and assistantships.

42. Enter the result of Worksheet C.

Questions 43–45: Student Asset Information

The following questions ask for information about the student's assets. Even if a family qualifies for the simplified Expected Family Contribution, in which assets are not counted, it is important to provide asset information, because many states and schools use this information for their own aid programs. Not providing the information may exclude the student from these programs.

What is an asset?

An asset is defined as property that has an exchange value. The purpose of collecting asset information is to determine whether the student's assets are substantial enough to support a contribution toward his or her cost of attendance. Only the net asset value is counted. To determine the net value of any asset, the student first determines the market value of the asset and then subtracts the amount of debt against that asset. The result is the net value.

Divided or contested assets

Part ownership of asset. If the student (or spouse) owns an asset with others and, therefore, owns only a portion or percentage of it, the student (or spouse) should report only the net asset value of his or her share of the asset.

Contested ownership. An asset should not be reported if its ownership is being legally contested. For example, if the student and his or her spouse are separated and the student may not sell or borrow against jointly owned property that is being contested, the FAFSA would not list any value for the property or any debts against it.

Lien against asset. If there is a lien or imminent foreclosure against an asset, the asset should be reported on the FAFSA until the party holding the lien or making the foreclosure completes legal action to take possession of the asset.

Unreported assets

Principal place of residence or family farm. The student's principal place of residence is not reported as an asset, nor is the student's family farm if the farm is the principal place of residence and it is claimed on Schedule F that the family "materially participated in the farm's operation."

A small business with 100 or fewer employees. If the student's family owns and controls a small business that has 100 or fewer full-time or full-time equivalent employees, the business should not be reported as an asset.

Personal possessions. Do not report possessions such as a car, stereo, clothes or furniture. By the same token, personal debts such as credit card debt may not be reported.

Pensions and whole-life insurance. The cash value or built-up equity of a life insurance (whole-life) policy should not be reported as an asset. However, any income distributed to the beneficiary should be reported as income.

Excluded assets from Native American students. Do not report any property received under the Per Capita Act, the Distribution of Judgment Funds Act, the Alaska Native Claims Settlement Act or the Maine Indian Claims Settlement Act.

Treatment of investments

Rental property. Generally, rental properties must be reported as investment assets rather than as business assets. To be reported as a business, a rental property would have to be part of a formally recognized business. Usually such a business would provide additional services, such as regular cleaning, linen or maid service.

Take-back mortgages. In a take-back mortgage, the seller takes back a portion of the mortgage from the buyer and arranges for the buyer to repay that portion directly to the seller. For IRS purposes, the seller must report the interest portion of any payments received from the buyer on Schedule B of IRS Form 1040. If an amount is reported on this line of the tax return, the student should report the outstanding balance of the remaining mortgage on the FAFSA as an investment asset.

Trust funds. If trust funds are in the student's (or spouse's) name, they should be reported as the student's (or spouse's) asset on the application. In the case of divorce or separation, where the trust is owned jointly and ownership is not being contested, the property and the debt are equally divided between the owners for reporting purposes, unless the terms of the trust specify some other method of division.

TIME SAVER . . . .

Filing the FAFSA electronically is faster than by paper. The whole world is moving online, and so is the Department of Education. If you use FAFSA on the Web and sign electronically, your application will be processed a week or two sooner than if you use the paper form.

How the trust must be reported varies according to whether the student (or spouse) receives or will receive the interest income, the trust principal or both. If the student (or spouse) receives only interest from the trust, any interest received in the base year must be reported as income. Even if interest accumulates in the trust and is not paid out during the year, if the student will receive the interest, the student must report an asset value for the interest to be received in the future. The trust officer can usually

Straight Talk with a Financial Aid Administrator ▶ **FAFSA tricks that failed**

Some tricks parents try are adding more people to the number in the household than for whom they actually provide more than half support; undervaluing assets, such as bank accounts; and putting incorrect marital status, such as stating separated and not married, in order to reduce the income in the household. We have become very good at spotting these types of tricks. For example, we can compare the reported number in the family's household with what they report on their tax form. We may also notice interest income is greater than the assets reported. In these instances we will need proof of the information via tax forms and/or written statements. There are also stiff penalties for knowingly providing false information.

Peggy Loewy-Wellisch, Associate Vice President for Student Financial Services, Nova Southeastern University

calculate the present value of interest the beneficiary will receive while the trust exists. This value represents the amount a third person would be willing to pay to receive the interest income the beneficiary will receive from the trust in the future.

The present value of the principal is the amount a third person would pay today for the right to receive the principal when the trust ends (basically, the amount that would have to deposited now to receive the amount of the principal when the trust ends, including the accumulated interest). Again, the trust officer can calculate the present value.

As a general rule, the student must report the present value of the trust as an asset, even if access to the trust is restricted. If the creator of a trust has voluntarily placed restrictions on the use of the trust, the student should report the trust as if there were no restrictions. If a trust has been restricted by court order, however, the student should not report it as an asset. An example of such a restricted trust is one set up by a court order to pay for future surgery for the victim of a car accident.

43. Total current cash, savings and checking account balance. The student must include the balance of all checking or savings accounts as of the date the FAFSA is signed. Do not include money from student financial aid.

44. Net worth of investments. Investments include real estate such as rental property, land and second or summer homes. Do not include the student's primary place of residence, but do include the value of portions of multifamily dwellings that are not the student's principal residence.

Investments also include trust funds, Uniform Transfers to Minors Act (UTMA)/ Uniform Gifts to Minors Act (UGMA) custodial accounts, money market funds, mutual funds, certificates of deposit, stocks, stock options, bonds, other securities, Coverdell savings accounts, college savings plans, the refund value of 529 prepaid tuition plans (if student is independent), installment and land sale contracts (including mortgages held), commodities and so on. Do not include the value of life insurance and retirement plans (pension funds, annuities, noneducation IRAs, Keogh plans, etc.)

The value of all qualified educational benefits or education savings accounts, such as Coverdell savings accounts, 529 college savings plans or the refund value of a 529 prepaid tuition plan should be reported in Question 44 if the student owns the account and is not reporting parental information on the application.

Remember, Investment Value - Investment Debt = Net Worth of Investments. Investment debt is how much the student (and/or his or her spouse) owes on real estate and investments other than the principal residence. Investment debt includes

---

Straight Talk with a Financial Aid Administrator	**Don't ever try to manipulate your information**

There are many opportunities for us to detect when a family is trying to manipulate their information. With a practiced eye, you can easily pick out these deceptions. When you see a house that has been owned for a long time but has no equity, that is a red flag that marks the case for more investigation. We also make assumptions based on the facts we do know. For example, if we see dividend or interest income of $1,000 but the family is reporting only a few hundred dollars in assets, we immediately know we need to dig deeper. Because we know approximately what interest rates the banks and savings and loans are paying, we have a pretty good sense of what it takes to generate a certain level of income, so we scrutinize assets carefully. Sometimes we can compare the family's lifestyle with the numbers they have  reported to figure out what is going on. This is an intuitive process but, ultimately, we get to the bottom line. If a family is caught being dishonest it tends to taint the process. I just don't think the risk is worth the reward—particularly if the dishonesty is spotted by the feds.

Jim Belvin, Director of Financial Aid, Duke University

only those debts that are related to the investments. Subtract the amount of debt on these assets from their value to determine the net worth.

45. Net worth of business and/or investment farm. Business or farm value includes the current market value of land, buildings, machinery, equipment, inventory and so on. Do not include the value of the student's primary home.

As with investments, remember, Business/Farm Value - Business/Farm Debt = Net Worth of Business/Farm. For business or investment farm value, first figure out how much the business or farm is worth today. Business or investment farm debts are what the student (and/or his or her spouse) owes on the business or farm. Include only debts for which the business or farm was used as collateral. Subtract the amount of debt from the value to determine the net worth of a business and/or investment farm.

To report current market value for a business, the student must use the amount for which the business could sell as of the date of the application. If the student is not the sole owner of the business, he or she should report only his or her share of its value and debt.

Questions 46–47: Veterans Education Benefits

46. Number of months veterans education benefits received. Enter the number of months during the award year (July 1-June 30), that the student expects to receive veterans education benefits. If the student does not receive veterans education benefits, enter zero.

47. Amount of veterans education benefits. Veterans education benefit information is not used in the financial aid calculation; however, a college will use it when putting together the aid package. If the student receives veterans education benefits, the amount of monthly benefits expected during the award year (July 1-June 30), must be reported. Do not include a spouse's veterans education benefits. Such benefits include, but are not limited to,

- Montgomery GI Bill—Active Duty (MGIB)
- Reserve Officer Training Corps (ROTC) scholarship
- Post Vietnam Veterans Educational Assistance Program (VEAP)
- Dependents Educational Assistance Program (DEA)
- Reservists Educational Assistance Program (REAP)

Questions 48–54: Dependency Status

The purpose of these questions is to determine whether the student is dependent or independent for purposes of financial aid. Students who answer "No" to all questions are considered dependent students, even if they do not live with their parents. Even if the student has unusual circumstances, this section must be answered. A school's financial aid administrator has the authority to override a student's dependency status on the initial application or by correcting the Student Aid Report if the financial aid administrator decides that a dependent student should be considered an independent student.

After completing this section, a dependent student moves to questions 56–89 and provides information about his or her parents. An independent student skips questions 56–89 and picks up with question 90 to continue through to the end of the application.

48. Was the student born before January 1, 1985? If the student was born on or after January 1, 1985 (for the 2008-09 school year), he or she should answer "No."

49. At the beginning of the school year, will the student be working on a master's or doctoral program (MA, MBA, MD, JD, PhD, EdD, graduate certificate, etc.)? The student should answer "Yes" if he or she will be enrolled in a master's or doctoral program. If the student will be finishing a bachelor's degree in the first term of the school year and then moving on to a master's or doctoral program, the student should answer "No." Once the student has completed the undergraduate degree, he or she must notify the financial aid office and change this answer to "Yes."

Be careful to answer this question correctly, as a graduate or professional student is not eligible for a Federal Pell Grant, Federal Supplemental Educational Opportunity Grant, an ACG Grant or a National SMART Grant.

50. As of today, is the student married? Answer "Yes" if the student is legally married on the date of the application. "Married" does not mean living together unless the student's state recognizes the relationship as a common-law marriage. Answer "Yes" if the student is separated but not divorced.

51. Does the student have children who receive more than half their support from the student? "Support" is defined as financial support. An applicant whose unborn child will be born before June 30 of the end of the award year may answer "Yes." This applies to both male and female students. The key to this question is financial support, not whether the child lives with the student.

52. Does the student have other dependents (besides a child or spouse) who live with the student and receive more than half their support from the student, now and through June 30 of the end of the award year? Again, the FAFSA is asking about financial support. For a "Yes" answer, the dependent must actually live with the student.

53. Are both of the student's parents deceased or is/was the student a ward or dependent of the court? The student should answer "Yes" if both parents are dead and the student does not have an adoptive parent. If both parents are dead and the student has a legal guardian, the student should still answer "Yes." Also, the student should answer "Yes" if he or she is currently a ward or dependent of the court or was a ward or dependent until age 18.

54. Is the student currently serving on active duty in the U.S. Armed Forces for purposes other than training? Answer "Yes" if the student is currently serving in the U.S. Armed Forces or is a National Guard or Reserves enlistee who is on active duty for other than training purposes. Answer "No" if the student is a National Guard or Reserves enlistee who is on active duty for state or training purposes.

55. Is the student a veteran of the U.S. armed forces? Answer "Yes" if the student has been on active duty in the Army, Navy, Air Force, Marines or Coast Guard; was a member of the National Guard or Reserves who was called to active duty for purposes other than training; or was a cadet or midshipman at one of the service academies. The student must have been released from service under a condition other than dishonorable. Box 24 of DD214, the military discharge form, indicates "Character of Service." If anything other than "dishonorable" appears in the box, the student should answer "Yes" to question 55. No minimum amount of service is required to be considered a veteran for federal student aid

BRIGHT IDEA . . . . . .

In a pinch, use estimates. Doing your taxes before you fill out the FAFSA is highly recommended. However, if you are unable to do that, use estimates. You may need to update these numbers after you've done your taxes. But if you wait until April to apply for financial aid, you may miss the college deadlines and jeopardize your child's chances of getting aid. It's far better to use estimates than to miss the deadlines.

purposes, but the service must be "active service." Answer "Yes" if the student is not a veteran now but will be one by June 30 of the end of the award year.

The student should answer "No" to this question if he or she is currently a member of ROTC, a cadet or midshipman at a service academy or a National Guard or Reserves enlistee activated only for training purposes, or is currently serving in the U.S. armed forces and scheduled to serve through June 30 of the end of the award year.

Dependent or independent

If your child answered "Yes" to any of questions 48–55, he or she is considered to be independent and may skip questions 56–89. (If your child is a health professions student, the school may require him or her to complete questions 56–89 even if the child answered "Yes" to any of the dependency questions.) Otherwise, if your child answered "No" to questions 48–55, continue with the following questions about **parent** income and assets.

Questions 56-89: Parents of Dependent Students

Parents must provide financial information for questions 56–89 if their child is a dependent student. As you learned in Chapter 3, a percentage of your income and assets will be used in the financial aid calculation.

Who is considered a parent?

The term "parent" is not restricted to biological parents. There are instances (such as when a grandparent *legally adopts* the applicant) in which a person other than a biological parent is treated as a parent. In these situations, the parental questions on the application must be answered. The following are the most common parental situations and how they impact the financial aid application.

Married parents. If both parents are living and are married to each other, they must answer the questions about each of them. If the parents are living together and have not been formally married but meet the criteria in their state for a common-law marriage, they should report their status as married on the application. If the state does not consider their situation to be a common-law marriage, they should follow the rules for divorced parents.

Adoptive parents. An adoptive parent is treated in the same manner as a biological parent on the FAFSA. A foster parent, legal guardian or grandparent or other relative, however, is not treated as a parent for purposes of filing a FAFSA unless that person has legally adopted the student.

Surviving parent. If one parent has died, the answers should be about the surviving parent. Do not report any financial information for the deceased parent. If the surviving parent dies after the FAFSA has been filed, the student must submit a correction to question 53, updating his or her dependency status to independent, and must correct all other information as appropriate. If the surviving parent is re-married as of the date on which the FAFSA is completed, the answers must include information from the new spouse (i.e., the student's stepparent).

Divorced or separated parents. If the parents are divorced or separated, answer the questions about the parent the student lived with more during the 12 months preceding the application. If a student did not live with one parent more than the other, give answers about the parent who provided more financial support during this 12-month period or during the most recent year that the student received support from a parent. If this parent has remarried as of the date of filing the FAFSA, answer the questions on the remaining sections of the application about this parent and the spouse (i.e., the student's stepparent).

If the parents are legally separated, the same rules that apply for a divorced couple are used to determine which parent's information must be reported. A couple doesn't have to be legally separated to be considered separated for purposes of the FAFSA. The couple may consider themselves informally separated when one of the partners has left the household permanently. If the partners live together, they are not considered informally separated.

Treatment of a stepparent. A stepparent is treated in the same manner as a biological parent if the stepparent is married, as of the date of application, to the biological parent whose information will be reported on the FAFSA or if the stepparent has legally adopted the student. There are no exceptions. Prenuptial agreements do not exempt the stepparent from providing required data on the FAFSA. The stepparent's income information for the entire base year must be reported, no matter when in the year the parent and stepparent got married.

Straight Talk with a Financial Aid Administrator ▶ **Beware of who you pay for help with the FAFSA**

One problem we encounter is when a family hires someone to fill out the FAFSA. Sometimes these people are unscrupulous. Families need to beware of anyone who promises a certain amount of aid or that the student will definitely get gift aid if their service is used. These people usually use incorrect information. This is illegal, and unfortunately for the family they are the ones who are liable. Often these supposed experts will only accept payment in cash so the family has no paper trail back to them. Several years ago our computer flagged 10 families who had identical information on their FAFSA. When we investigated, it turned out all the families had used the same paid service to complete their FAFSAs. And, of course, they had all paid in cash.

Courtney McAnuff, Vice President for Enrollment Services, Eastern Michigan University

Special situations. Any special circumstances must be brought to the attention of the financial aid office at the college, where the financial aid administrator will review the situation and issue a decision. For the purpose of completing the FAFSA, dependent students must provide parental information. **For special situations, it is best to file the FAFSA according to the instructions and then contact the financial aid office regarding the special situation.**

56. Parents' marital status as of today. The FAFSA asks about your marital status because it directly affects the treatment of income and assets in calculating the Expected Family Contribution.

57. Month and year parents were married, separated, divorced or widowed.

58. Father's/stepfather's Social Security number. All dependent applicants must provide the Social Security number of the parent providing financial data on the application. If a parent doesn't have a Social Security number, enter 000-00-0000.

59-61. Father's/stepfather's last name, first initial and date of birth. Use the name on the Social Security card. The name must match the information in the Social Security Administration's records.

62. Mother's/stepmother's Social Security number.

63-65. Mother's/stepmother's last name, first initial and date of birth.

66. Number in parents' household. The number of family members determines the amount of an allowance that protects a portion of the reported income; this amount is subtracted from the family's income in the Expected Family Contribution calculation. The following persons are included in household size:

- The student—even if not living with the parents
- The parents (the ones whose information is reported on the FAFSA)
- Parents' other children, as long as parents provide more than half their support from July 1 through June 30 of the award year, or if the other children could answer "No" to every question in questions 48–55, which means they are dependent students age 24 or younger
- Parents' unborn child, if that child will be born before July 1 of the end of the award year
- Other people who live with and receive more than half their support from the parents at the time of application and who will continue to receive that support from July 1 through June 30 of the award year

To determine whether to include children in household size, the support test is used rather than a residency requirement, because there may be situations in which a parent supports a child who does not live with the parent, especially in cases where the parent is divorced or separated. In such cases, the parent who provides more than half the child's support may claim the child in his or her household. It does not matter which parent claims the child as a dependent for tax purposes. If a parent receives benefits such as Social Security or Aid to Families with Dependent Children (AFDC) payments in the child's name, these benefits must be counted as parental support to the child. Support includes money, gifts, loans, housing, food, clothes, car payments or expenses, medical and dental care and payment of college costs.

67. Number of college students in parents' household. This question asks about the number of household members who, in the award year, are or will be enrolled in a postsecondary school. The student who is applying must include himself or herself in this number. Include others only if they will be attending at least half time in a program that leads to a degree or certificate at a postsecondary school eligible to participate in any of the federal student aid programs. Do not include yourself (the parent), even if you will be in school. Do not include students at a U.S. military academy, because their entire education is paid for.

68. State of legal residence. Give the two-letter abbreviation for your current state of residence. Legal residence is a true, fixed and permanent home. If you are separated or divorced, use the state of legal residence for the parent whose information is reported on the form. If you live in a foreign country, enter "FC" in the state abbreviation space.

69. Legal resident before 2003. States have varying criteria for determining whether you are a resident for purposes of state financial aid. If you established a true, fixed and permanent home in any state more than four years ago, you will meet the state's criteria. Select "Yes" if you became a resident of the state before January 1, 2003, and "No" if you became a resident on or after January 1, 2003 for the 2008-09 award year.

70. Date of legal residence. If a parent did not become a legal resident of the state before January 1, 2003 for the 2008-09 award year, provide the month and year legal residency began for the parent who has lived in the state longer.

71-75. Benefits you (or anyone in your household) received last year. Mark if you've received benefits from any of the federal benefits programs. Answering these questions will not reduce your eligibility for financial aid or reduce your eligibility for the federal benefits.

71 Supplemental Security Income Program
72 Food Stamp Program
73 Free or Reduced Price School Lunch Program
74 Temporary Assistance for Needy Families (TANF)

75 Special Supplemental Nutrition Program for Women, Infants and Children (WIC)

Questions 76–83: Parent Income

The easiest way to complete the next section is to refer to your completed federal income taxes. If you have not done your taxes yet, calculate your estimated adjusted gross income (AGI) and taxes. This estimate will be compared with the tax return(s) you actually file. If the financial information does not agree, you will have to correct the FAFSA information on the website or by mail. Resubmitting and reprocessing corrected data could mean a delay in getting student financial aid. So do yourself a favor and get your taxes done early.

If you are not required to file an income tax return, you still need to calculate your earnings for the year. Use W-2 forms and other records to answer the questions in this section. The base year for these income tax questions is 2007 for the 2008-09 award year.

Note: The tax form line numbers and exemption amounts in this section are from 2007 IRS tax rules. The 2008 rules were not established at the time of publication—be sure to confirm this information when completing the FAFSA.

Foreign income

Income earned in a foreign country is treated the same as income earned in the United States. Convert all figures to dollars, using the exchange rate in effect on the day you fill out the FAFSA. Exchange rates are listed at www.federalreserve.gov/releases/h10/update. Include the value of any taxes paid to the foreign government in the "U.S. income tax paid" line item. If income earned in the foreign country was not taxed by the central government of that country, the income should be reported as untaxed income.

In many cases, if you file a return with the IRS for a year in which foreign income was earned, a portion of the foreign income can be excluded on IRS Form 2555 for U.S. tax purposes. The figure reported on line 45 of Form 2555 (or line 18 of Form 2555EZ) should be reported on the "Foreign income exclusions" line on Worksheet B. **The final total for Form 2555 should not be reported as untaxed income, because it contains other exclusions.**

76. Filing return. Indicate whether you have already completed, are going to complete or will not file, a tax return for 2007.

77. Type of return filed. Indicate which tax form you filed or will file.

78. Eligible to file a 1040A or 1040EZ. If you are eligible to file a 1040A or 1040EZ, indicate this. Even if you file a 1040, if you are *eligible* to file a 1040A or 1040EZ, make sure to note that fact here. **Tax preparers often file a Form 1040 or an electronic 1040 on behalf of tax filers even though their income and tax filing circumstances would allow them to file a 1040A or 1040EZ.**

In general, a person is eligible to file a 1040A or 1040EZ if he or she makes less than $100,000, does not itemize deductions, does not receive income from his or her own business or farm and does not receive alimony. A person is not eligible to file a 1040A or a 1040 EZ form if he or she itemizes deductions, receives self-employment income or alimony or is required to file Schedule D for capital gains. **If you filed a 1040 only to claim Hope or Lifetime Learning credits and would otherwise have been eligible to file a 1040A or 1040EZ, answer "Yes" to this question.**

BRIGHT IDEA . . . . . .

Get help. You are not alone when you're filling out the FAFSA. If you have questions, you can contact the Federal Student Aid Information Center at 1-800-4-FED-AID (1-800-433-3243) for assistance. If you have a hearing impairment, use the TTY line at 1-800-730-8913. You can also get help from college financial aid offices, and many high schools offer information sessions, known as "financial aid nights," to help families complete the application.

79. Adjusted Gross Income. Provide your AGI. AGI is found on IRS 1040, line 37; 1040A, line 21 or 1040EZ, line 4. If you have not completed a tax form, calculate your AGI. Note that AGI includes more than just wages earned; it also includes interest, dividends, alimony, taxable portions of Social Security and business income.

80. Income tax. Enter the amount of income tax you paid from IRS 1040, line 57; 1040A, line 35 or 1040EZ, line 10. If you did not pay any income tax, enter zero. Do not copy the amount of federal income tax withheld from a W-2 form.

81. Exemptions. Enter your exemptions. Exemptions are on IRS Form 1040, line 6d, or 1040A, line 6d. If you answered "You" or "Spouse" on 1040EZ, line 5, use EZ worksheet line F to determine the number of exemptions ($3,400 equals one exemption). If you didn't check either box on line 5, enter "01" if single and "02" if married. If you are divorced, separated or widowed but have filed or will file a joint tax return, list only your portion of the exemptions.

82. Father's/stepfather's income earned. In calculating your Expected Family Contribution, certain allowances are deducted from your income for required and necessary expenses (such as taxes and basic living costs). Your income earned from work will be used in the calculation as an income factor when no tax form is filed.

**Straight Talk
with a Financial Aid
Administrator**

Community college will stretch your financial aid dollars further

No matter what college you attend—whether Harvard or Cincinnati State—if you qualify for a federal Pell Grant, you will receive it up to a maximum of $4,731. But if your tuition is $20,000, that grant is not going to go as far as if your tuition is $6,000. At some community colleges, getting a full Pell Grant will pay for full tuition and books! The same is true for other types of financial aid such as the Supplemental Educational Opportunity Grant (SEOG). If you have to borrow money, you will not have to borrow as much to pay for your community college education. Also, you don't have to be a full-time student to receive financial aid. We send all of our part-time students who qualify for aid an award letter and prorate their award based on their status.

Dawnia Smith, Director of Financial Aid,
Cincinnati State Technical and Community College

If you filed (or will file) a tax return, include only your individual share from IRS Form 1040, total of lines lines 7 + 12 + 18 + Box 14 of IRS Schedule K-1; 1040A, line 7 or 1040EZ, line 1. Even if you filed a joint return, report each of your earnings separately in questions 82 and 83. If you did not file a tax return, report your earnings from work. This information is on the W-2 form(s).

83. Mother's/stepmother's income earned. See instructions for line #82 above.

Parent Worksheets A, B and C

Parent Worksheets A, B and C will help you compute the answers for Questions 84-86. You can get these worksheets at www.fafsa.ed.gov by clicking on "FAFSA on the Web Worksheet" under "Before Beginning a FAFSA." The worksheets are also printed in the application booklet of the paper FAFSA.

The following income and benefits should **not** be reported on Worksheets A and B.

Combat Pay for non-tax filers. If you did not file a tax return, you must report any combat pay you received as income earned from work in Question 82 or 83. None of it should be reported on Worksheet B. This is because income earned from work is used in place of adjusted gross income (AGI) for non-tax filers, so putting combat pay on Worksheet B in this case would yield a double counting of funds.

Food stamps and other programs. Benefits received from federal, state or local government programs are not counted as untaxed income: Food Stamp Program; Special Supplemental Nutrition Program for Women, Infants and Children (WIC); Food Distribution Program; Commodity Supplemental Food Program; National School Lunch and School Breakfast Programs; Summer Food Service Program; and Special Milk Program for Children.

Dependent assistance. You may be eligible to exclude a limited amount of benefits received for dependent care assistance if certain requirements are met. Generally, up to $5,000 of benefits may be excluded from an employee's gross income, or $2,500 for a married employee who files a separate return from his or her spouse. This exclusion can't exceed the employee's (or the spouse's) earned income. (Note: Some states provide reimbursement for child care expenses incurred by welfare recipients through TANF. You must report this on the application, because you bill the state for child care costs incurred while you are on welfare and are reimbursed on that basis.)

Per capita payments to Native Americans. You should not report individual per capita payments received from the Per Capita Act or the Distribution of Judgment Funds Act unless any individual payment exceeds $2,000. Thus, if an individual payment were $1,500, you would not report it on the application; however, if a payment were $2,500, you would report the amount that exceeds $2,000: $500.

Heating/fuel assistance. Exclude from consideration as income or resources any payments or allowances received under the Low-Income Home Energy Assistance Act (LIHEA). Payments under LIHEA are made through state programs that may have different names.

Parent Worksheet A

Student/Spouse	Worksheet A	Parents
For question 40	Report Annual Amounts	For question 84
$	Earned income credit from IRS Form 1040—line 66a; 1040A—line 40a; or 1040EZ—line 8a.	$
$	Additional child tax credit from IRS Form 1040—line 68 or 1040A—line 41.	$
$	Welfare benefits, including Temporary Assistance for Needy Families (TANF). Don't include food stamps or subsidized housing.	$
$	Social Security benefits received, that were not taxed (such as SSI), for all household members reported in question 90 (or 66 for your parents). Report benefits paid to parents in the Parents column, and benefits paid directly to student (or spouse) in the Student/Spouse column.	$
$ —Enter in question 40.		Enter in question 84. — $

This worksheet helps you determine how much you received in untaxed benefits. This income will be added to your adjusted gross income. You will need the following information to complete Worksheet A.

Earned income credit. Enter the earned income credit from IRS Form 1040, line 66a; 1040A, line 40a or 1040EZ, line 8a.

Additional child tax credit. Report the amount from your IRS Form 1040, line 68, or 1040A, line 41.

Welfare benefits. Enter the total amount of welfare benefits you received, including TANF. Report the amount you received annually, not the monthly amounts. **Do not include the annual value of food stamps or subsidized housing.**

Untaxed Social Security benefits for all household members as reported in the parent's household. If Social Security benefits were paid to you on behalf of your dependents (because they were under 18 years old at the time), these benefits are reported as income. You must report benefits received on behalf of persons included in your household as your income. However, if a member of your household, such as an uncle or grandmother, receives benefits in his or her own name, you do not report those benefits in your income. The actual amount of benefits received for the year must be reported, even if that amount represents an underpayment or overpayment that may be adjusted in the next year. This conforms with the IRS treatment of overpayments of taxable income (such as salary) that must be reported and are taxed as any other income.

84. Enter the result of Worksheet A.

Parent Worksheet B

Worksheet B
Report Annual Amounts

For question 41		For question 85
$	Payments to tax-deferred pension and savings plans (paid directly or withheld from earnings), including, but not limited to, amounts reported on the W-2 Form in Boxes 12a through 12d, codes D, E, F, G, H and S.	$
$	IRA deductions and payments to self-employed SEP, SIMPLE, and Keogh and other qualified plans from IRS Form 1040—line 28 + line 32 or 1040A—line 17.	$
$	Child support received for all children. Don't include foster care or adoption payments.	$
$	Tax exempt interest income from IRS Form 1040—line 8b or 1040A—line 8b.	$
$	Foreign income exclusion from IRS Form 2555—line 45 or 2555EZ—line 18.	$
$	Untaxed portions of IRA distributions from IRS Form 1040—lines (15a minus 15b) or 1040A—lines (11a minus 11b). Exclude rollovers. If negative, enter a zero here.	$
$	Untaxed portions of pensions from IRS Form 1040—lines (16a minus 16b) or 1040A—lines (12a minus 12b). Exclude rollovers. If negative, enter a zero here.	$
$	Credit for federal tax on special fuels from IRS Form 4136—line 17 (nonfarmers only).	$
$	Housing, food and other living allowances paid to members of the military, clergy and others (including cash payments and cash value of benefits).	$
$	Veterans noneducation benefits such as Disability, Death Pension, or Dependency & Indemnity Compensation (DIC) and/or VA Educational Work-Study allowances.	$
$	Other untaxed income not reported elsewhere on Worksheets A and B, such as workers' compensation, untaxed portions of railroad retirement benefits, Black Lung Benefits, disability, etc. Tax filers only: report combat pay not included in AGI (FAFSA questions 35 and 79). Don't include student aid, Workforce Investment Act educational benefits, combat pay if you are not a tax filer, or benefits from flexible spending arrangements (e.g., cafeteria plans).	$
$	Money received, or paid on your behalf (e.g., bills), not reported elsewhere on this form.	XXXXXXXX
$ ——Enter in question 41.		Enter in question 85. —— $

This worksheet helps you determine how much you received in untaxed income, which will be added to your AGI. You will need the following information to complete Worksheet B.

Payments to tax-deferred pension and savings plans. You must report money paid into tax-sheltered or deferred annuities (whether it is paid directly or withheld from earnings), including, but not limited to, amounts reported on the W-2 form in boxes 12a–12d, codes D, E, F, G, H and S. You must include untaxed portions of your 401(k) and 403(b) plans. **Do not report employer contributions to tax-deferred pension and savings plans as an untaxed benefit.**

IRAs and other plans. Enter the amount of IRA deductions and payments to self-employed SEP, SIMPLE, Keogh and other qualified plans. These plan payments can be found on IRS Form 1040, total of lines 28 + 32, or 1040A, line 17.

Child support. Report child support received for all children. Do not include foster care or adoption payments.

Tax-exempt interest income. Enter the total amount of tax-exempt interest income you earned, as reported on Form 1040 or 1040A, line 8b.

Foreign income exclusion. The IRS allows eligible U.S. citizens and residents living in foreign countries to exclude a limited amount of income earned abroad. Although deducted for tax purposes, this amount is considered untaxed income for federal student aid purposes. Give the total amount of the foreign income exclusion you reported on Form 2555, line 45, or 2555EZ, line 18.

Untaxed portions of IRA distributions. This amount can be calculated from IRS Form 1040 (line 15a minus 15b) or 1040A (line 11a minus 11b). If the result is a negative number, enter zero.

Untaxed portions of pensions. This amount can be calculated from IRS Form 1040 (line 16a minus 16b) or 1040A (line 12a minus 12b). If the result is a negative number, enter zero.

You do not have to report IRA or pension distributions as income if these distributions were rolled over to another IRA or retirement plan within 60 days of the day on which you received the distribution from the initial IRA or retirement plan.

Special fuels credit. Enter the total amount of credit for federal tax on special fuels that you reported on IRS Form 4136, line 18 (nonfarmers only).

Housing, food and other living allowances. Allowances provided to you and reported on the W-2 form must be reported. These may be part of a compensation package that some people (such as clergy and military personnel) receive for their jobs. Include cash payments and cash value of benefits. (Rent subsidies for low-income housing are not included.)

Veterans noneducation benefits. Enter the total amount of veterans noneducation benefits you received. Include Disability, Death Pension, Dependency & Indemnity Compensation (DIC) and/or VA Educational Work-Study allowances.

Other untaxed income and benefits. List untaxed income or benefits not reported elsewhere on Worksheets A and B, such as worker's compensation, untaxed portions of railroad retirement benefits, untaxed portions of capital gains, Black Lung Benefits, Refugee Assistance, disability, foreign income that wasn't taxed by any government, etc. Do not include benefits from flexible spending arrangements (e.g., cafeteria plans), student aid or Workforce Investment Act (WIA, formerly JTPA) educational benefits.

Money received. You should not report anything for this question.

85. Enter the result of Worksheet B.

Parent Worksheet C

Worksheet C		
For question 42	Report Annual Amounts	For question 86
$	Education credits (Hope and Lifetime Learning tax credits) from IRS Form 1040—line 49 or 1040A—line 31.	$
$	Child support paid because of divorce or separation or as a result of a legal requirement. Don't include support for children in your (or your parents') household, as reported in question 90 (or question 66 for your parents).	$
$	Taxable earnings from need-based employment programs, such as Federal Work-Study and need-based employment portions of fellowships and assistantships.	$
$	Student grant and scholarship aid reported to the IRS in your (or your parents') adjusted gross income. Includes AmeriCorps benefits (awards, living allowances and interest accrual payments), as well as grant or scholarship portions of fellowships and assistantships.	$
$ ——Enter in question 42.	Enter in question 86. ——	$

This worksheet will help you determine what may be excluded from income for the purposes of financial aid. This amount will be subtracted from your adjusted gross income. Because the items listed in this worksheet will be excluded from income, do not subtract them from your responses to the previous income questions. These amounts should be calculated on the basis of what you received between January 1 and December 31, 2007 (for the 2008-09 award year), and not what you received during the school year. You will need the following information to complete Worksheet C.

Education credits. The Hope and Lifetime Learning tax credits benefit students or parents who pay tuition and related expenses for attendance at least half time

---

Straight Talk with a Financial Aid Administrator

Don't skip applying for financial aid just because a community college is affordable

Because a school like Cincinnati State is so affordable, some families choose not to apply for financial aid even though they may qualify. No matter what college you attend, you should always apply for financial aid. You could be eligible for a federal Pell Grant or the Supplemental Educational Opportunity Grant (SEOG). You can apply for the work-study program and take advantage of low-interest student loans. We also have state aid in the form of grants as well as our own institutional scholarships. It's important that families don't neglect applying for aid even if their college price tag is low or they have received an outside scholarship.

Dawnia Smith, Director of Financial Aid,
Cincinnati State Technical and Community College

---

in a degree-granting program. These credits are subtracted directly from the total federal tax on a tax return. Enter the total amount of Hope and Lifetime Learning credits you received, from Form 1040, line 49 or 1040A, line 31.

Child support payments. Report any child support payments you made because of divorce, separation or legal requirement. Do not include support for children in your household as reported in the "number in household" question on the FAFSA (question 66 for dependent students). For purposes of the FAFSA, a child is a member of your household if you provide more than half of the child's support, whether the child lives with you or not.

Taxable earnings from need-based employment programs. These are earnings from any need-based employment programs including Federal Work-Study and need-based employment portions of fellowships and assistantships.

Grants and other awards. Report any grant and scholarship aid that you reported to the IRS as income. This category includes AmeriCorps benefits (awards, living allowances and interest accrual payments) as well as grant and scholarship portions of fellowships and assistantships.

86. Enter the result of Worksheet C.

Straight Talk with a Financial Aid Administrator ▶ **There is no substitute for doing the right thing**

Much earlier in my career as a financial aid administrator I sat at my maternal grandfather's dinner table with my folks and one of my mother's cousins. This cousin was an engineer for the city. He earned a comfortable living and had several children who would be heading off to college. At some point during the dinner we started talking about financial aid. My mother's cousin began to speak at great length about how he was going to beat the system. He was planning to manipulate his income so he could get more money. I felt he was wrong and said so. A heated discussion soon broke out. It was one of the few times my father was silent during a conversation. We didn't come to an agreement that evening. This conversation took place in the early 1980s.

More than 20 years later my father called to tell me this same cousin visited them. The cousin brought up the conversation out of the blue, telling my father he realized after that evening I had been right. He said after that conversation he looked at the issue from the perspective that I put forward. He realized it was wrong to manipulate the system. To me, having heard this cousin admit this meant a lot. There really is a distinction between what's "legal" and what's "right."

James M. Bauer, Assistant Dean of Enrollment Management and Director of Financial Assistance Services, University of Miami

Questions 87–89: Parent Asset Information

An asset is defined as property that has an exchange value. The purpose of collecting asset information is to determine whether your family's assets are substantial enough to support a contribution toward the cost of college attendance. Only the net asset value is counted in the need analysis. To determine the net value of any asset, first determine the market value of the asset and then subtract the value by the amount of debt against the asset. The result is the net value.

Divided or contested assets

Part ownership. If you own an asset with others and, therefore, own only a portion or percentage of it, report the net asset value that represents your share. Determine the current market value of the asset, reduce the value by any outstanding debt and then multiply the net asset value by your ownership percentage. Report this number.

Contested ownership. An asset should not be reported if its ownership is being legally contested. For example, if you are separated and may not sell or borrow against jointly owned property that is being contested, do not list any value for the property or any debts against it. If ownership of the asset is resolved after you file the FAFSA, you may not update this information.

Lien against asset. If there is a lien or imminent foreclosure against an asset, the asset should be reported on the FAFSA until the party holding the lien or making the foreclosure completes legal action to take possession of the asset.

Unreported assets

Not all types of assets are used in the financial aid calculations. The following are examples of assets that are not reported:

Principal place of residence or family farm. Your principal place of residence is not reported as an asset, nor is your family farm if the farm is your principal place of residence and your family claimed on Schedule F of the tax return that it "materially participated in the farm's operation."

A small business with 100 or fewer employees. If you own and control a small business that has 100 or fewer full-time or full-time equivalent employees, do not report the net value of the business as an asset.

Personal possessions. Do not report possessions such as cars, stereos, clothes or furniture. By the same token, personal debts such as credit card debt may not be reported.

Pensions and whole-life insurance. The cash value or built-up equity of a life insurance (whole-life) policy should not be reported as an asset. However, any income distributed to the beneficiary should be reported as income.

Excluded assets from Native American students. Do not report any property received under the Per Capita Act, the Distribution of Judgment Funds Act, the Alaska Native Claims Settlement Act or the Maine Indian Claims Settlement Act.

Treatment of investments

Rental properties. Generally, rental properties must be reported as investment assets rather than business assets. To be reported as a business, a rental property would have to be part of a formally recognized business. Usually such a business would provide additional services, such as regular cleaning, linen or maid service.

Take-back mortgages. In a take-back mortgage, the seller takes back a portion of the mortgage from the buyer and arranges for the buyer to repay that portion directly to the seller. For IRS purposes, the seller must report the interest portion of any payments received from the buyer on Schedule B of IRS Form 1040. If an amount is reported on this line of the tax return, you should report the outstanding balance of the remaining mortgage on the FAFSA as an investment asset.

Trust funds. If a trust fund is in your name, it should be reported as an asset. In the case of divorce or separation, where the trust is owned jointly and ownership is not being contested, the property and the debt are equally divided between the owners for reporting purposes, unless the terms of the trust specify some other method of division.

How the trust must be reported varies according to whether you receive or will receive the interest income, the trust principal or both. If you receive only interest from the trust, any interest received in the base year must be reported as income. Even if interest accumulates in the trust and is not paid out during the year, if you will eventually receive it, you must report an asset value for the interest you will receive in the future. The trust officer can usually calculate the present value of interest you will receive while the trust exists. This value represents the amount a third person would be willing to pay to receive the interest income you will receive from the trust in the future.

The present value of the principal is the amount a third person would pay today for the right to receive the principal when the trust ends (basically, the amount that one would have to deposit now to receive the amount of the principal when the trust ends, including the accumulated interest). Again, the trust officer can calculate the present value.

As a general rule, you must report the present value of the trust as an asset, even if your access to the trust is restricted. If the creator of a trust has voluntarily placed restrictions on the use of the trust, report the trust as if there were no restrictions; however, if the trust has been restricted by court order, do not report it as an asset. An example of such a restricted trust is one set up by court order to pay for future surgery for the victim of a car accident.

87. Total current cash, savings and checking account balance. Include the balance in your checking and savings accounts as of the date the FAFSA is completed. Do not include money from student financial aid.

88. Net worth of investments. Investments include real estate such as rental property, land and second or summer homes. Do not include your primary home, but do include the value of portions of multifamily dwellings that are not your principal residence. Investments also include trust funds, Uniform Transfers to Minors Act (UTMA)/Uniform Gifts to Minors Act (UGMA) Custodial Accounts, money market funds, mutual funds, certificates of deposit, stocks, stock options, bonds, other securities, Coverdell savings accounts owned by you, 529 college savings plans, the refund value of 529 prepaid tuition plans, installment and land sale contracts (including mortgages held), commodities and so on. Do not include the value of life insurance and retirement plans (pension funds, annuities, noneducation IRAs, Keogh plans, etc.)

You must report in Question 88 all qualified educational benefits or education savings accounts, including Coverdell savings accounts, 529 college savings plans and the refund value of 529 prepaid tuition plans that you own. You should **not** report any accounts owned by a dependent student in this question.

Remember, Investment Value - Investment Debt = Net Worth of Investments. If you own real estate or investments other than your principal residence, the value equals the amount they are worth today. Investment debt is how much you owe on real estate and investments other than your principal place of residence. Subtract the amount of debt on these assets from their value.

89. Net worth of business and/or investment farm. Business or farm value includes the current market value of land, buildings, machinery, equipment, inventory and so on. Do not include your primary residence. Do not include the net worth of a family owned and controlled small business with not more than 100 full-time or full-time equivalent employees.

As with investment value, remember that Business/Farm Value - Business/Farm Debt = Net Worth of Business/Farm. For business or investment farm value, first figure out how much the business or farm is worth today. Business or investment farm debts are what you owe on the business or farm. Include only debts for which the business or farm was used as collateral. Subtract the amount of debt from the value to determine the net worth of a business and/or investment farm.

To report current market value for a business, use the amount for which the business could sell as of the date of the application. If you are not the sole owner of the business, report only your share of its value and debt.

Questions 90 and 91: Independent Students

If the student answered "Yes" to any of the dependency questions (48–55), he or she will need to respond to both of these questions.

90. Number in student's (and spouse's) household. The following persons are included in the household of an independent student:

- The student.
- Student's spouse, excluding a spouse not living in the household as a result of death, separation or divorce.

- Student's children, if they will receive more than half their support from the household between July 1 and June 30 of the award year.
- Student's unborn child, if that child will be born before July 1 of the end of the award year and the household will provide more than half of the child's support from the projected date of birth to the end of the award year. (If there is a medical determination of a multiple birth, include all expected children.)
- Other people, if they live with the student and will receive more than half their support from the household for the entire award year (July 1 through June 30 of the award year).

91. Number of college students in household. This question asks about the number of household members who, in the award year, are or will be enrolled in a post-secondary school. The student should count himself or herself as a college student. Include others only if they will be attending at least half time in a program that leads to a degree or certificate at a postsecondary school that is eligible to participate in any federal student aid programs.

Benefits the student (or his or her spouse or anyone in the household) received during 2007 (for the 2008-09 award year). If anyone received benefits from any of the federal benefits programs shown in the boxes below, mark the ovals to the corresponding questions on the paper form or use the corresponding drop-down menus online. Use the instructions for Question 90 to identify who is included in your household. Answering these questions will not reduce the student's eligibility for student aid. Nor will it reduce the student's, his or her spouse's or anyone in the household's eligibility for these federal benefits.

92 Supplemental Security Income Program
93 Food Stamp Program
94 Free or Reduced Price School Lunch Program
95 Temporary Assistance for Needy Families (TANF)
96 Special Supplemental Nutrition Program for Women, Infants and Children (WIC)

Question 97: School Codes and Housing Plans

This section allows your child to list up to four schools on the paper FAFSA or up to 10 schools online to receive information from the FAFSA. The Department of Education will send the information to all the schools listed. Include each school's Federal School Code; school codes can be found on www.fafsa.ed.gov in the "Federal School Code List." Generally, it does not matter in what order the schools are listed; however, several states require students to list state schools first to be eligible for state aid.

If your child wants information sent to different schools than those listed on the application, there are several ways to make sure that all schools receive the data:

- When you receive the Student Aid Report, replace some or all of the original schools with other schools. You or your child can make corrections to the FAFSA online at www.fafsa.ed.gov.
- After you receive the Student Aid Report (SAR), you or your child may call the Federal Student Aid Information Center (1-800-433-3243) to request changes to the school list.
- You or your child may provide the Data Release Number (DRN) printed on the Student Aid Report to any school not listed on the FAFSA. These additional schools can use the DRN to obtain an electronic copy of your student's application information.
- You can add or delete schools on the FAFSA online at www.fafsa. ed.gov. Select "Add or delete a School Code." Your PIN is required to access this information.

If you are unable to find the Federal School Code for a certain college, indicate clearly the complete name, address, city and state of each college. If a college is a branch campus, include the complete name of the branch. Also, indicate if it is a specific part of a university, such as the law school. Note, however, that the FAFSA will be processed faster if the Federal School Code is provided.

Straight Talk with a Financial Aid Administrator ▶ **Missing a deadline can cost you a bundle**

Like most schools, we have limited funds for campus-based and institutional financial aid. Therefore, these types of financial aid are awarded to those who get their applications to us before our priority deadline, which is February 15 for new students and March 1 for returning students. All applicants who submit a completed application by these dates are awarded money from our campus-based funds on a need and funds-available basis. Students who turn in their applications afterward typically don't receive campus-based aid because the funds will have been depleted. In fact, students will receive much more self-help aid like loans if we receive their applications late. In the past few years I think parents have become more aware of the importance of deadlines. As soon as you get your tax information, file your financial aid application. Use estimates if you have to. Only by getting your application in by the deadline will your student be considered for as much financial aid as possible.

Veronica J. Leech, Director of Financial Aid, Central State University

Housing plans. For each school listed, indicate your child's intended housing plan: on campus, off campus or with parents.

Questions 98–102: Date and Signatures

98. Date this form was completed. If you apply on paper, fill in the month, day and year. Note that all information you report on the FAFSA must be accurate as of the date you complete the form. If you apply online, the date you submit the application will automatically pre-fill this field.

The last task is to decide how to sign the application. On FAFSA on the Web, students and parents are able to sign electronically. Independent applicants (and a parent of a dependent applicant) must either use a PIN or print out, sign and submit a signature page. If you are completing a paper FAFSA, simply sign it. The application will not be processed without the proper signatures.

By signing the FAFSA, you also give permission to the state financial aid agency to obtain income tax information for all persons in your household who are required to report income and for all periods reported on this form.

Although parental information must be provided for a dependent student, a high school counselor or college financial aid administrator may sign the application in place of a parent in the following cases:

DEADLINES . . . . . .

Federal aid. Students should file the FAFSA as soon as possible after January 1 of the year in which they will need federal financial aid.

State aid. States also have deadlines for submitting applications. These deadlines may coincide with the federal deadline or may be earlier.

Institutional aid. Most college deadlines are earlier than state and federal deadlines. You can find these deadlines on the application or on the college's financial aid website.

■ Parents are not currently in the United States and cannot be contacted by normal means.
■ Parents' current address is not known.
■ Parents have been determined to be physically or mentally incapable of providing a signature.

A parent's unwillingness to sign the FAFSA or provide financial information is not a reason for the financial aid administrator to sign the form in place of him or her.

101–102. Preparer's name/Social Security number/signature and date. The law requires that if anyone other than the student, student's spouse or student's parent prepares the application, the preparer must write in his or her name, the company name (if applicable), the company address and either the company's employer identification number (EIN) or the preparer's Social Security number.

High school counselors, financial aid administrators and others who help students with their paper applications by actually filling out line items on the form or dictating responses to items on the form are considered preparers, even if they are not paid for their services.

Your Information Is Subject to Verification

The Department of Education has a verification program (similar to a tax audit) for FAFSAs. Each year, the department selects a group of FAFSAs for verification. The goal of the verification program is to prevent ineligible students from receiving aid by reporting false information and to ensure that eligible students receive all the aid for which they qualify. Some applications are selected for verification because of inconsistent information; others are chosen at random.

The CSS/PROFILE

The CSS/PROFILE is required by some private colleges, universities, graduate and professional schools and scholarship programs to determine eligibility for nonfederal financial aid—such as an institution's own grants, loans and scholarships. The PROFILE may be submitted as early as the fall (unlike the FAFSA, which may not be submitted until January 1).

As with the FAFSA, the easiest way to submit the CSS/PROFILE is online. You can register for the CSS/PROFILE at the College Board website (www.collegeboard.com) or by phone at 305-829-9793. The registration process requires answering basic questions and listing the schools to which your child plans to apply.

The CSS/PROFILE is customized, so you will be asked only the questions required by the schools your child is going to apply to. If you complete the PROFILE online, you will have access to "live" help from customer service advisors through chat or e-mail. If you prefer, you may use a paper application.

After you submit the CSS/PROFILE, you'll receive an acknowledgement that lists the schools and programs that received your information. You will also receive a CSS/PROFILE Data Confirmation Report for each school and program. Look for any discrepancies or errors in these reports and make corrections directly with the schools.

Requirements. The information you will need to complete the CSS/PROFILE is similar to that for the FAFSA. Although some schools have different requirements, at a minimum, you and your child will need to provide the following:

Students:

- ❏ Income (including untaxed income)
- ❏ Taxes paid
- ❏ Assets
- ❏ Trust fund information, if applicable

Parents:

- ❏ Income (including untaxed income)
- ❏ Taxes paid
- ❏ Assets (including home equity)
- ❏ Number of family members
- ❏ Number of children attending college
- ❏ Extraordinary medical/dental expenses
- ❏ Special circumstances—such as unemployment, change in family status, serious injury or natural disaster—that were not reflected in the previous year's income and that might affect your ability to pay college expenses. (The financial aid administrator may use this additional information to increase the amount of financial aid you receive.)

Unlike the FAFSA, the CSS/PROFILE is not free. You will pay a registration fee and fees for each school that needs to receive a copy of your information. The least expensive way to register for the CSS/PROFILE is online.

Colleges also may select applications for verification. Students whose applications are selected must provide the financial aid office with documentation that supports the information on the FAFSA.

Be sure you save all the records and other materials you use to complete the FAFSA. You may need them later to prove the information you reported is correct.

You're Finished!

While the FAFSA contains many questions, most are fairly straightforward, especially if you've already completed your tax return. Remember, $97 billion[1] in financial aid was awarded **last** year alone. The only way you will know if your child deserves some of this money is to fill out the FAFSA and/or CSS/PROFILE.

---

1. The College Board, *Trends in Student Aid 2007*, October 22, 2007.

CHAPTER 5

How Do We Choose the Best Financial Aid Package?

What you'll learn:

- What a financial aid award letter looks like
- How to evaluate offers to pick the best one
- What to do if you don't get enough aid
- How to achieve a successful reassessment

You open the mailbox and your heart skips a beat: Lying there is a letter from your child's dream college. You hand the letter to your child and wait nervously. The first word says it all: "Congratulations!"

A week later, another letter arrives. This is the award letter from the school's financial aid office. Now that your child has gotten into college, it's time to find out how much you'll have to pay.

Your child has been accepted at several schools, so you receive several award letters. Each offers a different blend of grants, loans, scholarships and work-study. Given the variety of offers, how do you make sense of it all? What is the true price difference between your child's top two college choices? And what if the financial aid package is not enough?

To answer these questions, you need to evaluate each financial aid offer, decipher the various programs and terms and weigh the advantages and disadvantages of each. Only by carefully analyzing the offers will you be able to choose the best one.

The Envelope, Please

The financial aid award letter is the official notice of how much financial support the school will provide your child for the coming year. Most parents go straight to the bottom line to see the total amount of aid the college is offering, but this can be misleading. It's important to break down the package and examine where the money comes from. Also, you are not obligated to accept the entire package; as with a buffet, you may pick and choose from what is offered.

What can you expect to find in your child's letter? A typical award letter may include money from

- Grants
- Scholarships
- Work-study
- Student loans

Almost all money comes with terms and conditions. A scholarship, for example, may require maintaining a minimum grade point average (GPA). Also, unless otherwise stated, the award letter applies only to the coming school year. The following is an example of a typical financial aid award letter:

Straight Talk
with a Financial Aid ▶
Administrator

What to look for in your award letters

When evaluating different financial aid offers, it's important to take a close look at a number of characteristics, such as:

- What are the enrollment requirements for grants and scholarships?

- Are the awards for one year or all four years?

- Is the required GPA to maintain the awards realistic?

- If student employment is part of the financial aid package, what types of jobs are available and what rate of pay is typical?

- When an institution describes the cost of education, is it providing the entire expense of attending the institution or only expressing those costs attributable to the college or university?

It is important to look at the NET out-of-pocket cost the family is expected to pay as well as any share of financial assistance in the form of loans versus grants and scholarships. Do not be surprised if a loan is part of a financial aid package you receive. Loans are the most common form of financial aid available. While the financial aid offers may appear straightforward, it's important every student understand in detail the specific requirements for each type of aid.

Dr. Lawrence Burt, Associate VP for Student Affairs & Director of Student Financial Services, University of Texas at Austin

ABC UNIVERSITY
Office of Student Financial Aid
Financial Aid Award

Joan A. Student   March 22, 2006
101 College Way   Award year: 2006-07
Anytown, VA 20000   SSN: 123-45-6789

Dear Student:

After reviewing your FAFSA, we are pleased to provide you with the following financial aid offer. This award is contingent upon anticipated annual renewal of funding from federal, state and private sources. You may accept or decline any of the awards offered.

Projected Cost of Education: $15,000
Expected Family Contribution: $5,000
Total Financial Need: $10,000

Type of Aid	Fall	Spring	Total	Accept	Decline
Pell Grant	$600	$600	$1,200	( )	( )
FSEOG	$800	$800	$1,600	( )	( )
ABC Univ. Grant	$1,000	$1,000	$2,000	( )	( )
Work-Study	$700	$700	$1,400	( )	( )
Perkins Loan	$600	$600	$1,200	( )	( )
Stafford Loan	$1,300	$1,300	$2,600	( )	( )
	$5,000	**$5,000**	**$10,000**		

Please sign this letter and return it to the financial aid office within two weeks. Read the enclosed information on how to apply for and receive the Federal Stafford loan offered. If you need additional funding to supplement this offer, please refer to the attachment for information on additional funding options.

Don't Rush to Accept

While you have only a few weeks to respond, don't sign on the dotted line until you understand exactly what is being offered. To help guide you through the letter, here is a description of the most common types of aid. Contact the financial aid office if you have questions.

Grants. All grants are good: They offer free cash that does not have to be repaid. If your child is offered a grant, accept it. Just remember that grants are usually guar-

CURRENT TRENDS .

Show me the money. The five largest sources of financial aid are federal loans (40%), institutional grants (21%), federal Pell grants (13%), state grants (8%) and education tax benefits (5%).

Source: College Board, *Trends in Student Aid 2007.*

anteed only for one year, and your child will have to reapply each year. A grant may include requirements, such as maintaining a minimum GPA.

Federal Pell Grant. This grant is for undergraduate study only, with the exception of postbaccalaureate teacher certification programs. Students enrolled less than half time are also eligible. The amounts vary depending on funding but the maximum amount is $4,731.

Federal Supplemental Educational Opportunity Grant (FSEOG). This grant is for undergraduates who demonstrate the most financial need on the basis of the information provided on the FAFSA. The federal government provides funds for individual schools to administer this program, and there is no guarantee that every eligible student will receive an FSEOG, or that every college a student applies to will offer that student the same amount. The amounts vary from $100 to $4,000 per year.

Academic Competitiveness Grants. These grants are for undergraduate students who are eligible for Federal Pell Grants and complete a rigorous high school program. The grants provide up to $750 for the first year of study and up to $1,300 for the second year.

National Science & Mathematics Access to Retain Talent Grants (National SMART Grants). These grants of up to $4,000 are for undergraduate students in the third and fourth year of undergraduate study who are eligible for the Federal Pell Grant and majoring in physical, life or computer science; mathematics; technology; engineering or a foreign language related to national security.

Teacher Education Assistance for College and Higher Education Grants (TEACH Grants). Providing up to $4,000 per year, these grants support students who agree to teach for at least four years in a public or private elementary or secondary school that serves students from low-income families.

Institutional and state grants. Most states administer grant programs for their residents. To find the program for your state, contact the higher education agency listed in Chapter 9. These programs may be based on need, merit or a combination of both. Most colleges also offer various

---

Straight Talk with a Financial Aid Administrator ▶

Work-study has the highest correlation with academic success

One of the best options for paying for college is work-study. A lot of parents assume work-study, which involves having a job on campus, will interfere with students' ability to study. But if Janie didn't study 80 hours a week when in high school she won't magically change and do so in college!

Parents, consider that the average student is in class 15 hours per week. If the student studies two hours a day, that's another 14 hours a week. Sleep may total 56 hours a week. That still leaves more than 80 hours in the week. Students definitely have time to work and study.

In addition, we have found work-study has one of the highest correlations with academic success. Participating in work-study changes students' peer groups since they are not just hanging out with students their age. They are working in a setting with other adults and graduate students. Their bosses and co-workers become mentors. Work-study also requires that the student maintain satisfactory academic progress. Their boss is keenly aware of this and will even provide the equivalent of "parental" oversight to make sure the student is doing well.

Work-study places a value on the students' time. When students don't work, it can seem like they have all the time in the world, when really they don't. Students who participate in work-study appreciate the value of both time and money. Work-study students tend not to be so cavalier about dropping classes. And, of course, work-study gives students some spending money, which makes life better.

Working off-campus, on the other hand, can be detrimental. Work-study is limited to 20 hours a week, and the understanding is that the students' studies come first. This isn't the case with off-campus jobs. Employers expect students to put work first, and students tend to get sucked into working more and more. Students who work off-campus do not do as well as those who work on-campus. Given all these benefits of work-study, I find it very strange only half of students accept it when offered. I'd like to see that change.

Courtney McAnuff, Vice President for Enrollment Services, Eastern Michigan University

grant programs; often the admissions application is used to determine who receives these awards.

Federal Work-Study. This program provides jobs for undergraduate students with financial need, allowing students to earn money to help pay their education expenses. The program encourages community service and work related to courses of study. Both on-campus and off-campus jobs are available. On-campus jobs may include working in the library or the dining hall or for a professor; off-campus employment is typically with a private nonprofit organization or a public agency.

The total Federal Work-Study award depends primarily on the level of need and the funding level of the college. Most students find campus employment rewarding. The jobs are flexible to accommodate students' schedules; in fact, employers and financial aid administrators usually consider class schedule and academic progress to make sure that work does not detract from academic performance. If your child qualifies for work-study, his or her salary will be at least the current federal minimum wage and perhaps higher, depending on the type of work and the skills

Straight Talk with a Financial Aid Administrator ▶ **How we package your financial aid**

At George Mason University we create an aid packaging policy even before we look at the first application. Once our policy is established, we process all applications that meet our "priority filing date," which is March 1. The policy we establish helps ensure our aid decisions are fair and equitable and our budget can assist the greatest number of students possible. We have different amounts of funds available for in-state and out-of-state students. In general, we have more money for in-state students since we are a state public institution, but we also have some funds reserved only for non-residents. Of course, everyone is considered for a Pell Grant and will receive one if they meet the federal guidelines. After we award grant funds, we use the federal Stafford and Perkins student loans. If the student still has financial need, we will then offer them federal work-study. In this way we expend all our grant funds first and then make up the balance of a student's financial need with self-help aid. This is why it's important for students to get the application in before the priority filing date. If an application arrives late, it is very possible our grant money will be gone.

Jevita R. de Freitas, Director, Office of Student Financial Aid, George Mason University required. However, your child may not earn more than the amount of the work-study award.

Scholarships. Any scholarships your child has won and informed the school about will be listed. In addition, the college may award its own scholarships. You can learn more about scholarships in Chapter 7. Like grants, scholarships are free money and should always be accepted.

Student Loans. Borrowing money is a serious decision: Although student loan programs offer competitive rates and flexible repayment schedules, you or your child will be paying back the loan for a number of years. However, many students view loans as a necessary investment in their education. In addition, having a financial stake in their own education can be powerful motivation to take their studies seriously.

> **Stafford loans.** These loans will be in your child's name. Dependent undergraduate students may borrow a maximum of

- $5,500 for the first year of study
- $6,500 for the second year of study
- $7,500 a year for all subsequent years of study

For independent undergraduate students or dependent students whose parents are not able to get a PLUS loan (see below), the maximums are

- $9,500 for first-year students in full academic year programs ($3,500 of this amount may be subsidized—see below)
- $10,500 for students who have completed the first year of study ($4,500 may be subsidized)
- $12,500 a year for students who have completed two years of study ($5,500 may be subsidized)
- $20,500 a year for graduate students ($8,500 may be subsidized)

Stafford loans come in two types: *subsidized* and *unsubsidized*. The difference between the two is significant. With a subsidized loan, the government pays the interest while your child is in school, so it is basically an interest-free loan—at least until your child graduates, withdraws or attends school less than half-time. The government also subsidizes the interest during the student's grace and deferment periods. With an unsubsidized loan, the interest accrues and is added to the total loan amount after graduation. In both cases repayment is not required until six months after graduation.

The interest rate is fixed at 6.8 percent. There is also a fee of up to 4 percent of the loan. The money must be used first for tuition, fees and room and board. After these expenses are paid, the student receives the remaining amount. Students must begin repaying the loan following a six month grace period which begins after they graduate, leave school or drop below half-time enrollment.

Parent Loans for Undergraduate Students (PLUS). These loans are available to parents who have good credit histories. The maximum amount you may borrow is the total cost of attending college for one year (the Cost of Attendance, or COA) minus any financial aid your child receives. For example, if the cost of attendance is $10,000 and your child receives $6,000 in financial aid, you may borrow up to $4,000.

The interest rate is fixed at 7.9 percent for Direct PLUS Loans and 8.5 percent for FFEL PLUS Loans. There is also a fee of up to 4 percent of the loan. The money is disbursed to the school and must first be used for tuition, fees and room and board. After these expenses are paid, you will receive the remaining amount. Repayment begins within 60 days after the loan is fully disbursed.

Straight Talk with a Financial Aid Administrator ▶ # Financial aid is not a bottomless well

Some families assume we have an unlimited amount of money to give away as financial aid. This is absolutely not true. Every college has a budget and limited funds. Therefore, one of my jobs is to make sure our limited funds go to those who need it the most based on an objective standard that is fairly applied to everyone. My job is to make college possible for every family, but that doesn't necessarily mean it will be easy. If I were to do something special to make it more than possible for one family to pay for college, I am also making it less possible for another family. As financial aid administrators we will only give as much as we can in order to be able to help the next in line. We need to ensure we make the money we do have go as far as it possibly can.

James M. Bauer, Assistant Dean of Enrollment Management and Director of Financial Assistance Services, University of Miami

---

Note: *PLUS Loans are available even if not mentioned in the award letter.*

Federal Perkins Loans. These are low-interest loans for undergraduate and graduate students with extreme financial need. The college provides the loan with funds from the federal government and its own funds. The maximum amount a student may borrow is $4,000 a year as an undergraduate and $6,000 a year as a graduate student. The interest rate is 5 percent, and there are no additional fees. Your child starts repaying the money nine months after graduating, leaving school or dropping below half-time enrollment.

USEFUL TERM . . . . .

Unmet financial need. This occurs when the college can't provide enough aid to cover a family's entire financial need. When there is unmet financial need, the family will have to pay more than its Expected Family Contribution. While colleges do their best to meet students' financial need, not all schools have the funds to do so. Of course, this situation can also arise because the student has turned in the financial aid application late and there is no more money.

State and college loan programs. Some states sponsor student loan programs, and these may be listed on the award letter. The terms and conditions of these loans are governed by the state. The college may offer its own student loan programs. Be sure you understand the details of these loans, as they may be different from those of federal student loans.

Evaluating the Award Letter

To evaluate the financial aid offer, look at the big picture, including what the college costs, your Expected Family Contribution and, of course, the composition of the aid package. The following worksheet will help you itemize each component of the equation and will reveal any unmet financial need, which occurs when the total value of the financial aid package plus your Expected Family Contribution still does not cover the entire cost of the college. If a college can't meet 100 percent of your financial need, you will have to get the money elsewhere—either through personal savings or by taking out additional loans.

Use your child's financial aid award letters to fill out the following worksheets. Once you have a worksheet for each college, you'll be able to compare apples to apples.

WORKSHEET

College Name:

Tuition:	$
+ Additional required fees:	$
+ Books/supplies:	$
+ Other expenses:	$
+ Room and board:	$
+ Transportation:	$
= Total Cost of Attendance:	$
- **Expected Family Contribution:**	**$**

The Expected Family Contribution is the amount your family is expected to pay toward education-related expenses. In other words, this money will come from your own pocket.

= **Financial Need:**	**$**
Scholarships / grants:	$
+ Work-study:	$
+ Perkins:	$
+ Subsidized Stafford:	$
+ Unsubsidized Stafford:	$
+ PLUS loan:	$
+ Private loans:	$
+ Other loans:	$
= **Total Financial Aid:**	**$**
Unmet Financial Need:	**$**

WORKSHEET

College Name:

Tuition:	$
+ Additional required fees:	$
+ Books/supplies:	$
+ Other expenses:	$
+ Room and board:	$
+ Transportation:	$
= Total Cost of Attendance:	$
- **Expected Family Contribution:**	**$**

The Expected Family Contribution is the amount your family is expected to pay toward education-related expenses. In other words, this money will come from your own pocket.

= **Financial Need:**	**$**
Scholarships / grants:	$
+ Work-study:	$
+ Perkins:	$
+ Subsidized Stafford:	$
+ Unsubsidized Stafford:	$
+ PLUS loan:	$
+ Private loans:	$
+ Other loans:	$
= **Total Financial Aid:**	**$**
Unmet Financial Need:	**$**

WORKSHEET

College Name:

Tuition:	$	
+ Additional required fees:	$	
+ Books/supplies:	$	
+ Other expenses:	$	
+ Room and board:	$	
+ Transportation:	$	
= Total Cost of Attendance:	$	
- Expected Family Contribution:	**$**	

The Expected Family Contribution is the amount your family is expected to pay toward education-related expenses. In other words, this money will come from your own pocket.

= Financial Need:	**$**	
Scholarships / grants:	$	
+ Work-study:	$	
+ Perkins:	$	
+ Subsidized Stafford:	$	
+ Unsubsidized Stafford:	$	
+ PLUS loan:	$	
+ Private loans:	$	
+ Other loans:	$	
= Total Financial Aid:	**$**	
Unmet Financial Need:	**$**	

Straight Talk with a Financial Aid Administrator ▶ **We have the legal right to use professional judgment**

Financial aid is based on your previous year's income taxes, but a lot can change between the time you did your taxes and filed the FAFSA. A death in the immediate family, a divorce or change in marital status, unemployment or the end of unemployment benefits or if the president declares a national disaster area are all reasons for a reassessment.

As financial aid administrators we have the power to use what is known as "professional judgment" based on extenuating circumstances. But to use it we need proof. For example, if your family lived in an apartment and there was a fire that destroyed everything and you didn't have insurance, you would need to document this so we can use professional judgment to make a change.

One of the most difficult things to document is when a student claims to be independent. In such a case, a letter from a member of the clergy or social worker could be important.

So, one important piece of advice for all families is to keep a file and save everything. Families that have good documentation make it easy for us to use professional judgment to reassess their situation.

Courtney McAnuff, Vice President for Enrollment Services, Eastern Michigan University

Online Award Analyzer

These worksheets are available on the Sallie Mae website (www.salliemae.com). The online tool goes one step further by analyzing your personal savings and calculating the cost of borrowing additional money if your savings are not enough. It even estimates the monthly payments associated with borrowing various loan amounts.

Comparing Award Letters

The hardest part of comparing award letters is that you can't just look at the bottom line; you have to determine how the money is packaged. As you compare offers, focus on these key areas:

Sticker price. Compare each college's tuition, required fees and room and board. For some schools, your child may want to explore options such as off-campus housing or even living at home as a way to reduce these costs.

**Straight Talk
with a Financial Aid
Administrator**

At our university, the first $5,000 is generally self-help

As with many private institutions, at Duke we have what we call a "threshold package strategy." This means the first X dollars will generally be in the form of self-help, which includes work or student loans. Once we pass this limit—the threshold—the remainder will be in grants.

If our cost of attendance is $35,000 and a student has an EFC of $5,000, that student's financial need is $30,000. Since Duke has a policy to meet 100 percent of a student's need we will develop a package that covers this entire need. The first $5,000 we award will generally be in the form of campus employment and student loans. The remaining $25,000 will be in the form of grants. This system holds true as well for a student who has an EFC of $20,000, but in this case the first $5,000 is self-help and $15,000 is grants.

The idea behind the threshold strategy is this: We believe every student should help himself or herself through either work or student loans before we commit our grant money. We want the student to be financially invested in education. We also want the student to know we are in this together. Therefore, we expect every student to borrow a little and work a little. After the student fulfills this obligation, we commit our grant money to cover the rest. In this way we make our university both accessible and affordable.

Jim Belvin, Director of Financial Aid, Duke University

Expected Family Contribution (EFC). Financial aid is designed to cover the difference between your Expected Family Contribution and what the college costs. However, colleges may use different Expected Family Contributions for the same family. For example, one college may use the Federal Methodology, while another uses the institutional methodology. Or you may have special financial circumstances, such as unemployment or unusual medical expenses, that will require financial aid administrators to use their professional judgment. Any of these factors could explain why one college would calculate a different EFC than another.

Unsubsidized Stafford Loans and PLUS Loans. Loans can help families cover their EFC. In other words, if a college reports your EFC to be $5,000, but you don't have that money available, unsubsidized Stafford and PLUS loans make up the difference. Perkins and subsidized Stafford loans also help bridge the gap between the EFC and the cost of college, but they are considered a different type of financial aid. On award letters, colleges may lump unsubsidized and subsidized loans together.

If they do, you should separate them, because they really are two distinct forms of financial aid.

Gift aid versus self-help. Look at the amount of gift aid your child receives (money that does not need to be paid back) versus self-help money, such as student loans. Work-study, while technically self-help, is probably better thought of as gift aid, since it does not need to be repaid.

When comparing gift aid and self-help, don't assume that a college that awards more gift aid is better. Even if the college awards more gift aid, it may still expect your family to pay more out of pocket. It's important to look at the financial aid offer as a whole, especially how student debt will affect your child after graduation.

Unmet financial need. A college is not necessarily obligated to cover your entire financial need. Any amount not covered is considered unmet need, and you are responsible for it.

Don't focus on the total size of the aid package. In the case of award letters, bigger is not always better. It's crucial to look at the total cost of the college, your Expected Family Contribution, how the money is packaged and whether the aid package covers your entire financial need.

Test Your Evaluating Skills

The following are three fictional financial aid award letters. Imagine that these are from your child's colleges and you must decide which is really the best offer:

College A
Cost of Attendance (COA): $25,000
Expected Family Contribution (EFC): $12,000
Financial need: $13,000

Financial Aid Package
Grants: $6,000
Scholarships: $2,000
Subsidized loans: $2,500
Work-study: $1,500
Total aid package: $12,000
Unmet need: $1,000

Analysis of College A's Offer

With an EFC of $12,000, your family is expected to contribute nearly half the one-

BRIGHT IDEA . . . . . .

Analyze aid awards electronically. Use the Sallie Mae (www.salliemae.com) Online Award Analyzer to evaluate your child's financial aid packages. This tool will help you compare different financial aid packages and calculate the cost of borrowing additional money.

year cost of attendance at this college, and the financial aid package leaves $1,000 in unmet need. So you will have to come up with $13,000 for your part. If you don't have this money, you will have to borrow it.

For College A, total gift aid is $8,000 plus $1,500 from work-study. Your child will also have to borrow $2,500 in student loans.

College B

COA: $21,000
EFC: $10,000
Financial need: $11,000

Financial Aid Package

Grants: $5,500
Scholarships: $2,500
Subsidized loans: $2,000
Work-study: $1,000
Total aid package: $11,000
Unmet need: 0

Straight Talk with a Financial Aid Administrator ▶ **Colleges don't usually play "Let's Make a Deal"**

Formal "negotiation" between parent and college only happens on the margin and is not a typical occurrence. This is not meant to imply that parents don't try to deal; many do. But schools normally do not make substantial changes in award packages. It's best to think of "negotiating" more as establishing an accurate comparison from one institution to another. If the financial aid offer is significantly higher at one institution than another, it's certainly appropriate for the parents to bring the discrepancy to the attention of other educational institutions the student is thinking of attending. Do we make mistakes? Sure. Do we make many mistakes? No. So unless your circumstances have changed, be prepared for colleges and universities to decline matching other institutions' financial aid packages. Certainly all parents should look to ensure the awards made are fair and equitable and that their child is viewed in the best light possible. Parents should not expect to play "Let's Make a Deal" with the college. It's exceedingly rare any institutions will play this game.

Dr. Lawrence Burt, Associate VP for Student Affairs & Director of Student Financial Services, University of Texas at Austin

Analysis of College B's Offer

In addition to being a few thousands dollars cheaper than College A, College B expects you to contribute only $10,000 of your own money. Why is College B's EFC different from that of College A? The two colleges may have used different formulas, or perhaps they evaluated your special circumstances in different ways. This college does not leave you with any unmet need.

BRIGHT IDEA . . . . . .

Don't judge financial aid packages only by the bottom line. Remember that scholarships and grants don't need to be repaid, loans do and work-study requires time to work. Even if a financial aid package totals up to less, it may be more valuable if much of it does not need to be repaid.

Total gift aid is $8,000 (same as College A), plus $1,000 from work-study. Although the amount of work-study is less than College A's offer, it means that your child will be able to work less and have more time to study. Your child will have to borrow $2,000 rather than $2,500. (Borrowing $500 less may not seem like much, but the total savings will be more than $500 because of the interest avoided.)

College C
COA: $16,000
EFC: $10,000
Financial need: $6,000

Financial Aid Package
Grants: $1,000
Scholarships: $2,000
Subsidized loans: $2,500
Work-study: $500
Total aid package: $6,000
Unmet need: 0

Analysis of College C's Offer

The cheapest college in the group, College C expects you to contribute $10,000 of your own money—the same as College B and $2,000 less than College A. This college does not leave you with any unmet need. It is interesting to note that even though College C is much cheaper than College B, what comes out of your own pocket is the same.

Total gift aid is $3,000, plus $500 from work-study. Your child will have to borrow $2,500 in student loans.

And the Winner Is…

Which package is best? Colleges B and C will take less out of your pocket than College A. College B may even allow your child to borrow less, which is partially offset by the fact that your child will have to work more.

However, the answer to this question may have less to do with finances and more to do with the quality and desirability of Colleges A, B and C. You and your child may decide that—on the basis of factors such as educational quality, location and campus environment—it is worth paying more to attend one college over another. How much a college costs is important, but it's rarely the only consideration.

Straight Talk with a Financial Aid Administrator ▶ **Keys to a successful reassessment**

Financial aid offices across the country are well prepared to respond to special circumstances. Financial aid professionals understand that during the time from when the application is completed to when a student enrolls, unfortunate circumstances can arise. We also understand the FAFSA application is designed to solicit information from families across the United States and there are some unique circumstances that are not easily communicated on the form.

Many years ago when I just started in the financial aid profession I had a student bring her mother and father to her appointment. She was requesting a revision in her financial aid award and brought in not only the necessary documentation from the insurance company and hospital but also a copy of the newspaper article describing how her parents' store literally blew up. This unfortunate incident dramatically reduced any income opportunity for the family and caused unemployment and additional medical bills. The student's father was still wearing a cast when they arrived in my office. Such dramatic documentation is not required to get a positive response, but when circumstances arise be thoughtful about bringing such things such as police records if something of value was stolen, unemployment documentation or hospital bills. A clearly written letter describing the change in circumstance and what the family's expected income will be in the coming months and for how long the income will be reduced is very helpful. This is the best way to help us provide you with the most assistance.

Dr. Lawrence Burt, Associate VP for Student Affairs & Director of Student Financial Services, University of Texas at Austin

Straight Talk with a Financial Aid Administrator ▶ **Sorry, we don't negotiate**

Our policy is simple. We don't ever negotiate a financial aid offer or match another school's offer. This is not to say that other schools will not since each school operates differently. We sometimes get a parent who calls and says, "Oatmeal Tech gave my son $5,000 more in aid, so can you match that offer?" Our answer is, "No, but if you truly can't afford our school, let's talk." If there are circumstances that we didn't originally consider, we are more than happy to adjust the aid package. But there must be new information before we will consider making an adjustment. Just because another college made a better offer is not a reason. We don't use need-based financial aid to "lure" or to "buy" students. Financial aid is meant to facilitate the family's ability to afford college. If the information we used in our initial calculation is a true representation of the family's circumstance, then our decision is fair. If parents call for more money, we will listen and make sure our original calculations were correct. But we certainly don't take the position we will do whatever it takes. We don't provide additional aid because one student's parent called and another didn't.

Jim Belvin, Director of Financial Aid, Duke University

If you pick College A, you know that it will cost $3,000 more out of pocket and $500 more in student loans than College B. The higher price may be entirely worth it to you and your child. Comparing award letters shows you what each college truly costs. This financial analysis, along with all the other intangible factors, will allow you and your child to make the most informed decision possible.

What If It's Not Enough?

Paying for college is not like buying a car, where you can haggle over the cost of floor mats and how much you're willing to pay. Through the award letter, the college presents a firm offer that it believes is fair, given your financial situation. Nevertheless, there may be room for improvement.

If your financial situation has changed significantly since you filled out the forms, contact the school's financial aid office and ask for a reassessment. This is a request to the financial aid administrator to take a second look at the financial aid package. Be sure you can present concrete reasons why the calculations are not accurate and you deserve more aid. Special circumstances or changes to your family's finances may include the following:

- Unusual or unexpected medical expenses
- Tuition for a child, including private secondary or elementary school expenses
- Unemployment of a spouse or parent
- Ongoing divorce or separation
- Care for an aging relative
- Significant change in income that is not reflected in last year's tax return. (Remember, you used last year's return to complete this year's FAFSA.)

DEADLINE . . . .

Respond promptly to the award letter. Every college has a deadline by which you need to accept their offer of financial aid. Be sure to respond before the deadline. Many students need financial aid—if the college doesn't hear from your child before the deadline, that money will go to someone else.

Explain the circumstances to the financial aid administrator in detail in a letter or in person. Don't just describe the event; provide the numbers that show how it affects your family's finances. Financial aid administrators prefer to deal with numbers.

If you ask for a reassessment, keep the following points in mind.

Be pleasant; never threaten. Some parents take an aggressive approach to asking for more aid; this usually backfires. Financial aid administrators are professionals who believe in the aid packages they create. They know they can make mistakes and are happy to take a second look if you present a good reason. However, if you are aggressive, abrasive or confrontational, they will have little desire to help. Remain cordial, present the facts and listen to their reasons.

Know what you need. The financial aid administrator may ask how much more aid you need. Be ready to state an exact amount, with whatever details you need to back it up.

Be honest about your financial situation. Don't be self-conscious about your financial problems. Trying to hide embarrassing facts, such as bad credit that prevents you from taking out a loan, will only hurt your case. Financial aid administrators have seen and heard it all. They are there to help, so let them.

Don't wait for something bad to happen if you know it will. If you know that a change in your employment or an unavoidable expenditure is coming, inform the financial aid office now. Like any organization, the college has a limited budget. If you wait until the last minute, it might be too late for the college to respond. If you give them advance notice, they may be able to help you when the inevitable occurs.

A Reassessment Request That Worked

You may ask for a reassessment at any time during your child's college years if there is a change in your family's finances. Following is an actual letter a student wrote to the financial aid office. Before she wrote the letter, she had received only a small loan, despite the fact that her father had been laid off for more than a year. She composed this letter to explain her family's extenuating circumstances, describing their actual income and expenses. It paid off—she got a $6,500 grant per semester for the rest of the year.

Dear Sir or Madam:

I am writing to request that my financial aid package for the fall semester be reconsidered. My family and I were disappointed with the amount we were offered because, in addition to my father having been unemployed for over a

Straight Talk with a Financial Aid Administrator ▶ **For special circumstances, documentation is paramount**

Whenever a parent asks us to consider special circumstances we require documentation. For example, if a parent earned $50,000 last year but got laid off at the end of the year, we require documentation such as a letter from the employer or unemployment records. We don't want to pry into a family's private affairs, but by getting this documentation it enables us to provide more aid.

Another example is when a student requests to be treated as an independent student. While a parent may believe a child is independent at age 18, the federal regulations state, for financial aid purposes a child is only independent at age 24 or if they meet one of the other criteria stated on the FAFSA. Therefore, to overrule the federal guidelines we need documentation from three sources, only one of which can be a relative. The other two could be sources like a school counselor, police officer, social worker or member of the clergy. Every special circumstance needs to be reviewed individually, and the more documentation a family can provide, the easier it will be for us to help.

Veronica J. Leech, Director of Financial Aid, Central State University

year, my older sister will be a sophomore in college and my mother, a part-time teacher, has received no income since June because of summer break.

We understand that nearly every family must undergo an amount of hardship to send its members to college. However, because my parents wish to continue financing my sister's and my education, they are worried about how they will pay for their own expenses. They have been using my mother's income to basically cover their mortgage payments and their savings to pay for everything else. In February, my parents had $33,000 in savings. In the last six months, their savings has decreased by about $15,000. They now have about $18,000 to contribute to my sister's and my college expenses as well as to spend on their and my younger brother's food and basic necessities. They don't know how long their savings will last without a change in the amount of aid I receive.

At the end of this month, my sister will begin her sophomore year at USC. The cost will be $26,998, and she has received $18,758 in financial aid. This makes my parents' contribution amount to $8,240, of which they will borrow $2,625.

Straight Talk with a Financial Aid Administrator ▶ **Keep grades up to keep financial aid**

Most financial aid programs have a critical stipulation: To continue to receive the aid a student needs to maintain "satisfactory academic progress." Imagine that typical freshmen start with 17 or 18 credits. They start having a good time living on their own and away from mom and dad. After consulting their roommate they decide to drop 15 credits and just keep the easy classes. At this new pace it will take them 18 years to graduate! That's not "satisfactory academic progress," and the students (surprise!) will lose their aid package. We see this happen to hundreds of students every year. Students need to understand that every grade counts. Every class counts. Every withdrawal or incomplete counts. If you drop too many classes, it will push your projected graduation beyond the acceptable five years and you will lose your financial aid.

Courtney McAnuff, Vice President for Enrollment Services, Eastern Michigan University

Since July of last year, my father has been unemployed. His severance pay ended in October, and his unemployment benefits have been depleted since February. Although he has applied for over a dozen positions, his prospects for finding a job in his specialty are slim.

My parents and I have discussed the possibility of having me take a year off so that I may work to help pay for tuition, but we'd much rather that I finish school now and work after I have received my degree.

Please contact my parents or me with any further questions you may have. Thank you very much for your time and consideration. I hope that this information is helpful in your review of my application.

Sincerely Yours,

There's no guarantee that a letter like this will work, but it can't hurt to ask when the financial situation of your family changes significantly and you can show how the change has affected your ability to pay. If the financial aid office says no, nothing changes; if it says yes, life gets better and easier.

> **KEY CONCEPT . . . .**
>
> **When asking for a reassessment, make your case in numbers.** It's not enough to say that your financial aid package is not enough. Financial aid decisions are based on calculations and rules that are applied equally to all families. Therefore, changes can't be made unless they are backed by actual numbers. If you can support your request for more aid (e.g., documenting that your family just paid a $5,000 medical bill), you will help the college justify giving you more.

Accepting the Award

The clock is ticking! Note the deadline for responding to the financial aid award letter. Don't miss this deadline, or the award could be in jeopardy. As soon as your child decides which college to attend, let both the admissions and financial aid offices know.

And congratulations on making it through the process.

Straight Talk
with a Financial Aid
Administrator

How to ask for a financial aid reassessment

Various circumstances may lead to a reassessment of the financial aid package. These include, but are not limited to, drastic change in income, divorce, high medical bills, child care costs and dependency status. To be reassessed, parents or students must complete the Request for Professional Judgment, after reading the Professional Judgment Information Statement, and submit it to the financial aid counselor. There is also a Child Care Form and Employer Form that must be completed for certain scenarios. When reassessing a package we look at everything on a case-by-case basis. Therefore, it's important families provide as much information and documentation as possible to help us understand the specifics of their situation.

Peggy Loewy-Wellisch, Associate Vice President for Student Financial Services, Nova Southeastern University

CHAPTER 6

Should We Borrow Money to Pay for College?

What you'll learn:

- How to apply for a low-interest student loan
- How borrower benefits can save you money
- Advantages and disadvantages of each type of student loan
- Where else to borrow money for college
- When to use loan forgiveness programs

Most 17- or 18-year-olds have no real credit or collateral to draw on. Your child may not even have a part-time job. Despite this, your son or daughter would have no trouble borrowing more than $35,000 to pay for college—all guaranteed by the federal government. That's how much faith the government has in every college-bound high school student.

The government-backed programs are available to you as well. As the parent of a college student—and if you have a good credit rating or a creditworthy endorser—you can borrow whatever you need to make up the difference between what college costs and the amount of financial aid your child receives. The program is known as the Parent Loan for Undergraduate Students (PLUS), and this loan also is backed by the federal government.

Equally impressive are the incredibly favorable terms and student-friendly repayment policies of student loans. With low interest rates and protections against rising rates, student loans are often the cheapest source of borrowed money. With all these advantages, it's no surprise that more than 70 percent of students take advantage of student loans to help pay for college.

College: A Worthy Investment

College is an investment in your child's future. As with any worthwhile investment, you may need to borrow money to help pay for it. Consider borrowing through the student loan programs, as they are often the most affordable.

Borrowing Responsibly

For years you have been telling your child to be responsible. That lesson is never more appropriate than in borrowing money. Responsible management of student loans can be easy, can help your child establish a good credit rating and can protect him or her from experiencing the negative effects of too much debt. But make sure your child understands the responsibility.

If for some reason your child doesn't complete his or her education or is unsatisfied with it, the loan still must be repaid. Failing to pay back a loan will put your child in default, which can scar a credit rating for years. This concept may be easy for you to understand, but your child may not realize how severe the ramifications of defaulting can be.

Get to Know the Student Loan VIPs

The first step to learning about loans is to get to know the entities that make them. Unlike the case of a home mortgage, for which you usually only deal with one lender, many parties are involved in student loans.

Straight Talk
with a Financial Aid
Administrator ▶

Loans let you buy more by paying over time

If you think about it, you can usually buy more if you pay over time. This is true with a car when you finance it or with a home when you take out a mortgage. It is also true with college. If you can spread the costs over time, you can afford more. (Of course, spending more does not necessarily mean you get a better education.) Student loans essentially let you pay for college beyond the four years you are there. In fact, with a loan you can stretch the cost of college over 10 or more years.

Jim Belvin, Director of Financial Aid, Duke University

Federal government. The U.S. Department of Education oversees the federal student loan programs. For some types of loans, it also serves as the lender.

Lenders. These are the organizations that actually provide the money, own the loans and take your regular payments. Most schools have developed relationships with various lenders and even provide a list of "preferred" lenders. In most cases, the lender is a bank, although it could also be a school, credit union, pension fund, insurance company, consumer finance company or the federal government itself.

KEY CONCEPT . . . .

Never borrow more than you need. Borrowing too much is a big mistake of first-time borrowers. For many students, repaying their loans seems far away, which can lead to irresponsible borrowing. Encourage your child to borrow only what he or she absolutely needs to pay for school. For miscellaneous expenses—"fun money"—encourage your child to work during the summer or find a part-time job at school.

College. Colleges play a major role in the student loan process. The financial aid office determines the amount a student needs to borrow, recommends lenders and answers questions about loans.

Guarantor. A guarantor is a state or private nonprofit agency, approved by the federal government, that ensures lenders will be repaid for most of the loan and are the reason why students with no credit histories are able to receive loans. If a borrower defaults on a federal student loan, the guarantor reimburses the lender and then pursues the borrower (you or your child) for collection. For loan programs in which the federal government is the lender, a guarantor is not required.

Servicer. Lenders usually hire companies to "service" student loans. A servicer may perform tasks on behalf of the lender, such as processing loan applications, answering customer service phone calls, processing loan payments and collecting delinquent accounts.

Credit bureau. Credit bureaus gather and store credit information on individuals. A credit report is not necessary for students to receive a federal student loan, but it is required for parents who are applying for PLUS loans as well as for most private student loans.

Borrower. This is your child (or, in the case of a PLUS loan, you)—the person who actually borrows the money. For federal student loans, your child is the borrower. This means your child is fully responsible for repayment.

The Loan Life Cycle

Federal student loans are available from two sources: 1) the Federal Family Education Loan Program (FFELP) in which private financial institutions are the lenders and 2) the Federal Direct Loan Program (FDLP) in which the federal government is the lender. These programs are very similar and a school can decide to participate in one or both. The following describes the typical life cycle of a federal student loan.

Phase 1: Identifying Need

Students and parents:

- Complete and submit the Free Application for Federal Student Aid (FAFSA). This form will help determine your eligibility for aid.

- Review the Student Aid Report (SAR). Your SAR will summarize the information you provided on the FAFSA and indicates your Expected Family Contribution (EFC).

- Compare the financial aid award letters received from schools.

Phase 2: Loan Application

- Borrower requests loan by submitting a loan application.

- School certifies student eligibility.

- Lender approves borrower loan application.

- In the case of the FFELP loans, a guarantor provides guarantee that the loan will be repaid.

Phase 3: Disbursement

- Lender sends loan proceeds to the school by check or electronic funds transfer.

- School may contact borrower for check endorsement.

- School applies loan proceeds to student's outstanding bill and turns over any remaining funds to the borrower.

- Under most federal loan programs, loan proceeds are not disbursed to first year undergraduates who are also first-time borrowers until the student completes the first 30 days of his or her program of study

- Lender sends parent borrower a repayment disclosure statement for federal PLUS loan.

■ Parent borrower with federal PLUS loans begins repayment after full disbursement. The first payment is due no later than 60 days after disbursement.

■ For loans requiring credit, the lender notifies credit bureaus that loan proceeds have been disbursed.

Phase 4: In School

■ Student attends school. Student borrower is not required to make federal loan payments during this time.

● Under some federal loan programs, accrued interest on loan during this period is paid by the federal government (interest subsidy).

● Under other programs, the borrower is responsible for paying the interest that accrues while the student is in school.

● Student borrowers who have Federal Stafford or Federal Perkins loans are considered "in-school" unless they are enrolled less than half-time, graduate, or withdraw. Parent borrowers with one or more Federal PLUS loans do not have an "in-school" phase.

Phase 5: Grace Period

■ Student graduates, enrolls for less than half time, or withdraws.

■ Student borrower receives a single "grace period" of 6-9 months (depending on the type of federal loan) before repayment of any federal loan begins.

Parent borrowers do not receive a "grace period" with federal PLUS loans. Borrowers of private loans may or may not receive a "grace period."

■ Lender sends student borrower a repayment disclosure statement detailing the date payments must start, monthly payment amount, number of payments, and interest rate for the student loan(s).

HEAD START . . . .

You must file a FAFSA to get a federal student loan. You may not know whether you need a loan until the start of the school year; however, if you haven't completed the FAFSA, you and your child will not be eligible to receive a federal student loan. Think of the FAFSA as an insurance policy: If you need to borrow money, you'll be able to do so. Also, filing the FAFSA will make your child eligible for grants and work-study.

Phase 6: Repayment

- Student begins repaying Federal Stafford or Federal Perkins loans when the grace period ends.

- Parent begins repaying Federal PLUS loans immediately after full disbursement and must make initial payment within 60 days of disbursement.

- Student and/or parent begin repaying private loans according to the terms of the loan.

- For federal loans, your child (and you) may switch from one repayment plan to another once a year as long

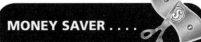

MONEY SAVER . . . .

Loan consolidation allows borrowers to consolidate all of their eligible loans into a new single loan. This provides borrowers with the advantage of having only one monthly student loan payment and the convenience of working with a single service provider. In addition, consolidation allows a borrower, depending upon their total education loan debt, to extend their loan repayments term up to 30 years thus providing borrowers extended monthly payment relief.

as the maximum loan term for the new plan is longer than the amount of time left under the current plan. To choose the best repayment plan or compare plans, use one of the calculators on the Sallie Mae website (www.salliemae.com). With the Repayment Calculator, you can estimate monthly loan payments and see the impact of required minimum monthly payments.

Although the most common method of repayment is to pay the same amount each month until the loan is paid in full, many lenders offer alternatives. Depending on the type of loan, your child may be able to choose from the following options:

Standard repayment plan. Standard repayment usually offers borrowers the lowest total loan cost. Regular payments of both principal and interest are due monthly, excluding periods of *deferment* and *forbearance* (see below under Ways to Postpone Payment). The term is 10 years for Stafford and PLUS loans.

Extended repayment plan. This plan extends the term of the loan up to 25 years. Extending repayment reduces monthly payments but also means more interest. This plan may be a good option if your child has borrowed such a large amount that the standard monthly payments would be close to impossible. This plan is also available for PLUS loans.

Graduated repayment plan. Graduated repayment plans are designed to make initial monthly payments more affordable. These plans typically allow borrowers to sharply reduce their monthly payments by making interest only payments for a specific period of time. The initial payments are small—as much as 50 percent less than under the standard plan—and then gradually increase over the term of the loan. Your child will pay more interest than under the standard plan, but this method helps new graduates because payments start small and increase as salary grows. The plan is also available for PLUS loans. These plans can usually be combined with an extended repayment plan for even greater relief.

Income-sensitive repayment plan (Federal Family Education Loan Program). Available for Stafford, PLUS, and Consolidation loans, an income-sensitive plan allows borrowers to make monthly payments in an amount between 4 percent and 25 percent of their monthly gross income and has a maximum repayment period of ten years.

Income-contingent repayment plan (Federal Direct Loan Program). An income-contingent plan sets monthly payments according to the borrower's income, and payments are adjusted each year as income goes up or down. The term of the loan is up to 25 years; after 25 years, any remaining balance on the loan is discharged. This plan is not available for PLUS loans.

All federally sponsored loans and most private loans allow borrowers to pay part or all of the outstanding balance at any time without penalty. Prepaying can greatly reduce the total cost of borrowing.

Phase 7: Paid in Full

- Borrower makes final loan payment.

- Lender sends notice confirming to borrower that loan is paid in full.

- Lender notifies credit bureaus that borrower has fully repaid the loan.

How to Borrow Money

The student loan application may be the first contract your child ever signs, and that's exactly what it is: a contract. The application is a legal agreement between the borrower and the lender and should be taken seriously. Like most contracts, it includes fine print and "legalese." Here are some of the terms you need to know to understand a loan application:

- Promissory note
- Master promissory note (MPN)
- Repayment options
- Disclosure statement

- Accrued interest
- Capitalized interest
- Collection
- Late charge
- Change of status
- Default

Promissory note. This is the contract, containing everything your child needs to know about the loan. The "prom note" is what your child signs, meaning that he or she agrees to all terms, and should be read carefully.

Master promissory note. The master promissory note covers multiple Stafford loans over the duration of your child's education at any participating four-year college or graduate school. Your child will need to sign only one master promissory note for federal Stafford loan borrowing. In the past, he or she would have had to sign a note for loans in each academic year. The same is true for your PLUS loans. Only one master promissory note is now needed instead of a new promissory note for each year.

Straight Talk with a Financial Aid Administrator ▶

College debt is an investment; consumer debt is just debt

Student loans are the dominant source of financial assistance because the federal government, which provides the largest amount of assistance, understands that significantly more funds can be made available to families through loans than grants or scholarships. When considering borrowing money, it is very important to view educational debt as an investment versus borrowing for a consumer item such as taking a car loan or carrying a credit card debt. Consumer debt allows access to goods and services that are, as the name implies, consumed. Capital investments, such as educational loans, yield benefits throughout the student's life. In this country it is typical for college graduates to earn a million dollars more over their lifetime than non-college graduates. If a student or a family has to borrow a moderate amount to get that million-dollar payback and the significant increase in quality of life that comes from having a career instead of a job, it becomes somewhat easier to understand and accept the necessity of taking on educational debt.

Dr. Lawrence Burt, Associate VP for Student Affairs & Director of Student Financial Services, University of Texas at Austin

---

Disclosure statement. Whichever repayment option your child selects, the disclosure statement will outline the facts and figures for that option, including the interest rate of the loan, the number of monthly payments required to pay the loan in full and the amount(s) of the payments. The statement includes the estimated amount that will be repaid—principal and interest—if your child follows the schedule in the disclosure.

USEFUL TERM . . . . .

Entrance counseling. The federal government requires all Stafford and Perkins borrowers to participate in entrance counseling. The information-packed session reviews the basic facts about the loan, including the rights and responsibilities of the borrower. The counseling is usually provided on campus by the college.

Interest. Interest is the fee or charge paid to a lender for the use of their money and to cover their costs for servicing the loan until it is paid in full. The amount is based on the amount of the loan, the rate and the total amount of time to repay. Typically, the interest rate and how it is applied are defined in the promissory note and the disclosure statement. The interest rate percentage is established when your child receives the money. For federal student loans, the rate is fixed. Interest rates for private loans vary among lenders.

Interest is computed on a daily basis. It is important that your child understand that late payments mean extra interest. Except for subsidized loans, the interest accrues and is added to the loan balance once your child starts repayment. To reduce costs, your child might start repaying the loan—or at least making payments on interest—before he or she graduates. Most lenders allow interest-only payments on a monthly, quarterly or annual basis while borrowers are still in school.

Capitalized interest. For most loans, including student loans, interest is repaid before the principal. If your child is unable to make payments for a reason such as unemployment, he or she may qualify to suspend the payments. During that time, though, interest continues to accrue. With a subsidized loan, the federal government may cover that amount, depending on the reason for not paying. If your child doesn't qualify for this interest subsidy, there are two options: make interest-only payments or have the interest added to the outstanding loan principal when repayment is resumed. See the Accrued Interest Calculator on the Sallie Mae website (www.salliemae.com) for help in analyzing these options.

Collection. If your child doesn't repay the loan on time, he or she will get calls and letters from the lender or servicer. Before this happens, have your child contact the servicer(s). They may be able to help or make suggestions for dealing with financial troubles.

Late charges. Failure to pay all or a portion of a required payment on time may trigger late charges of varying amounts.

Change of status. Your child must provide changes in name, address, phone number or Social Security number to the school, lender or servicer. Your child's signature on the promissory note signifies that he or she has agreed to this borrower responsibility.

Default. Don't do it. The terms of the loan hold your child responsible for repaying it in full and on time, with serious consequences for failing to do so. Not paying, or defaulting, on a loan can have a significant impact on your child's future.

MONEY SAVER . . . .

Before taking out a second mortgage, consider the PLUS. As a parent, if you have good credit, you can take advantage of a federal student loan program called the Parent Loan for Undergraduate Students. The PLUS allows you to borrow money for each child, and you do not have to prove financial need. In general, PLUS loans have lower interest rates than other forms of consumer borrowing, as well as protections against rising rates. Be sure to include the PLUS among your borrowing options.

Exploring the Federal Student Loan Program

Federal loans are the largest source of educational financing. Because they have very attractive terms compared with most other borrowing options, these loans should be considered first. Among the benefits are

- Less stringent credit requirements for parents and none for students
- Lower interest rates
- Longer repayment terms
- The possibility of having interest subsidized by the federal government while the borrower is in school, grace and deferment
- The option to postpone making payments

Following are descriptions of the various types of federal student loans available and their criteria.

Federal Stafford Loans

Stafford loans are among the most common low-interest loans for undergraduate and graduate students—and for good reason: They are guaranteed by the government, so even students with low or no credit will have no problem getting a loan. Borrowers must attend an accredited school at least half time and must use the money only for qualified expenses such as tuition and fees, room and board, books and supplies, transportation and living expenses. These loans have a fixed interest rate of 6.8 percent. There are two types of Stafford loans: subsidized and unsubsidized.

Subsidized Stafford loans. Subsidized Stafford loans are awarded to students who demonstrate financial need. The Department of Education subsidizes the interest on the loans—borrowers are not charged interest while they are enrolled in school at least half time and during grace and deferment periods.

Unsubsidized Stafford loans. Unsubsidized Stafford loans are available to students regardless of financial need. Borrowers are responsible for the interest that accrues during any period including periods when the student is in school.

Where does the money come from? Either the Federal Family Education Loan Program or the Federal Direct Loan Program. The college chooses to participate in

---

Straight Talk with a Financial Aid Administrator ▶ # Why colleges have preferred lenders

Financial aid offices across the country have found there are many dependable lenders as well as a few lenders with poorer credentials. Lenders that are very new to student lending can be inexperienced and less reliable. Taking on educational debt is a serious issue, and it is critical that funds are reliably delivered and that both the disbursement and repayment process are handled well.

To help you choose a reliable lender, colleges have what are known as "preferred" lender lists. The lenders that appear on an institution's lender list typically have been involved in student lending for many years and have a substantial track record. These lenders have consistently shown themselves to be on the cutting edge of electronic innovation, ease of process and are very reliable and compatible with educational institutions and the clientele they serve. Lender lists make it easy for families to evaluate a relatively small number of lenders out of the hundreds that may be processing student loans.

For instance, it may be important that electronic funds transfer is used for distributing funds. This is common for the experienced lenders. Families may be interested in knowing whether the lending institution or a business partner will collect the loan. Things called "borrower benefits" such as interest rate reduction for a good payment experience and a high level of customer service are important for many families. We have done the legwork of evaluating these areas prior to allowing a lender to appear on our preferred lender list.

Dr. Lawrence Burt, Associate VP for Student Affairs & Director of Student Financial Services, University of Texas at Austin

one or both of these programs. The programs are similar; the differences are in the application process and repayment options.

Eligibility. No credit check is required for a Stafford loan. The applicant must be a U.S. citizen or eligible noncitizen and must be enrolled as a full- or half-time undergraduate or graduate student.

Interest rate. The rate is fixed at 6.8 percent.

Loan limits. Loan limits vary depending on student status. Independent students generally may borrow more than dependent students. Grade level is also a factor. Typically, the Stafford annual limits are as follows:

	Dependent Undergraduate Student	Independent Undergraduate Student	Graduate Student
First Year	$5,500	$9,500	$20,500
	$3,500 of this amount may be in subsidized loans	*$3,500 of this amount may be in subsidized loans*	*$8,500 of this may be subsidized*
Second Year	$6,500	$10,500	Same as above
	$4,500 of this amount may be in subsidized loans	*$4,500 of this amount may be in subsidized loans*	
Third Year or Later	$7,500	$12,500	Same as above
	$5,500 of this amount may be in subsidized loans	*$5,500 of this amount may be in subsidized loans*	

Note: Loan amounts are current as of date of publication.

Maximum total debt from Stafford loans upon graduation:

- $31,000 for dependent undergraduate students (only $23,000 of this amount may be in subsidized loans)
- $57,500 for independent undergraduate students (only $23,000 of this amount may be in subsidized loans)
- $138,500 for graduate or professional students (only $65,500 of this amount may be in subsidized loans). Graduate debt limit includes Stafford loans received for undergraduate study.

PLUS Loans

With most college loans, the student is the borrower; with the PLUS loan, the parent is the borrower. These loans are available through both the Federal Family Education Loan Program and the Federal Direct Loan Program. PLUS loans:

- Are available regardless of income or assets
- May be up to the full cost of each student's education each academic year (minus any grants and financial aid)
- Require no collateral
- Have a low fixed interest rate of 7.9 percent for Direct PLUS Loans and 8.5 percent for FFEL PLUS Loans
- Offer interest that may be tax deductible
- Have no prepayment penalty

Eligibility. Parents must meet these requirements to be eligible for a PLUS loan:

- Have a dependent undergraduate student enrolled in college full or half time
- Be a U.S. citizen or eligible noncitizen
- Pass a basic credit check and have no adverse credit history (parents with adverse credit may be eligible with a "co-borrower", referred to as an "endorser" for PLUS loans or by proving extenuating circumstances that are acceptable to the lender)

While the federal government does not require that you file a FAFSA to qualify for a PLUS loan, some schools require the FAFSA for PLUS borrowers.

If you have adverse credit, you will need an endorser—someone who is responsible for making your payments if you are unable to repay the loan. Endorsers must pass a PLUS credit review and must live in the United States. All payments made by an endorser must be in dollars. Make sure your endorser understands the responsibility involved.

Limits. With no minimum or maximum loan amounts, a parent can borrow up to the total cost of a child's education (minus other aid received). Here are two examples:

	College A	College B
Annual college cost	$10,000	$25,000
Student financial aid received	(2,625)	(9,625)
PLUS loan eligibility	$7,375	$15,375

Fees. Fees of up to 4 percent may be charged and are deducted from the total amount of the loan.

Use Sallie Mae's Online Repayment Calculator to estimate monthly loan payments based on the principal balance, interest rate and loan term.

Federal Perkins Loans

The Perkins loan is a guaranteed loan carrying a 5 percent interest rate for both undergraduate and graduate students with exceptional financial need. The Department of Education provides colleges with a specific amount of funding, and the schools determine which students have the greatest need. Schools usually add their own funds to the federal funds they receive. The student must complete the FAFSA to be eligible for this loan.

The school pays the student directly, usually by check, or applies the loan to school charges. The loan is disbursed in at least two payments during the academic year. Repayment doesn't begin until nine months after the student graduates, leaves school or attends less than half time. During the time the student is in college, interest does not accrue on the loan.

Perkins loans share many of the characteristics of subsidized Stafford loans, but the Perkins loan has no fees and has a longer grace period.

Consolidation Loans

Loan consolidation is a great way to reduce monthly payments by up to 50 percent. With consolidation, your child refinances one or more eligible education loans. The original loans are paid in full, and a new loan for the combined balance is originated, for a new term and often with a lower interest rate and lower monthly payment. The only drawback is that because it will take longer to pay off the new loan, your child would most likely pay more in interest.

Consolidation can be helpful if your child

- Has a heavy education debt
- Wants to lock in a fixed interest rate
- Wants to reduce monthly payment, paperwork and check-writing responsibilities

TIME SAVER . . . .

Apply online. Sallie Mae (www. salliemae.com) offers the convenience of applying for federal and private student loans online. The process takes only about 15 minutes, and some schools allow you to electronically sign for the loan with E-Sign. Using the Internet simplifies the loan application process.

With a consolidated loan, your child may choose among various repayment plans: level repayment (monthly payment is fixed over the life of the loan), graduated repayment, extended repayment or income-sensitive repayment. The plans can assist borrowers by creating flexibility and possibly further reducing their monthly payment. To learn more, visit Sallie Mae at www.salliemae.com.

Private Loans

Not all student loans are backed by the government. Many banks and financial institutions provide loans that are similar to federal student loans; however, since these loans are private and not guaranteed by the government, the terms are set by the individual lenders. These loans can be extremely useful if you have exhausted federal sources of aid, and you or your child may apply for them at any time during the school year.

You apply for private loans in one of two ways:

> **1. From the school.** Some loans are available from the school (which has obtained funds from private lenders on your behalf). The FAA will be able to tell you which private loans are available.

> **2. From a lender.** Other loans are available from a lender, in which case funds will be sent to you.

Sallie Mae's partner lenders offer comprehensive and affordable private loans, including:

■ **The Signature Student Loan®** offers undergraduate and graduate students financing beyond what federal programs can offer. These loans must be approved by your school's financial aid office.

■ **The Tuition Answer Loan**[SM] is a practical, affordable education loan that allows creditworthy students with income to borrow to cover any education-related expense. Parents also are eligible to apply for this loan. These loans do not require approval by your financial aid office, but do require proof of enrollment.

■ **EXCEL Loan** programs help students and their families cover the cost of attendance. StudentEXCEL®, Grad-EXCEL® and discipline-specific loans are for student borrowers, while creditworthy parents may borrow an EXCEL Loan on a student's behalf. EXCEL loans offer competitive rates and benefits.

■ **MEDLOANS®, LAWLOANS® and MBA LOANS®** offer professional graduate students a package of federal and private loans to cover the entire cost of their studies.

■ **The Career Training Loan**[SM] Program assists in financing technical training or trade school, distance learning or other continuing education programs to cover the total cost of education and certain related expenses.

■ **Continuing Education Loan**[SM] is specifically designed to provide financing for postsecondary students not seeking degrees and for part-time students seeking degrees.

(In addition, some loan programs may be available from both the school and a private lender.)

The interest rate for private loans is often based on your credit history—the better your credit rating, the lower the interest rate. Some private loans for education allow you to defer interest and principal payments until after graduation. In selecting a private loan, compare the interest rates, repayment options, loan terms, fees and borrower benefits.

Choosing a Lender

Too often parents think the lender decision is not important; that one loan is the same as another. Wrong. Differences in loans can

- Simplify and shorten the application process
- Save you and your child money
- Ensure better service over the life of the loan

Since your child is entering a relationship with a lender that might last many years, he or she should learn about these differences.

Evaluate Lenders

Most schools have a preferred list of lenders that

- Are trustworthy, are reliable and have proven track records
- Provide attractive loan terms and benefits to borrowers

Straight Talk with a Financial Aid Administrator ▶ **Address bad credit issues early**

The federal Parent Loan for Undergraduate Students (PLUS), which is a part of financial aid, can be a real lifesaver. But since it's based on credit score, some parents are denied a PLUS loan. Therefore, parents should work on their credit issues as soon as possible. While students do not need credit to borrow, parents do. We advise all parents to request a copy of their credit score and identify and correct any problems. The PLUS loan is one of the cheapest ways to borrow money, but it won't do parents any good if they don't qualify.

Veronica J. Leech, Director of Financial Aid, Central State University

■ Provide excellent service to the borrower

It's a good idea to pick a lender from the list since you will be assured the school has an established relationship with the lender.

Consider the following factors when you choose a lender:

■ Compare interest rates and terms; for federal programs, they are generally very similar, but some lenders offer discounts, and private programs can vary significantly
■ Compare borrower benefits, such as those offered for paying on time and making loan payments electronically
■ Compare repayment plans
■ Compare loan application processes—many lenders offer online applications and instant loan approval
■ Compare levels of customer service

As a borrower, your child can get valuable benefits by choosing one lender over another. Often these benefits are money-saving incentives for things such as making on-time payments, making payments via automatic debit or signing up for other services provided by the bank or loan servicer. These incentives may include interest rate reductions or even reductions to the principal balance of the outstanding loan. Usually nothing needs to change in the way your child repays the loan when an incentive is applied to the account. The monthly payment amount remains the same, but your child saves money by paying off the loan faster. Be sure to explore these money-saving borrower benefits. All things being equal, pick the lender that offers the best benefits.

Streamline with One Lender

Putting all your eggs in one basket is usually not a good idea, but in the case of student loans, using one lender can have major benefits. For example, if you use one lender, there is a better chance that the loans will stay together through repayment. The lender will likely service the loans as a group, sell them to a secondary market as a group or allow a servicer to service them as a group. Keeping the loans together will simplify the repayment process.

If your child gets loans from different lenders, he or she will have several monthly bills and payment schedules to track and several checks to write each month. Updates—such as a change of address—will have to be sent to all lenders. Having one lender means one bill, one place to send payments, one lender to keep updated and one source for assistance. Doesn't that sound easier?

Choose a Loan Amount Carefully

Some students borrow as much money as possible, to make sure they have enough for spring break getaways and other extras. While tempting, it can have bad consequences when it comes time for repayment. Your child should borrow only what is absolutely necessary to cover the cost of education. Be conservative and take only what is necessary to cover tuition and fees, housing, meals, books, personal expenses and transportation. When it's time to repay the loans, your child will have other financial obligations as well—living expenses, taxes and other debts—and could easily feel overwhelmed by large student loan payments.

MONEY SAVER . . . .

Do a repayment reality check. A great way to ensure that you and your child are borrowing responsibly is to use the Repayment Calculator on the Sallie Mae website (www.salliemae. com) to see how much will need to be repaid each month and for how many years to pay off the loan. Seeing the loan payment in monthly terms can help you gain perspective on the real impact of borrowing money.

Before your child borrows, encourage him or her to calculate the monthly loan payments after graduation and how many years it will take to repay the loans. Will he or she be able to make the loan payments, cover basic living expenses, have fun and still save some money? This is an important reality check before your child decides how much to borrow.

Ways to Have a Student Loan Forgiven

You may dream that your child's college loans are miraculously forgiven, but this happens in only a few special circumstances. Federal student loan debt is cancelled entirely if a student loan or PLUS borrower becomes totally and permanently disabled or dies. Other conditions in which student loan debt may be discharged either partially or in full include bankruptcy filing, school closure, false loan certification (school admitted you when you did not meet requirements for admission or signed your name on the loan application without your authorization) or an unpaid refund from the school. As you can see, the cure is worse than the disease—you wouldn't want any of these situations to befall your child.

Ways to Postpone Payment: Stafford Loans

Deferment and Forbearance. There may be times in your child's life when student loan payments need to be put on hold or deferred. For subsidized Stafford loans, the government will continue to make the interest payments for your child during deferment. For unsubsidized Stafford loans, your child will be responsible for all interest that accrues during deferment. To qualify for deferment, your child must meet one of the following requirements:

- Decide to go back to school at least half time
- Become unemployed
- Experience severe economic hardship
- Enter a graduate fellowship program

Straight Talk with a Financial Aid Administrator ▶

How to choose the right student loan

Due to the high cost of education, it is very difficult for most students in a private institution to attend college without some type of loan. Grants and scholarships, under most circumstances, can't cover the entire cost of education. That being said, loans should be taken out as a last resort and only if the family needs the money to attend college. It is very easy to take the maximum funds, but remember loans must be repaid. It's important not to get into too much debt, especially as an undergraduate student. Students and parents should make sure that when they graduate, they will be able to cover the repayment, and this is usually based on the future profession of the student. Students should definitely attend a debt-management workshop to have a clear understanding of how a loan will affect them.

When choosing a loan it is important that parents and students are well informed about loans by reading the financial aid website, Department of Education Student Guide (www.ed.gov) and other loan information, as well as attending financial aid orientations and other loan workshops. The best loan is the subsidized Stafford. With this loan the student does not have to repay until six months after graduation or dropping below half-time status, and there is no interest accrued while the student is in school or during the grace period. In addition, some students may be eligible for the federal Perkins Loan, which has a 5 percent interest rate and nine-month grace period after the student graduates or drops below half-time status. If the student is not eligible, parents can apply for the PLUS loan. These loans usually have better interest rates and deferment options than private loans. It is also important to find out what repayment options and benefits lenders have after repayment begins. This could save the students money when they are ready to repay the loans.

Peggy Loewy-Wellisch, Associate Vice President for Student Financial Services, Nova Southeastern University

- Be involved in rehabilitation training (provided by the Veterans Administration or by a state agency that oversees vocational rehabilitation, drug abuse treatment, mental health services or alcohol abuse treatment)

Deferment does not mean that your child never has to repay the loan; when the deferment period ends, payments must resume.

For borrowers who don't qualify for deferment, forbearance may be granted to those with temporary financial difficulties, under specific circumstances and for defined periods in increments of up to one year. During this time, the borrower is responsible for interest and may pay it as it accrues. Any unpaid interest is added to the principal balance.

If your child has taken out the loan, he or she must apply for forbearance from the lender. You may not do it for the child. A lender may grant forbearance if your child:

- Encounters economic hardship or personal problems that affect his or her ability to make regular payments
- Becomes unemployed and has already used the maximum time allowed for deferment
- Has poor health or a disability
- Has debt payments that exceeds total monthly income
- Files for bankruptcy
- Serves in a public service organization such as AmeriCorps
- Serves in the military
- Lives in an area that suffers a natural disaster or a local or national emergency

These are not the only reasons forbearance may be granted. Your child should consult the lender or loan servicer if he or she encounters any special circumstances that make it difficult to make the monthly payments. Forbearance is preferable to defaulting.

Ways to Postpone Payment: PLUS

Deferment and Forbearance. Similar to the Stafford loan, as a PLUS borrower you may also apply for deferment or forbearance under certain circumstances. You may qualify for deferment if you:

- Decide to go back to school at least half time
- Enter a graduate program
- Are engaged in an approved rehabilitation training program

■ Become unemployed
■ Experience severe economic hardship

If you do not meet the above requirements, you may still be eligible for forbearance. For both deferment and forbearance you must contact the loan servicer and continue to make payments until the request is approved. While deferment or forbearance does not relieve your responsibility to pay back the loan, they can be extremely useful should circumstances arise that prevent you from making the payments. Being able to temporarily reduce or suspend your loan payments—without defaulting—is a major advantage of the PLUS.

Defaulting Will Haunt Your Child for a Long Time

Defaulting on a student loan is a very bad idea. If your child starts to miss monthly payments, the loan may go into default. This affects his or her credit rating and makes it hard to take out a consumer loan, car loan or mortgage, or even to pass a simple credit check when renting an apartment. He or she will not be eligible to receive any form of financial aid in the future. Defaulted loans may result in the garnishment of your child's wages, subtracting up to 10 percent of salary to pay for the loan. If your child is unable to make the scheduled payments, make sure he or she calls the lender or servicer immediately. Often steps can be taken to avoid default.

Straight Talk with a Financial Aid Administrator ▶ **Don't confuse need and want**

My first recommendation when it comes to loans is to apply for them last. You want to exhaust all your other sources—grants, scholarships and work-study—before you accept a loan.

For parents it's important to teach your child the difference between wants and needs. Many young people have a hard time making this distinction. They want a single room, new stereo and car. Do they need all of them? No. We see this confusion all the time. The danger is it can lead students to borrow more than they need. Or, if they put all these "wants" on plastic, they may be tempted to borrow more to help pay off their credit card debts. When it comes to loans, families really need to borrow only what they need.

Courtney McAnuff, Vice President for Enrollment Services, Eastern Michigan University

---

Other Loan Forgiveness and Scholarships for Service Programs

Generally, only death or disability cancels a student loan. However, there is one other option: loan forgiveness or repayment programs. Many of these programs are run by state governments to encourage students to enter a specific profession or work in an underserved area. Typical fields are teaching, medicine and law enforcement; some states also have programs in business, technology and law. For each year that your child participates in the program, the state pays a percentage of his or her student loan. Typically, after four or five years, the loans are completely paid off.

Some, but not all, state-supported loan repayment programs are reserved for residents of the state; others allow anyone to participate as long as they work in the state. Your child may attend college in one state, then move to another state to work in one of these programs, so check out programs in your own state as well as other states. (For more details on state loan repayment programs, see Chapter 9.)

Closely related to loan forgiveness programs are national and state scholarships for service. These awards are contingent on performing a specific duty, such as studying and working in a specific field or doing volunteer work and community service.

One possible drawback to loan forgiveness programs and scholarships for service is that both require your child to study specific subjects, enter certain occupations or perform volunteer duties. But if this path fits your child's plans for the future, these programs are an excellent way to cut college costs.

The following are the large national programs. They are designed to encourage your child to give a year or two of his or her life to volunteer work. Many students consider this an invaluable experience, and, as a reward for giving their time, these programs offer educational benefits that help defray the cost of college.

AmeriCorps

AmeriCorps (www.americorps.org) is managed by the Corporation for National and Community Service. Volunteers serve through more than 2,100 nonprofits, public agencies and faith-based organizations, performing a range of services that include tutoring, building affordable housing, cleaning parks and streams and helping communities respond to disasters. Volunteers serve either full or part time over a 10- to 12-month period.

Full-time volunteers receive $4,725 to pay for college or graduate school or to repay student loans. They receive health insurance, training and student loan deferment and, depending on the service, even a living allowance. Part-time volunteers receive a partial education award. Volunteers can earn up to two awards; by serving for two years, a student can earn nearly $10,000 for college or graduate school.

Volunteers in Service to America (VISTA)

Part of AmeriCorps, VISTA (www.friendsofvista.org) focuses on empowering people in low-income areas. By volunteering at least 1,700 hours with private, nonprofit groups that help eradicate hunger, homelessness, poverty and illiteracy, students can receive $4,725 from VISTA toward repayment of student loans, as well as a living allowance and deferment of their loans. Volunteers work as community organizers, recruiting volunteers, raising funds or helping develop new programs.

Teach for America

Each year, Teach for America (www.teachforamerica.org) selects 2,000 recent college graduates for training to become full-time teachers in urban and rural public schools. These teachers receive a salary, health benefits and insurance similar to that of other beginning teachers. They also qualify to receive forbearance on student loans and an education award of $4,725 for each year of service, which can be used for student loans or toward future education.

National Health Service Corps

This program pays for tuition, fees, a stipend and supplies for health professional students who work in underserved areas after graduating. Applicants must be enrolled, or accepted for enrollment, in a fully accredited U.S.:

Straight Talk with a Financial Aid Administrator ▸

Loans force many to appreciate the value of their education

At Central State University a lot of students are rightfully concerned about accumulating too much debt. This is a good thing. What we see is once students get a loan, they really think about the long-term implications of paying it back. These students do whatever they can to borrow the least amount possible. After finishing their first year, many seek employment—either on their own or through our student employment office, which is part of the financial aid office. In this respect loans seem to make students take more responsibility for their own education. I think students adopt the attitude, "If I'm paying for it, I'd better make the most of it."

Veronica J. Leech, Director of Financial Aid, Central State University

---

- Allopathic or osteopathic medical school
- Family nurse practitioner program (master's degree in nursing, post-master's or post-baccalaureate certificate)
- Nurse-midwifery program (master's degree in nursing, post-master's or post-baccalaureate certificate)
- Physician assistant program (certificate, associate, baccalaureate or master's program)
- Dental school

Students attending medical school are expected to complete residency programs in one of the following specialties:

- Family medicine
- General pediatrics
- General internal medicine
- Obstetrics/gynecology
- Psychiatry
- Rotating internship (D.O.s only) with a request to complete one of the above specialties

Dental students may do residencies in general practice or pediatric dentistry.

Recipients must serve full time, commit to working in an underserved area for at least two years and be U.S. citizens. For more information, go to http://nhsc.bhpr.hrsa.gov.

Other Places to Borrow Money

Anyone who watches late night television or reads junk mail knows that many, many companies are soliciting to lend money. Most of these deals are not a good way to finance your child's education. However, you do have some legitimate alternatives to student loan programs.

Home Equity

Homeowners may be able to use their equity as collateral on a loan to pay for college. You can borrow a lump sum and make monthly payments or establish a line of credit and borrow money as you need it. When you establish a line of credit, you pay interest only on the amount of money you actually borrow. Interest rates may be fixed or variable, depending on the loan.

Home equity loans have some advantages over other types of consumer borrowing. The biggest is that you may be able to deduct interest payments from your taxes on loans up to $100,000. The downside is that if you default on a home equity loan, the lender could foreclose on your home. There may also be fees and closing costs for setting up the loan, applying for the loan, recording the loan and performing a property survey and title search.

Whole-Life Insurance

If you have a whole-life (as opposed to term-life) insurance policy, you may have built up some cash value that you can borrow against. Usually your beneficiaries would receive this cash value after you die, but some policies let you withdraw some of this money or borrow against it. Unless you pay it back, this amount will be deducted from your death benefits, decreasing the amount your beneficiaries will receive.

IRA or 401(k)

You may make withdrawals from traditional IRAs and SIMPLE IRAs and avoid the 10 percent early withdrawal penalty if you use the funds for qualified educational expenses. You will still have to pay income tax on the amount withdrawn. Since Roth IRAs are funded with after-tax dollars, withdrawals of the contributions (not the gains) are subject to neither early withdrawal penalty or income tax.

If you have a 401(k) retirement plan, you may borrow money from it and repay the principal and interest within a five-year period. The risk is that if you lose your job, you will have to repay the loan immediately or face the double expense of income tax and a penalty on the amount you borrowed. Check with your plan administrator to see how this might work for your child's education.

Generous Relatives

Maybe you have a wealthy relative who will give or lend you money to pay for your child's education. A person may gift up to $12,000 a year without tax consequences ($60,000 if it is contributed to your child's 529 plan—see Chapter 10 for details). Or this relative may be willing to lend you the money with either no or low interest. Be careful here, as loans over $10,000 must follow IRS rules on minimum interest charged, and there are tax implications for both lender and borrower. Even more risky is the effect a personal loan can have on family relations. What will happen if you miss a payment or can't pay back all the money?

If you are going to borrow money that you intend to pay back with interest, put the terms in writing. Even if it's your favorite uncle, put it on paper. Include when you will begin repayment (usually some time after your child graduates and can find a job), as well as the consequences of missing a payment (usually a penalty fee).

If you are borrowing a large amount, you might want to pay a service to manage the loan. There are companies that accept money from one relative and lend it to another for a fee. They also manage the collection of payments and ensure that the interest rate meets IRS minimums. Having an intermediary between you and Uncle Joe can help keep your financial relationship separate from your personal relationship.

Grandparents

To avoid the estate tax implications of a large gift of cash, the child's grandparents can write a check directly to the college. Even if they write a check for the entire cost of your child's tuition, they will not face any estate taxes.

Borrowed Money to the Rescue

Borrowed money fills the gap between what college costs and what your family can afford. For some students, a loan makes the difference between going to their top-choice college or not. While borrowing money is a major decision and a big responsibility, it is frequently necessary. The key to making it work is to thoroughly research your options, understand both the costs and the responsibility of borrowing and, most important, never borrow more than you or your child can comfortably repay. Following these rules will allow your child to get a great education and enable you and the student to repay the loans within a reasonable time.

CHAPTER 7

How Can My Child Win a Scholarship?

What you'll learn:

- Why scholarships are not just for athletes and brains
- Where to find the best awards
- Seven steps to winning a scholarship
- How to write a winning scholarship essay
- How to ace the interview

Looking for a scholarship may seem like a game of hide-and-seek. You've heard stories of vast amounts of free dollars waiting to be claimed, but when you try to find this money, it seems to have disappeared. Or you may find a scholarship but have no idea how your child can win it. In this situation, many students and parents simply give up.

Don't let this happen to you.

There are plenty of scholarships that are perfect for your child. And once you identify them, you can dramatically increase your child's chances of winning by following a few simple strategies. Finding and winning scholarships can go from a tantalizing dream to a reality.

Dancing the Scholarship Two-Step

With homework, after-school activities, socializing, sleeping and the occasional household chore, it's a miracle if your child has any time left. Since it can be all too easy to put off, it's important that you make applying for scholarships a priority.

It may be hard for a teenager to grasp how much college costs. Have a serious conversation about college costs with your student and make sure he or she understands the importance of finding scholarship money. This isn't something Mom or Dad should take care of; it is a family project, and your child should play an active role. The student's efforts to find and apply for scholarships are a vital part of the family's overall plan to pay for college.

Winning the lottery and getting a college scholarship are two opportunities for free money. But, unlike the astronomical odds against hitting a lottery jackpot, winning a scholarship is not out of reach. Your child does not have to be the class valedictorian or a sports superstar—financial awards are available for nearly every background, talent and achievement imaginable.

Once you and your child agree on the importance of scholarships, create a schedule. When will your child work on scholarships? It's best to dedicate a certain amount of time each day or week, such as an hour a day or three hours every weekend. The key is to make researching and applying for scholarships part of your child's routine, just like doing homework or practicing the piano.

But first, let's address some common misconceptions about who wins scholarships.

Scholarships Are Not Only for Athletes and Brains

A persistent myth about scholarships is that they go to straight-A students and star athletes. While there certainly are scholarships that reward such achievements, the vast majority are not based on grades or athletic prowess.

In fact, when it comes to the grade point average (GPA), most scholarships either do not consider it or use it only to establish a minimum criterion for applying. For example, a scholarship might require applicants to have a 2.0 GPA or higher, but every applicant who meets or exceeds that requirement has a chance of winning.

Even when grades and test scores are required on an application, they often do not carry the greatest weight in determining the winner. Students may obsess over grades, but they may not be very important to scholarship judges. Imagine this situation:

> *You are a successful businessperson. As a teen, you were an avid skateboarder and even now you are a member of a skateboarding association. Through this group you contribute money to fund a scholarship for a high school skateboarder. Do you think this scholarship should go to a student with a 4.0 GPA? Even though you might ask for the applicants' grades and set a minimum GPA for applying, you're looking for an applicant who has been heavily involved with skateboarding and can describe how skateboarding has influenced his or her life.*

This example is based on an actual scholarship for high school skateboarders. It illustrates the fact that most scholarship judges view grades as only part of the overall mix. The lesson: You don't need a 4.0 GPA to apply for scholarships.

Don't count your child out when it comes to athletics either. Many scholarships are offered by colleges, sporting organizations and sports equipment manufacturers. Except for the big-name college programs (for example, the University of Southern California in football or Stanford University in tennis), it is not necessary to be a nationally ranked athlete. You'd be surprised at the level of ability required for an athletic scholarship. In fact, it's possible that your child could be second string in high school but a starting player in college—it all depends on how strong the college and your high school are in the particular sport.

HEAD START . . . .

Start applying for scholarships as early as possible. Many students assume that they must be seniors before they can apply for scholarships. While the majority of scholarships are for seniors some do exist for underclassmen. If a student wins a scholarship as a high school sophomore, the money is usually held by the organization until the student heads off to college. What better situation to be in than to have some money in the bank before graduation?

Scholarships Are Not Only for the Financially Needy

Generally, your child may compete for two types of scholarships: those based on *need* and those based on *merit*.

Need-based scholarships. These awards are limited to students who can show financial need, which can be measured by family income, assets or Expected Family Contribution, as determined from the Free Application for Federal Student Aid (FAFSA). However, there is no universal definition of what constitutes need. One scholarship may target families earning less than $30,000 a year, while another award may set the limit at $80,000 a year. Don't assume that your family does not qualify for a particular need-based scholarship until you know how financial need is defined.

Meeting the requirements for a need-based scholarship does not mean that your child will automatically win. The need requirement simply admits your child into the competition. To win, the student must compete on other criteria, such as academic achievement, community service or leadership.

Merit-based scholarships. These awards are based on a student's achievements, ambitions and potential. Family finances are not considered.

The term "merit" is broadly defined and does not necessarily mean academic achievement. Merit may include participation in extracurricular activities and sports, personal qualities such as leadership or character, intended major or career aspirations, or talent in the arts, sciences, music, dance or a foreign language. Merit-based scholarships are even available for being left-handed, extremely tall or skilled at using duct tape! In short, there are merit-based awards for almost every academic, career, talent or interest area that you can imagine.

Between need- and merit-based scholarships, your child should find plenty of opportunities to get some free cash for college.

Starting the Scholarship Hunt

For most students, the hunt for scholarships is a short one. Many start with a scholarship book or head to the Internet. Unfortunately, most students end their search after exhausting these two sources.

Big mistake!

Books and the Internet are only the tip of the iceberg, and neither comes close to listing all the available scholarships. If you do your own detective work and canvass the community, you will uncover additional awards. Since few families do this, the scholarships you find will have much less competition. Here's where to begin:

High school. The first stop in your scholarship hunt should be the high school counseling office. When an organization establishes a new scholarship (awards are created every year), high schools are the first places to get a notice. Over the years, most counseling offices have assembled a long list of scholarships. Some schools have a binder for students to peruse, while others post their list on the school website or even publish a regular scholarship newsletter. Don't reinvent the wheel if the counselor has already collected the information.

Prospective colleges. Have your child contact the financial aid office at every school he or she is interested in attending. Your child should explain that he or she is a prospective student and would like to know more about scholarship opportunities. Not only do the colleges themselves offer scholarships, but their financial aid offices also maintain lists of outside opportunities. Sit back and watch the deluge in your mailbox.

Civic and community organizations. Every community is home to dozens of civic organizations, such as the Rotary Club, Lions Club, Knights of Columbus, American Legion, Elks Club and VFW. Part of their mission is to support the community by awarding scholarships. To benefit, start by using the phone book and your city's website to identify all the organizations that are active in your community. Visit community centers, as many groups operate through these facilities. Your local library also may have a list of active clubs. Once you have a list of organizations, start calling. Ask if they offer any scholarships to high school students and whether they know of other community groups that do.

Businesses big and small. Many businesses—such as newspapers, shopping malls, supermarkets and retailers—offer scholarships to local students. For example, every Wal-Mart and Target store awards scholarships to students in the community. To find these opportunities, contact the manager at these businesses. You can get a list of businesses from the chamber of commerce or in the reference section of the public library.

On the national level, many large corporations (including Toyota, Chevrolet, Coca-Cola and Henkel—the makers of duct tape) award scholarships. If your city is home to a big corporation, contact its public relations or communications department and ask about scholarship opportunities for local residents.

Professional sports teams. If your city has a professional sports team, contact the front office to see if they offer scholarships. The San Francisco Giants, for example, sponsor the Junior Giants Scholarship. Not to be outdone by their northern neighbors, the Los Angeles Dodgers also fund scholarships through their community foundation, most recently teaming up with Boeing. Neither scholarship is based on your batting average; in fact, they have nothing to do with baseball. Teams from the National Football League (NFL) to the National Basketball Association (NBA)

| Straight Talk with a Financial Aid Administrator | **Winning a scholarship begins before high school** |

One of the keys to winning scholarships is for parents to make sure their child is well-centered educationally before starting high school. Colleges provide a lot of scholarships that have nothing to do with a family's finances. Many are based on academic performance. While some students (and parents) think it's normal and even acceptable to slack early on in high school, turning grades around senior year may be too late. Not only does this make admissions more difficult, but it may also hurt the student's chances of receiving a scholarship later on. Parents should make sure their child has good study habits and understands the importance of doing well in high school. This will not only make for a better student but can lead to scholarship dollars down the road.

James M. Bauer, Assistant Dean of Enrollment Management and Director of Financial Assistance Services, University of Miami also sponsor scholarships for students in their cities. Contact these teams or their community foundations.

Employers. If you work for a large company, ask the human resources department about scholarships. If they are limited to the children of employees, there may be little competition for these awards. In addition to your own or your partner's employer, have your child look into opportunities based on summer or part-time employment. Popular teen employers such as McDonald's, Burger King and Subway offer scholarships for students who have worked for them.

Unions. If you are a member of a union, ask the union representative or national union organization about scholarships. The AFL-CIO website (www.aflcio.org) has a massive database of union-related awards.

Professional or trade associations. From accounting to zoology, every profession has its own associations, and many of these professional associations use scholarships to encourage students to enter the field. Start by looking at groups related to your child's future career. If your child is thinking of entering the medical or health professions, look at awards from the American Medical Association. If law interests your child, try the American Bar Association. Don't forget to inquire with groups you belong to—some associations don't require applicants to have an interest in the industry but only to be the dependents of members.

Religious organizations. Your church or temple may offer scholarships to support members. If your local church does not have a scholarship program, check with the national headquarters.

KEY CONCEPT . . . .

Scholarships are not only for valedictorians and athletes. Literally millions of scholarships are available that reward almost every talent, background and interest imaginable. They are based on career plans, leadership, community service and talents such as debate, art, music and even the ability to bake an apple pie. The key is to identify your child's strengths and find the appropriate awards. Having straight As or a killer bank shot is not a prerequisite for winning a scholarship.

Ethnic and cultural organizations. To promote a certain culture, develop leaders or encourage members to pursue higher education, many ethnic organizations sponsor scholarships. From the Organization of Chinese Americans to the Hispanic Heritage Awards Foundation, you can probably find an organization related to your ethnic and cultural heritage.

Political parties and politicians. Some political parties provide scholarships to the children of members or to students who have volunteered for the party. Also, local politicians have a long tradition of giving scholarships to students in their district (regardless of political affiliation) as a way to thank voters and generate positive publicity for themselves.

Military associations. Serving in the military entitles you to certain educational benefits, but a lesser known bonus is that the benefits may extend to your children. Military and veterans organizations offer awards to the dependents of active duty members, Reserve members and veterans. Start with the websites of the American Legion (www.legion.org), American Legion Auxiliary (www.legion-aux.org) and AMVETS (www.amvets.org). See Chapter 13 for more information.

BRIGHT IDEA . . . . . .

Don't look for scholarships alone. Successful scholarship winners do not search by themselves. They team up with other students to create a network to look for scholarships, which helps them find many more awards. Don't be afraid of sharing what you find with others, as long as they reciprocate. The one sure way to lose a scholarship is not to know it exists.

State and local governments. Make those tax dollars work for you by taking advantage of financial aid from state and local governments. Each state has a higher education agency that provides information on financial aid, and many administer state-based grant and loan programs. (See Chapter 9 for contact information for your state's higher education agency.) Closer to home, your county or city government may have awards for students in the community. Get in touch with each to inquire about these opportunities.

Private foundations and charities. As part of their mission to help the community, private foundations and charities often offer scholarships. For example, the San Diego Foundation (www.sdfoundation.org) provides more than 40 scholarships for students in the county. To find these scholarships, visit your library and ask the reference librarian for a directory of local charities and foundations. Every time you speak to a charity, ask if they can refer you to other groups that you should contact. You can also use these websites:

- Community Foundation Locator (www.cof.org/Locator/)
- Network for Good (www.networkforgood.org)
- Volunteer Match (www.volunteermatch.org)

Friends and family. The more people who know your child is looking for scholarships, the better. Friends and family members can be invaluable scholarship scouts as they go about their daily business. Scholarship opportunities have been uncovered on supermarket bulletin boards, standing in line at a bank, even on a bottle of aspirin. You never know where a scholarship will be publicized and who can help you to find it. It's important that you get the whole family involved, and your friends and neighbors, too.

Straight Talk with a Financial Aid Administrator ▶ **You need to be proactive to find scholarships**

Thousands of scholarships are available on every college campus. At Eastern Michigan, most of our scholarships are tied to specific majors. Our largest major is education, and we have a lot of scholarship money in this area. Besides money from the university, private donors establish scholarships. For some you don't even need a minimum GPA.

You may also have heard that each year there are unclaimed scholarships. To a certain extent that is true. Virtually every school has scholarships they don't spend because the criterion is so specific. The scholarship might be restricted to a student from a specific high school or who participates in a particular activity. The college usually has no way of knowing which students are eligible. Therefore, students will need to self-select themselves by finding these scholarships and making sure the college is aware they are eligible. The best way to do this is by visiting the financial aid section of the school's website. Here you will often find a list of institutional scholarships. It's important that students are proactive and stand up to be counted.

Courtney McAnuff, Vice President for Enrollment Services, Eastern Michigan University

The Internet. Thousands of scholarships are just a click away. Don't fall into the common trap, however, of thinking that if you can't find the information on the Net, it isn't there. The Internet is vast, so here are some tips to make the search less overwhelming.

Dedicated scholarship databases. Websites such as the Sallie Mae website (www.salliemae.com) make it easy to find scholarships free-of-charge. If you provide some information about your child's academic, career and personal background, the database will display awards that fit. You can then visit the awarding organizations' websites to get information on how to request applications or apply online.

Organization websites. Using search engines, you can go directly to an organization's website to find awards. Look for the websites of clubs, foundations and professional associations that are active in your community or related to your child's interests. Going directly to an organization's website is an excellent way to gather intelligence and uncover the characteristics the organization is seeking in winners.

High school websites. In addition to using your own high school as a resource, make use of surrounding high schools. Most high school websites are accessible to anyone. Pick a few of the larger schools in your area and surf over to the college counseling sections. Many high schools publish lists of scholarships.

College websites. Colleges post scholarships that they offer, and some even have databases of regional or national awards. It's helpful to look at many colleges' websites, even those your son or daughter will not attend. You never know which college will provide the most useful online resources.

Although the Internet is a valuable resource, it is not a magic solution. Remember to use all the resources available to you.

Seven Steps to Winning a Scholarship

Winning a scholarship is not easy. Scholarship applications require essays, recommendations and interviews. A student may spend a lot of time finding scholarships only to spend very little time crafting the applications. To win a scholarship, the student must create a powerful application that helps him or her stand out from the competition. When your child applies for scholarships, it is vital that he or she not rush through the process and submit a mediocre application.

To win a scholarship, your child needs to make a fantastic first impression with a powerful and compelling application. While there is no fail-safe method to do this, the following general principles will greatly increase your child's chances of winning.

Step 1: Prioritize the List of Scholarships

A thorough search will almost certainly yield a long list of potential scholarships. The worst way to tackle this plethora of possibilities is first-come, first-served. In other words, don't let your child complete the applications in the order in which he or she finds them. Instead, prioritize. This will enable your child to focus on the competitions that he or she has the best chance of winning, and will save the time (and the inevitable disappointment) he or she might otherwise waste applying for long shots.

How do you prioritize? The key is to remember that every organization that gives away money does so for a reason. Imagine that you were offering a $1,000 scholarship. How would you pick the winner? You probably would have some specific ideas in mind. Maybe you would give your money to a student who contributes positively to the community, has overcome a challenge or dreams of becoming a teacher. The student who wins your scholarship will be the one who best shows how he or she fulfills your reason for giving away the money.

Therefore, the most efficient way to prioritize your list is to match the purpose of the scholarship with the attributes of your child. Put the awards that best fit his or her background, talents and achievements at the top of the list. If your child's strengths are chemistry, volunteering and tennis, focus on awards in those areas. Don't waste time on awards for future business leaders if your child is not interested in business and has no business-related experience.

Step 2: Take an Up Close and Personal Look at the Scholarship and Your Child

Some students adopt the throwing-Jell-O-against-the-wall approach to applying for scholarships. They blast the same application to as many scholarship competitions as possible, in the hope that one of them will stick. This rarely works. Winning requires a targeted approach. Each scholarship should be viewed as a unique opportunity, and the message in the application should be tailored accordingly.

Assume that you are giving $1,000 to help a student who wants to be a teacher. In reviewing the applications, you would probably look for students who have volunteered in the classroom or plan to major in education. An applicant who focused on student council and dreams of becoming a U.S. Senator may be impressive but would not fit your requirements.

To tailor an application that will excite the scholarship judges, your child needs to begin by researching the organization that is giving away the money. It's helpful to know what the organization is about, what issues it champions and who its members are. Look at the organization's website, publications and press coverage. They contain important information about the organization's history and mission. If the group is local, speak with a member or even attend a meeting.

After learning as much as possible about the scholarship organization, your child needs to build a case for why he or she is the best candidate for the award. This means examining experience, background, achievements, talents and aspirations to find relevant examples to share in the application, essay or interview.

Imagine that your son is applying for the Most Valuable Student Scholarship sponsored by the Elks National Foundation. From research, he learns that this award is based on academics, leadership and financial need. He also learns that the mission of the Elks is to promote charity, justice, brotherly love and patriotism. In his application for this scholarship, your son would first highlight his academic accomplishments, including challenging classes taken, high grades received and honors won. To demonstrate his experience as a leader, he would describe his involvement with a youth group and his job as a summer camp counselor. Knowing that the Elks value charity and patriotism, your son

Straight Talk with a Financial Aid Administrator ▶

Help the college give you more money

Every college offers scholarships. Some are based on financial need, others on such criteria as public service or intended major. Each scholarship also requires different materials to apply. Some are just an application form, while others require an essay.

At Cincinnati State we offer a Presidential Scholarship for students with high GPAs and an honors scholarship for students with strong GPAs. We also have a foundation that awards scholarships to students in various majors.

We even have scholarships that go unawarded because no one applies. It's important that students not assume they can't win and thus not apply. At Cincinnati State we look at a student's application not only for the scholarship they are applying to but also for any other scholarships we might have. A student may send in an application for a nursing scholarship but not meet the criteria. However, we may award that student another scholarship for which he or she meets the requirements. This is why it's always a good idea to attach an essay to the scholarship application even if it's not required since other scholarships we may consider you for do require one. By providing us with everything we may possibly need, you are helping us to give you a scholarship—even though it may not be the one you explicitly applied for. The bottom line is you need to help us to help you.

Dawnia Smith, Director of Financial Aid,
Cincinnati State Technical and Community College

would mention his volunteer work with the city's Fourth of July celebration. By putting together an application that clearly shows how his background and achievements align with the mission of the awarding organization, your son markedly improves his chance of winning the scholarship.

For each application, list any relevant experiences and accomplishments—those that match the purpose of the award and the mission of the organization. Give the judges some reasons to choose your child.

Step 3: Complete the Application

Most scholarships involve filling out a short application form. This form is a vital part of winning. Scholarship judges weed through hundreds—even thousands—of applications to determine which students will move on to the next stage. To ensure that your child's application makes the first cut, remember these key points:

Be a neat freak. Neatness counts on applications. If an application is illegible, sloppy or filled with errors, it will be discarded.

Fill in those blanks! Blank spaces on an application tend to make the student appear less qualified. If the application provides three lines for extracurricular activities, your child should try to list three activities. While you should never lie, you can think creatively. If there is a place to list employment and your child has never held a job, leave it blank. But if your child painted your house one summer and was paid for it, this can legitimately be listed as a job.

Don't save the best for last. The application will be one of many reviewed by the scholarship judges, so put the most impressive points first. If the application asks for five extracurricular activities, put the activities that directly relate to the scholarship's goal first. Next, list those that have affected a number of people or an honor that was given to only a few.

Nip and tuck every sentence. When it comes to scholarship applications, every word counts. There is not much room, so make the most of it. Instead of "I was president of the Science Club in 10th grade," write "Science Club Pres. (10th)." Use abbreviations where appropriate, and keep sentences short. Judges will scan the application for key points. If they want an essay, they'll ask for it.

Throw modesty out the window. When your child applies for a scholarship, he or she will have to "brag" about accomplishments. Instead of writing that she was a member of the robotics team that placed first in a competition, your daughter should highlight the fact that she was the lead designer for the robot's control system. In describing membership in the Key Club, your son should mention that he led the club's holiday toy drive. If your child stars in a sport, he or she should include being voted MVP by the team. It's important to be specific.

Show instead of tell. Actions speak louder than words. In a scholarship application your child shouldn't write "church volunteer (7th–12th grade)" when he or she could write "church volunteer (7th–12th grade): 8 hrs/wk; organized canned food drive that collected 2,000+ cans." Again, the more specifics, the better. Be sure to include projects, hours, results and other relevant details that add strength to the application.

A scholarship application is much more than a sheet of paper. In the eyes of the scholarship judges, it is a reflection of your child. It may be the only impression the judges will have of each applicant. Give it top priority as you make your way through the scholarship process.

Step 4: Get Great Recommendations

Scholarship judges like recommendation letters because they verify your child's abilities. Your child may say that he or she is a strong leader and give some examples, but written support from a person in authority is very powerful. Students usually ask teachers, counselors, coaches and employers to write these letters. Follow these three tips to get great recommendation letters:

1. Ask in advance. People are busy, and the last thing you want is a letter of recommendation that's a rush job. Ask for recommendations as far in advance as possible—at least three weeks. Teachers, counselors, coaches and employers may be writing references for many students, so give them a long lead time. They will appreciate the courtesy, and their appreciation may be reflected in their letters.

Straight Talk with a Financial Aid Administrator ▶ **Scholarships play an increasingly important role**

As colleges have increased tuition, it is sometimes impossible to cover all educational costs. Outside scholarships are an excellent source of additional aid. A variety is available to students both internally and externally. There are general scholarships, scholarships based on students in a specific program, academic scholarships and athletic scholarships. Students and parents need to be aware that for some scholarships just having high SAT scores and a high GPA can result in more money.

At Nova Southeastern University we select students for scholarships based on such criteria as financial need, GPA, SAT/ACT scores and community involvement. Each program and academic department also has its own criteria. The best place to learn about which scholarships are available from the college is to visit the school's website. On the NSU financial aid website we provide information detailing criteria and deadlines on institutional and external scholarships, as well as links to scholarship searches. In addition, we provide a publication called the Scholarship Resource Guide, which includes institutional and external scholarships, tips on applying for scholarships, a sample thank you letter and other scholarship information.

At NSU we have a scholarship coordinator who is available to assist students and departments and works in liaison with various program and university administrators within the university. Also, some of our financial aid counselors are designated to assist new freshman students with the scholarship process.

Peggy Loewy-Wellisch, Associate Vice President for Student Financial Services, Nova Southeastern University

---

2. Ask people who really know your child. Which teacher, coach, leader, boss or other adult knows your child well enough to write a strong letter of recommendation? What will this person say? For example, if your child is applying for an award based on public service, he or she should ask the adviser of a public service organization. That adviser's letter would naturally focus on the student's contribution to the community through service projects. On the other hand, if your child is applying for an academic award, he or she should ask a teacher. Asking the right person to recommend your child for a particular scholarship is critical to winning the scholarship.

3. Help write the recommendation. The secret to a great letter is to make sure the person writing it is familiar with the student's recent accomplishments. Your child should give the recommenders a letter that describes the purpose of the scholarship, suggests some points they may want to include in their letters and outlines the student's educational and extracurricular background. Recommenders appreciate this material because it makes their job easier. It helps them include specific examples and write stronger letters.

Step 5: Create a Scholarship Resume

Although some applications do not ask for a resume, your child should always include one. A resume highlights activities and achievements and allows for more detailed explanations. A good resume can be very impressive.

There is no single correct way to write a resume. Many styles and formats are appropriate. But, in general, every scholarship resume should include the following:

- Educational background
- Extracurricular activities
- Honors and awards
- Work experience
- Interests and hobbies

Encourage your child to describe accomplishments and their significance.

Instead of this:

Matt's Tutoring: Started business to tutor students in math and science.

Try this:

Matt's Tutoring: Founder of business to tutor students in math and the sciences. Recruited and managed six student workers. Annual revenue of $3,000.

The following is an example of a scholarship resume.

Matt Anderson
1234 Rose Street
Los Altos, CA 94022
(650) 555-1212

Educational Background

Los Altos High School   **Los Altos, CA**
Expected graduation 2009. 3.7 GPA. Honor roll, 9th grade–present. Winner: Outstanding Student in English (awarded to one student in class of 350), 2006.

Foothill College   **Los Altos Hills, CA**
Summer courses in creative writing and Spanish, summers 2006 and 2007.

Extracurricular Activities

Los Altos High School Newspaper   **Los Altos, CA**
Editorial page editor. Manage team of two writers. Assign and edit articles on local and national issues. 2006–present.

Key Club   **Los Altos, CA**
Community clean-up chairperson. Organized annual community clean-up. Mobilized 35 volunteers to remove 85 bags of garbage from city. 2005–present.

Los Altos High School Tennis Team   **Los Altos, CA**
Team won district title, 2006 and 2007. Won Most Valuable Player, 2007. Won Most Improved Player, 2006.

Work Experience

Los Altos Public Library   **Los Altos, CA**
Senior library page. Help patrons locate resources, provide computer customer support and shelve books. Promoted after six months of service. 2007–present.

Subway   **Mountain View, CA**
Sandwich artist. Responsible for customer service, training new employees and closing shop. 2006–2007.

Other Talents and Hobbies

Fluent in French and Spanish. Enjoy mountain biking, computer programming and snowboarding.

Step 6: Write a Winning Scholarship Essay

Imagine that you are a scholarship judge, wading through an enormous pile of applications. Although the information—grades, test scores and brief descriptions of activities—helps, it is not enough. Without meeting the applicants, how can you get a sense of who they are and whether they deserve your money? Enter the personal essay.

The personal essay is critical to winning a scholarship because it offers judges a window into each applicant. It is their way of getting to know the student beyond the stats in the application. It is also the best opportunity for students to make a strong and lasting impression.

Writing a good essay is not easy. It takes time to put words on paper and finesse each sentence to convey the correct meaning. While there is no right or wrong way to write a great essay, all good scholarship essays share certain qualities. The following are some of them:

Be clear about why you deserve to win. For most scholarships, the essay question is a springboard. A professional business association might ask, "Why do you want to study business?" A good answer will describe the motivations for entering business but will go on to demonstrate why this particular student has the most potential among all the applicants.

Reveal something about yourself. Regardless of the essay's topic, it should focus on the student. Whether your child is writing about an influential person, a career field or a research project, the essay must reveal something personal. For example, in an essay about an influential person, the scholarship judges don't want a biography; rather, they want to know how this person has affected your child's outlook or been an inspiration.

KEY CONCEPT . . . .

Don't stop applying for scholarships after high school graduation. Most students do exactly this, yet there are many (and in some cases, more) scholarships for college students. The department of your child's major, professional associations, companies and civic organizations all provide funds to support college students.

In most cases, the scholarship judges never meet the applicants. The personal essay is the only "photograph" the judges have of the student. When they finish reading an essay, the judges should have a clear idea of exactly who the student is.

Have a main point. Before your child starts writing, he or she should identify the central point of the essay. Too many students lose sight of what they are trying to communicate. Good essays are not rambling stories or disjointed collections of thoughts. There should be a main idea with a clear thesis statement and several paragraphs that support that statement.

Give specifics. "Education is the key to success" may be a good first sentence, but it is not enough. Students need to go beyond general statements. For example, if your child is writing about public service, he or she could describe a service project that was particularly meaningful. Details and examples make the essay come to life and, most important, make it memorable.

TIME SAVER . . . .

Save stamps and zap applications. In the old days, you had to send a self-addressed, stamped envelope to receive a scholarship application. Today, most organizations have websites where applications can be downloaded. Some even let you submit the application online. The online route is both faster and more reliable.

Be original. Imagine how many essays the judges for a medical foundation scholarship will read about why students want to become doctors. After awhile, they all sound alike.

Encourage your child to approach an ordinary topic in an original way. Instead of writing that he wants to become a doctor to help others, your son could describe how he first became interested in medicine when he volunteered at a hospital and watched the interactions between doctors and patients.

Not sure if your child's essay is original? Try the "thumb test." Cover the name at the top of the essay with your thumb. If you could insert any other child's name there, the essay is not personal. If your child's name is the only one that could be there, it is personal.

Expand on accomplishments. If your child has an impressive activity or accomplishment, the essay is the best place to elaborate. Don't just repeat what is already on the application; provide details and explain the importance of the achievement.

Avoid meaningless facts. Some students approach the essay as they would a research paper, cramming it with statistics and dates. If your child is trying to woo a corporation, using facts from the corporation's own website will not impress the judges. Don't repeat statistics without a reason.

Don't write a sob story. Essays filled with family tragedies and hardships may evoke sympathy, but they will not necessarily win scholarships. Judges are interested in personal challenges only insofar as how the student overcame or plans to overcome the hardship. Make sure the essay includes plans to succeed despite challenges and is not just a catalog of misfortunes.

Create positive energy. Everyone likes an uplifting story, especially from young people whose futures lie ahead. Scholarship judges enjoy reading essays that show enthusiasm and excitement for life. Avoid sounding pessimistic, antagonistic or critical. Your child does not have to put a happy face on every sentence, but if your teen is writing about a problem, he or she should offer solutions. Organizations respond to optimism and a positive outlook, and are more likely to give money to young people who have dreams of changing the world.

Get Editors for the Essay

Most writers—even those who write best sellers—have a trash can full of crumpled drafts. Masterpieces are not written the first time around. They also aren't written without the input of others.

Emphasize to your child that he or she doesn't have to write the final draft on the first attempt. Encourage your child not to worry about grammar, punctuation or spelling at first, but to focus on getting the important points down. He or she can go back later and correct any errors. It may help to write a first draft, put it aside for a few days and then return to edit it.

Your child should also get feedback from others, such as a teacher, a friend or… you! Ask for feedback on the overall message of the essay, not just spelling or grammar. Ask the editor to point out any unclear or disjointed paragraphs and to comment on how persuasive the essay is in showing why your child deserves to win the scholarship.

Straight Talk with a Financial Aid Administrator ▶ **Grants and scholarships won't necessarily harm your aid package**

Students should not be worried about outside scholarships hurting their financial aid. At Central State University, if a student receives a grant or scholarship it will typically decrease the self-help portion of their aid package, which means money from student loans or work. Most students would agree that it's much better to lose a dollar of borrowed money that needs to be repaid by having it replaced with a dollar of free money from scholarships.

Veronica J. Leech, Director of Financial Aid, Central State University

Remember, though, that you don't have to incorporate every piece of advice into the essay; your child should follow his or her own instincts. Also, an essay can't be written by committee. It's usually enough to get feedback from one or two people.

Recycling Essays

Over the years, students write dozens of essays for school classes. Think of these essays as a library from which your child can borrow. He or she may be able to use parts of various essays written for English class or for another scholarship or college application. This kind of recycling can save your child a lot of time.

BRIGHT IDEA . . . . . .

Win a $1,000 scholarship from Sallie Mae. Every month, Sallie Mae (www.salliemae.com) holds a drawing to award a $1,000 scholarship. To be eligible, simply visit the website and register. Complete details are posted on-line. Good luck!

Have your child review all the essays he or she has written over the past few years. Then look at the scholarship essay questions. Can any of the questions be answered by one of the essays?

The danger of recycling is that an essay may not actually answer the scholarship question. Make sure that the revised essay fits the question; otherwise, your child should write a new essay.

Step 7: Ace the Scholarship Interview

The thought of sitting in a chair facing a group of judges who fire questions faster than a Texas auctioneer at a cattle sale can be downright terrifying. While not every scholarship requires an interview, for those that do it is often the deciding factor in picking winners. Interviews give the judges the opportunity to get to know and interact with the applicants, and to learn more about the applicants' goals and achievements.

Fortunately, most scholarship interviews are not third-degree examinations; in fact, many interviews are informal and friendly. But this does not mean that your child can be unprepared. With a little bit of groundwork and practice, your child can confidently walk into a scholarship interview and (with luck) walk out with some college money. Here's how:

Do your homework. Each year, the Rotary Club awards more than 1,000 scholarships in amounts worth up to $25,000. Students apply through local clubs and advance to higher levels. The judges have high expectations for finalists, as they have already beaten out dozens of others at the local level.

BRIGHT IDEA . . . . . .

Be the deadline keeper for your child. For most teenagers, organization is not a strong point. One of the best ways you can help your child with scholarships is to keep track of the deadlines to make sure the applications are submitted on time. The best application in the world will not win if it is received after the deadline.

A Rotary Club judge told the story of one especially promising applicant. He attended a prestigious college, had excellent grades and wrote a superb essay. The Rotary judges started the interview with the standard opening question: "What do you think the Rotary Club stands for?" Despite this student's Ivy League education and impressive credentials, he couldn't answer the question. By not doing his homework, the applicant lost the scholarship.

Don't let your child make the same mistake. Before he or she steps into the interview room, make sure your child researches the awarding organization. It's easy to gather this information from the organization's website or the scholarship literature.

Practice, practice and more practice. You wouldn't go onstage without rehearsing your lines. Similarly, your child should not go to an interview without answering some practice questions. A mock interview will help your child construct good answers and become more comfortable with the process.

To practice, sit down with your child and pretend you are a scholarship judge. Ask questions the judges may ask. Give constructive feedback after the answers. Let your child know what you liked about the responses.

As important as what your child says is *how* he or she says it. Your child should speak with confidence and maturity. Work to eliminate filler words such as "like," "um" or "you know." Videotaping the mock interview may help. Remind your child to practice sitting up straight and making eye contact—body language conveys a message that is louder than words.

Throughout the practice interview, be positive and encouraging. Your child may not be used to sharing thoughts and opinions in this format. The more comfortable you can make your son or daughter feel in the practice environment, the better he or she will do in the real interview.

Dress for success. Here's yet another reason to request that your son or daughter not wear low-slung jeans or belly-baring tops. Whether it's fair or not, people judge on the basis of what they see. How your child looks is as important as what he or she says in an interview.

Clothing makes a strong first impression. Your child should wear what he or she might wear to a job interview or to church. Boys should wear a dress shirt and sports jacket or at least a dress shirt and tie. Girls should wear a dress, or pants and a blouse or a skirt and blouse that are appropriate for a business setting. It is better to be overdressed than underdressed, although your child also needs to be comfortable. Have him or her try on the interview outfit in advance.

Scholarships for Special Groups

The following are a few tips for scholarships aimed at a specific group of students or students with a particular talent.

Minorities. Minority organizations offer scholarships to encourage students to seek higher education and to promote leadership qualities. Some of these scholarships require only that one parent or grandparent have the ethnic background.

Student athletes. The National Collegiate Athletic Association (NCAA) oversees the administration of athletic scholarships at more than 1,250 colleges. You can take the following actions to help your child win an athletic scholarship.

The most important action is to build a case to the college. Unless you're talking about a state- or national-level superstar, assume that a recruiter will not observe your child in person; so it's important to provide as much evidence of your child's abilities as possible. Keep a record of statistics, awards and records. Clip articles from the newspaper. Videotape games to create a highlights tape. Put these pieces together to create a portfolio of your child's athletic accomplishments.

The high school coach can help by contacting the college coach to speak about your son's or daughter's abilities and by writing a letter of recommendation. College coaches are usually interested in getting the perspective of high school coaches who have worked closely with student athletes.

The college coach can be your greatest ally, as he or she often works with the admissions office to identify students for scholarships. It is important to give the college coach all the information you can. Get more details about athletic scholarships at the NCAA website at www.ncaa.org.

Leaders. To make the greatest impact with their awards, many scholarship organizations seek students whom they believe will become community leaders. Leaders in student government, clubs or organizations

TIME SAVER . . . .

Harness the power of the Internet to find scholarships. Many free websites will help you search for scholarships from the comfort of your home. For example, Sallie Mae (www.salliemae.com) has a database with more than 2.4 million awards—all free to search.

or activities outside school are prime candidates for these scholarships. Prudential, Coca-Cola and Target are among the companies that offer leadership awards.

In applying for these scholarships, your child should not just list the leadership positions he or she has held but should describe the effects of the leadership: what he or she achieved as a leader as well as what he or she gained from the experience. This kind of insight will illustrate your child's abilities and accomplishments.

Artists, performers and musicians. Scholarships for visual and performing artists are offered by symphonies, dance studios, museums and artistic foundations. Your child can find these awards by contacting such organizations on the local and national level. The awards are usually based on a competition that requires students to submit portfolios or tapes or to perform. Unlike other scholarship competitions, these may require an entry fee because of the amount of time it takes to review the portfolios or tapes.

Volunteers. Some organizations focus on students' contributions to their communities. On the national level, Toyota seeks students who have made extraordinary contributions; for example, one student created an education curriculum for organ donation in her community. On the local level, Walmart honors many students who have helped their communities through volunteer work.

With this type of scholarship, it is vital to demonstrate the results of the child's efforts, not just the number of hours he or she volunteered. Your child must be able to describe what was accomplished, what was learned and why this cause is important. The child's insight into the effects of the contribution will make the application stronger.

Bringing Back the Money

Scholarships are neither hard to find nor impossible to win. True, your child will be competing with others to prove to the judges that he or she is the most deserving of the award. And no student wins every time. But by applying for as many awards as possible and investing the effort to create strong applications and interviews, your child will have a chance of receiving a significant amount of money to help pay for college.

CHAPTER 8

How Can the College Help Us Pay?

What you'll learn:

- Why guaranteed scholarships exist
- Where to find tuition discounts
- How out-of-state students can pay in-state tuition
- How to take advantage of legacy awards and waivers
- Where to get emergency funds

For most parents, the relationship with a college is simple: The college sends a tuition bill, and the parent writes a check. What if the roles were reversed and the college wrote a check to you? Does this sound like a "Twilight Zone" episode? It happens more often than you might think.

Colleges use grants and scholarships to attract certain students. Because a school's reputation is based on the quality of its students, it is in the school's interest to make sure that students who meet certain criteria—such as having high grades or special talents—attend. Some schools go so far as to guarantee that all students who meet the requirements will get a scholarship. Colleges also offer numerous discounts: reduced tuition for in-state residents, tuition waivers for students from neighboring states and two-for-one deals for siblings.

When it comes to your bottom line, the college can be your most valuable partner in helping to pay the bills. Regardless of the form it takes, any award or discount from the college will feel like a check deposited directly into your bank account.

Dollars from Your College

We see newspaper headlines when a star quarterback or basketball forward receives a full-tuition scholarship, but, in fact, most money is given to students for much less exciting reasons, such as financial need, academic achievement and extracurricular involvement. These awards don't make headlines, but they provide a wealth of college money.

Merit Scholarships: Proof of Financial Need Not Required

Many colleges offer merit scholarships, which have nothing to do with a family's finances, as a way of attracting students. Students who will add to the campus community and reputation are highly sought after. These students might have high grade point averages (GPAs) or test scores; special talents in academics, music or the arts or strong leadership abilities.

At Duke University in Durham, North Carolina, the Angier B. Duke Memorial Scholarship provides full-tuition awards to students who display "academic and intellectual ambition." The college uses students' applications for admission to identify those who excel in an area of study. These students are then invited to compete for the full-tuition awards.

The University of Southern California (USC) in Los Angeles takes a similar approach by awarding up to 120 full-tuition Trustee Scholarships each year. Recipients typically have high GPAs in challenging courses and score in the top 1 to 2

Straight Talk with a Financial Aid Administrator ▶ **The financial aid administrator is on your side**

The financial aid administrator's job is to assist students in meeting their educational costs within the specific guidelines and regulations established by the school and federal government. If parents have a question, they can always contact a financial aid counselor or even the director. Parents (and students) should know there is always someone available to assist them.

It is also important parents understand the financial aid system. By viewing the financial aid office as the "enemy," the parent may stop listening to what the administrator has to say, even though it will explain the process. Of course, if a parent has a problem with a particular counselor, it is best to request assistance from a supervisor to assure the financial aid counselor or other staff is made aware of the situation and it can be corrected in the future. It is always to the benefit of both the parent and the financial aid administrator to have a good professional relationship.

Peggy Loewy-Wellisch, Associate Vice President for Student Financial Services, Nova Southeastern University

percent on the SAT or ACT. In addition to academic performance, the university considers talent, involvement in extracurricular activities and leadership.

These are just two examples of merit-based awards. Most colleges automatically use your child's application for admission as a scholarship application, so it's doubly important that your student submit the strongest application possible. How much better would it be for your child to be offered not only admission to his or her top choice college but a generous scholarship to boot?

BRIGHT IDEA . . . . . .

Don't miss out on college- and department-based awards. Some people think scholarships only come from companies and service organizations, but many opportunities originate with campus organizations, including the college and department of your child's major. The financial aid office usually maintains a list of scholarships available to current students. Check directly with the major department to uncover department-level scholarships and grants.

Need-based Scholarship Combos

As you learned in Chapter 3, by completing the Free Application for Federal Student Aid (FAFSA) or the CSS/PROFILE from the College Board, your child is eligible to receive need-based scholarships and grants. Beyond pure need-based awards, many colleges have programs that combine need and merit.

The Norman Topping Student Aid Fund at USC makes awards to low-income and first-generation college students. But financial need is not enough to get this money. Students must also exhibit community awareness, which is usually shown through participation in community service.

Combination need- and merit-based awards can add thousands of dollars to your college fund. Don't assume that turning in the FAFSA or CSS/PROFILE is the only way to get financial aid. Be sure your child actively pursues additional awards on the basis of your financial status.

Money for Your Child's Major

Don't stop with the resources of the college's financial aid office. Individual academic departments also offer funds. Because these scholarships are available only to students in a particular major, there is less competition.

A good example is the School of Music and Dance at San Francisco State University, which awards tens of thousands of dollars to students majoring in music. The awards are based on a combination of academic and musical performance.

Of course, many students enter college unsure of their major. But once your child declares a major, make sure he or she speaks with professors and administrative personnel in the department—they can point the way to scholarship opportunities.

Guaranteed College Scholarships

Normally, if you hear the words "guaranteed" and "scholarship" in the same sentence, it is a scam. (For more on scams, see Chapter 14.) The one exception is when a college is making the guarantee. A growing trend is for colleges to establish scholarships with specific, quantifiable criteria—any student who meets the criteria automatically gets the award. This removes much of the guesswork and allows families to know if they can count on a certain award. The following are examples of guaranteed scholarships.

Awards Based on GPA or Test Scores

Finally! A payoff for all those years you spent encouraging your child to study. Guaranteed scholarships based on GPA and ACT or SAT test scores are perhaps the most common of these awards. Many are offered on a sliding scale: The higher the grades and test scores, the more money is granted. Usually no scholarship application is necessary. Using the information in the application for admission, the college will automatically award the money to any student who qualifies.

Wilmington College of Ohio offers guaranteed scholarships to all incoming students who meet the following criteria:

- $4,500–$9,000 for students with a minimum 3.25 GPA and variable ACT/SAT score
- $1,500–$6,000 for students with up to a 3.25 GPA and variable ACT/SAT score

Saint Joseph's College in Rensselaer, Indiana, offers scholarships worth up to $13,000 to all accepted students based on their test scores and GPA. For example, students will receive:

- An Honors Scholarship of up to $13,000 with a minimum SAT score of 1300 and 3.25 GPA
- A Deans Scholarship of up to $11,000 with a minimum SAT score of 1200 and 3.2 GPA
- An SJC Scholarship of up to $9,000 with a minimum SAT score of 1000 and 3.0 GPA
- A Puma Opportunity Grant of up to $7,000 with a minimum SAT score of 810 and 2.8 GPA

- An Access Grant of up to $5,000 with a minimum SAT score of 810 and 2.0 GPA

The website has a calculator to determine students' eligibility for these awards.

Guaranteed scholarships remove the guesswork and can be a great motivator to earn good grades and high test scores in high school.

Transfer Student Awards

If your child is already in college and is considering transferring, it's important to know whether the financial aid package will transfer, too. In most cases, it won't. Your child will need to apply for financial aid all over again. You might be able to ease the transition with a guaranteed scholarship offered for transfer students. Often these awards are based on the student's performance at the previous college.

Spalding University in Kentucky offers a scholarship for transfer students according to the following scale:

- 29 percent of tuition for students with 3.5–4.0 GPAs
- 25 percent of tuition for students with 3.2–3.49 GPAs
- 22 percent of tuition for students with 3.0–3.19 GPAs

These funds help reduce the financial burden of transferring, especially if your child is moving from a less expensive community college to a pricier four-year university.

National Merit Scholarships

Do you remember that weekend during your child's junior year when he or she got up early to take the PSAT? You may have thought it was just a practice run for the SAT, but it had another purpose: establishing eligibility to win a National Merit Scholarship. If your child scored high enough on the PSAT, he or she was named a National Merit Commended Scholar or Semifinalist. While this is an impressive honor, it does not come with any money. However, doing extremely well on the PSAT brings an invitation to compete for a National Merit Scholarship. Each year, approximately 50,000 students are honored

KEY CONCEPT . . . .

Colleges offer many resources to help. The school itself is often your best ally in paying for college. In addition to financial aid, many offer their own scholarships, grants and work-study programs, as well as assistance in finding private scholarships. The financial aid office is a gold mine of information, with knowledgeable counselors who can answer your questions and help you create a plan for financing your child's education. If you are not taking advantage of all that the college offers, you are missing out on a huge opportunity.

as Commended Scholars or Semifinalists. Of those, approximately 15,000 go on to become National Merit Scholars with approximately 8,200 of these receiving a $2,500 award.

Even Commended Scholar or Semifinalist status may qualify your child for some extra scholarship dollars. Texas A&M University offers the Merit Plus Scholarship, a $2,000 award for National Merit Scholarship Semifinalists. In addition, these students may compete for Texas A&M's academic scholarships, which are worth an additional $10,000–$12,000 a year.

If your child achieves any level of National Merit distinction, notify the college. He or she may be eligible for a scholarship.

Double Your Dollars with Matching Grants

Would you like to see your child's scholarship money doubled? Ask the financial aid office if the college has a policy of matching grants, which means that the college will match outside scholarships dollar for dollar. For example, a matched $1,000 scholarship from the Lions Club turns into a $2,000 award. Most colleges set limits on how much they will match, but it is worth the effort to ask the financial aid office if the school is willing to match outside awards.

Create a Family Tradition with Legacy Awards

If your child is attending your alma mater, he or she may qualify for a scholarship. College alumni associations have long sponsored scholarship competitions for the children of members, although it is never a sure thing that any one student will win. Today, however, some colleges have guaranteed scholarships that reward second-generation students.

A few colleges go one step further and give money to the grandchildren of alumni. If your child intends to continue a family tradition, be sure to inquire about any awards that will help fund this legacy.

In-State Tuition Discounts

If you're hoping to keep your child close to home a little while longer, here is a financial incentive: All students who attend a public college in their home state receive an in-state tuition discount. In-state tuition can be significantly less than out-of-state tuition.

On the other hand, if your child is anxious to cut loose and move away, or just prefers a college elsewhere, you are not automatically stuck with paying the premium charge for nonresidents.

Straight Talk with a Financial Aid Administrator ▶ **Attend a financial aid night at your high school**

One of the best resources for parents is to attend a local financial aid night. These are usually held at high schools, community centers, churches and colleges. At Eastern Michigan we do more than 100 every January. A representative from our office explains the different types of financial aid, the concept of need and the various student and parent loan options. We introduce the FAFSA and give parents tips on filling it out. Common mistakes and misconceptions about how aid is awarded are covered. We explain savings plans and how they impact financial aid. We also review the deadlines and of course, we answer a lot of questions. Financial aid nights are an excellent resource open to all parents.

Courtney McAnuff, Vice President for Enrollment Services, Eastern Michigan University

Ask the college about the process for being considered a state resident. While some states make this difficult, others make it as easy as getting a driver's license. Most states have different requirements for residency for paying in-state tuition and residency for paying state taxes. Even if your child cannot get residency status immediately, there may be other ways to cut tuition prices, including reciprocity agreements, tuition waivers and nonresident scholarships.

Reciprocity Agreements: The Good Neighbor Policy

You may be able to avoid out-of-state tuition rates in a neighboring state through the goodwill program known as reciprocity agreements. These pacts between states offer each other's residents discounted or in-state tuition rates.

The Western Undergraduate Exchange provides reduced tuition rates for students in 15 western states. Through this program, residents of participating states are eligible for scholarships that allow them to pay 150 percent of the in-state tuition rate, which is a huge savings over the standard nonresident rate. The participating states are Alaska, Arizona, California, Colorado, Hawaii, Idaho, Montana, Nevada, New Mexico, North Dakota, Oregon, South Dakota, Utah, Washington and Wyoming.

Similarly, Minnesota, North Dakota, South Dakota and Wisconsin have a reciprocity agreement that reduces or eliminates nonresident fees for students who live in any of the four states. The Midwest Student Exchange provides discounts of at least

KEY CONCEPT . . . .

Strict rules govern how to become a resident to pay in-state tuition. States give discounts to residents who attend public universities; there are specific requirements for out-of-state students to gain residency. Factors include length of residency in the state, financial independence from parents and even intention of remaining in the state after graduation. Understand the state's specific rules for becoming a resident—they often involve more than just living in the state and getting a driver's license.

10 percent at participating community colleges, colleges or universities in Kansas, Michigan, Minnesota, Missouri, Nebraska and North Dakota.

The chances are good that your child can find a reciprocity agreement to help him or her attend a public school in a neighboring state.

In-State Tuition Waivers

If you are not able to take advantage of a reciprocity agreement, you may be able to save with an in-state tuition waiver on the basis of academic records, scholarships won and special circumstances. Some colleges grant a limited number of these waivers, which provide discounted tuition to out-of-state students. In applying for an in-state tuition waiver, your child should explain his or her academic record and describe the family's financial situation.

Nonresident Scholarships

Some colleges have scholarships specifically for nonresident students. For example, the University of Arkansas offers nonresident tuition awards for students from the neighboring states of Texas, Mississippi, Louisiana, Kansas, Missouri, Oklahoma and Tennessee.

Going to college out of state does not mean you will automatically be obligated to pay more. As these programs illustrate, out-of-state students can share the wealth of in-state tuition.

Tuition Discounts

Besides scholarships and grants, colleges may offer a limited number of special discounts. The following are examples of the kinds of discounts commonly available. Always check with the college's financial aid office to make sure you are not passing up any potential money-savers.

Sibling Discounts

Famous twins Mary-Kate and Ashley Olsen would have received a 50 percent discount if they had attended Sterling College in Kansas. While the multimillionaire entertainers don't exactly need a discount, it could make a big difference for your family. If your children are close in age and want to attend the same college, you may qualify for a two-for-one deal.

George Washington University in Washington, DC, offers the GW Family Grant for undergraduate siblings who attend the university at the same time. While one student pays the full price, the second student receives a 50 percent discount on tuition. At Lake Erie College in Ohio, the Twins Scholarship provides a full-tuition scholarship for the second twin enrolled. This means that both twins attend for the price of one.

Tuition Remission

Parents who work at a college or university are entitled to a tuition discount for their children. These employee discounts, called tuition remission programs, can save a ton of money. At Loyola Marymount University in Los Angeles, full-time employees who work a minimum of three years are eligible for full-time remission for their dependents.

But what if your child does not want to attend the college where you work? No problem. More than 550 colleges participate in a program called Tuition Exchange. Through this program, the families of faculty and staff receive scholarships to attend member institutions. Each year, approximately 4,000 scholarships are awarded. The awards are competitive, but they provide a significant discount to attend a college other than the one at which the parent works.

Alumni Referrals

Finding a job is not the only time alumni connections come in handy—at some colleges, alumni refer students to receive scholarships. At the College of St. Catherine in St. Paul and Minneapolis, Minnesota, alums may refer prospective students to receive application fee waivers as well as scholarships of up to $600. Check your network of friends and family to see if any are alums of the schools your child is applying to.

Pay for College in Installments

For many families, it is far easier to pay for college tuition in smaller, monthly amounts than in one big lump sum at the start of each semester. Some schools allow you to spread your payments over the academic year. Check with the college to see if it offers this payment option. One program that works with a number of colleges is called TuitionPay, a payment program from Sallie Mae's Business Office Suite. For a low annual enrollment fee, your tuition is divided into several payments, with no interest. Currently more than 1,500 schools participate in this plan. To see if your school does, visit www.tuitionpayenroll.com.

Emergency Aid: Money When You Need It Most

Colleges know that the unexpected can happen, and many offer emergency loans to students who have sudden medical, transportation or other expenses that interfere with their ability to pay tuition. These are short-term loans and are meant to be repaid quickly. Skidmore College in New York State grants emergency loans of $200, and Fort Lewis College in Colorado offers emergency loans of up to $500. It may not sound like much, but quick emergency cash can be a lifesaver in a crisis.

Don't Be Afraid to Ask for Help

Colleges have to send tuition bills, but they can be creative in helping you pay them. If you do a little digging and ask the right questions, you'll be able to take advantage of all the help that the school has to offer.

CHAPTER 9

How Can My State Help?

What you'll learn:

- Where to find your state higher education agency
- How to discover state grant programs
- Which loan repayment programs will forgive your loans

When Thomas Jefferson declared that "a democratic society depends on an informed and educated citizenry," he established a philosophy that can help you pay for college today. Your quest to create a well-educated child aligns perfectly with the national goal of an informed citizenry.

But, unlike many countries, the United States does not have a university system managed by the federal government. Instead, the individual states have taken responsibility for creating the world's best institutions of higher education. As you prepare to help your child become a well-educated citizen, find out how the state can help you do so affordably.

State Scholarships and Grants

All states offer scholarships and grants. Some are based on financial need (usually determined through the Free Application for Federal Student Aid, or FAFSA), and others are based on academic performance and other criteria. Some states require that the awards be used only at in-state colleges, while others allow students to spend the money in other states. The following are a few examples of the various kinds of state scholarships and grants:

Robert C. Byrd Honors Scholarship Program. Named for the senator from West Virginia, this program provides awards to students in all 50 states, the District of Columbia, the Commonwealth of Puerto Rico, Guam, the Commonwealth of the Northern Mariana Islands and the Virgin Islands. It is federally funded and is administered by each state to reward outstanding high school seniors. Applicants must be graduates of secondary schools or have earned a general equivalency di-

---

Straight Talk with a Financial Aid Administrator ▶

Contact your state higher education agency today!

One of the first things you should do is to contact your state's higher education council or agency. Almost every state has a website or toll-free number to get a lot of your questions answered. Here you can find out if your state offers any incentive grants or scholarships. Especially if you plan to attend college in your state, there could be grant programs that can help. But, even if you plan to go to an out-of-state college there may be funds available. Your state council or agency will be able to educate you about these programs—some of which are not well known by the general public.

In Virginia we have a program called the Academic Common Market offered through the Southern Regional Education Board (www.sreb.org). This program allows students who want to major in a degree program not offered at their state school to attend an out-of-state school at in-state tuition rates. For example, George Mason University has academic programs such as a Bachelor's of Integrated Studies or a PhD in Bioinformatics that are not offered in state schools in Maryland. Therefore, if students in this state want to attend our program, they can be billed in-state tuition rates even though their state of residence is not Virginia. It's very important to learn about the programs available through your state.

Jevita R. de Freitas, Director, Office of Student Financial Aid,
George Mason University

---

ploma (GED); be U.S. citizens or permanent residents and attend an institution of higher education. The average award is $1,500, and some awards are renewable. For more information, go to the Department of Education website at www.ed.gov/programs/iduesbyrd.

Leveraging Educational Assistance Partnership (LEAP). Through LEAP, students who demonstrate financial need may receive grants for higher education. For example, the Arizona LEAP program provides grants of up to $2,500 to Arizona students who demonstrate financial need and attend public or private Arizona postsecondary institutions.

CalGrants. Each year, California awards more than $500 million in CalGrants to California residents to help low- and middle-income families pay for college. The grants are based on financial need and high school academic performance. Students whose families meet the income and asset qualifications and the minimum academic standards and are attending a California school receive a grant.

Ohio War Orphans Scholarship Program. The War Orphans Scholarship program provides tuition assistance (up to full tuition at two- and four-year public colleges and universities, and partial tuition for private institutions) to the children of deceased or severely disabled Ohio veterans who served in the armed forces during a period of declared war or conflict. Eligible students must be residents of Ohio and enrolled in a full-time undergraduate program at an eligible Ohio college or university.

There are as many state scholarships and grants as there are states. Learn about the programs in your area and make sure your child meets the requirements to receive these awards. Start by contacting your state's higher education commission or agency (listed at the end of this chapter). Also, have your child speak to his or her college counselor to learn more about these programs.

State Loan Repayment Programs

If your child is thinking of becoming a teacher, doctor, nurse, dentist, police officer, firefighter, engineer or lawyer, college funds may be available through loan repayment programs. In some cases, by working in careers with shortages or in underserved areas, students can have all their student loans repaid by the state. Quite a deal!

Through California's State Loan Repayment Program, students who work in health care in areas where there is a shortage may have up to $120,000 of their loans forgiven. Georgia offers the Intellectual Capital Partnership Program for students who earn degrees or certificates to work as computer programmers, medical transcriptionists or Web designers or administrators. The program forgives up to $10,000 in loans. Georgia also offers the Scholarship for Engineering Education for engineering students who work in Georgia after they graduate.

To find your state's loan repayment programs, start by contacting your state higher education agency. Also, refer to Chapter 6 for a list of national loan repayment programs for teachers, health care professionals, volunteers, child care providers and others.

CURRENT TRENDS .

States give away more money each year. States are expanding their grant programs and helping more families pay for college. Between 1997 and 2007, the amount awarded in state grants increased a whopping 144 percent!

Source: College Board, *Trends in Student Aid 2007.*

State Work-Study

Work-study programs subsidize your student's salary for part-time work in college. The advantages of work-study are that your child will gain work experience while in college, have a convenient job that is usually located on campus and earn a fair wage. Typical jobs are working in the library, dining hall or research laboratories.

To apply for work-study, your child will have to fill out the FAFSA. If he or she is eligible, state work-study programs will be listed on financial aid award letters as part of the overall financial aid package.

State Higher Education Agencies

The best place to find state resources for financial aid is to contact your state's higher education agency or commission. These government bodies act as clearinghouses for information on state financial aid programs. Most maintain websites that explain the various programs and have links to other resources. Contact your agency today!

Alabama

Alabama Commission on Higher Education
P.O. Box 302000
Montgomery, AL 36130-2000
Phone: 334-242-1998
In-state toll-free: 1-800-960-7773
Fax: 334-242-0268
Website: www.ache.alabama.gov

Alaska

Alaska Commission on Postsecondary Education
P.O. Box 110505
Juneau, AK 99811-0505
Phone: 907-465-2962
Toll-free: 1-800-441-2962
Fax: 907-465-5316
TTY: 907-465-3143
E-mail: customer_service@acpe.state.ak.us
Website: www.alaskaadvantage.state.ak.us

Arizona

Arizona Commission for Postsecondary Education
2020 North Central Avenue, Suite 550
Phoenix, AZ 85004-4503
Phone: 602-258-2435
Fax: 602-258-2483
Website: www.azhighered.gov

Arkansas

Arkansas Department of Higher Education
114 East Capitol
Little Rock, AR 72201-3818
Phone: 501-371-2000
Fax: 501-371-2001
Website: www.adhe.edu

California

California Student Aid Commission
P.O. Box 419027
Rancho Cordova, CA 95741-9027
Phone: 916-526-7590
Toll-free: 1-888-224-7268
Fax: 916-526-8004
E-mail: studentsupport@csac.ca.gov
Website: www.csac.ca.gov

Colorado

Colorado Department of Higher Education
1380 Lawrence Street, Suite 1200
Denver, CO 80204
Phone: 303-866-2723
Fax: 303-866-4266
E-mail: executivedirector@cche.state.co.us
Website: www.state.co.us/cche/

Connecticut

Connecticut Department of Higher Education
61 Woodland Street
Hartford, CT 06105-2326
Phone: 860-947-1800
Toll-free: 1-800-842-0229
Fax: 860-947-1310
E-mail: info@ctdhe.org
Website: www.ctdhe.org

Delaware

Delaware Higher Education Commission
Carvel State Office Building, Fifth Floor
820 North French Street
Wilmington, DE 19801
Phone: 302-577-5240
Toll-free: 1-800-292-7935
Fax: 302-577-6765
E-mail: dhec@doe.k12.de.us
Website: www.doe.state.de.us/high-ed/

District of Columbia

Office of the State Superintendent of Education (District of Columbia)
441 4th Street, NW
Suite 350 North
Washington, DC 20001
Phone: 202-727-6436
Toll-free: 1-877-485-6751
Fax: 202-727-2834
TTY: 202-727-1675
E-mail: osse@dc.gov
Website: http://seo.dc.gov

Florida

Florida Department of Education
Office of Student Financial Assistance
1940 North Monroe Street, Suite 70
Tallahassee, FL 32303-4759
Phone: 850-410-5180
Toll-free: 1-888-827-2004
E-mail: osfa@fldoe.org
Website: www.floridastudentfinancialaid.org

Georgia

Georgia Student Finance Commission
Loan Services
2082 East Exchange Place
Tucker, GA 30084
Phone: 770-724-9000
Toll-free: 1-800-505-4732
Fax: 770-724-9089
E-mail: info@gsfc.org
Website: www.gsfc.org

Hawaii

Hawaii State Postsecondary Education Commission
Office of the Board of Regents
2444 Dole Street, Room 209
Honolulu, HI 96822-2302
Phone: 808-956-8213
Fax: 808-956-5156
E-mail: bor@hawaii.edu
Website: www.hawaii.edu/offices/bor/

Idaho

Idaho State Board of Education
P.O. Box 83720
650 West State Street
Boise, ID 83720-0037
Phone: 208-334-2270
Fax: 208-334-2632
E-mail: board@osbe.idaho.gov
Website: www.boardofed.idaho.gov

Illinois

Illinois Student Assistance Commission
1755 Lake Cook Road
Deerfield, IL 60015-5209
Phone: 847-948-8500
Toll-free: 1-800-899-4722
Fax: 847-831-8549
TTY: 847-831-8326
E-mail: collegezone@isac.org
Website: www.collegezone.com

Indiana

State Student Assistance Commission of Indiana
150 West Market Street, Suite 500
Indianapolis, IN 46204-2811
Phone: 317-232-2350
In-state toll-free: 1-888-528-4719
Fax: 317-232-3260
E-mail: grants@ssaci.state.in.us
Website: www.ssaci.in.gov

Straight Talk with a Financial Aid Administrator ▶ # Take advantage of your state savings plans

Most states offer a college savings plan. If you have enough time before your child starts school, seriously consider these plans since they can save a lot of money. For example, the Michigan Education Trust offers plans for families who want to save. One of the non-monetary benefits of these plans is that they help to ease the mental burden of worrying about tuition. But even if you don't use a savings plan, you need to plan for paying for college. Some families think financial aid will save them from poor planning. It will not. Often it just means their child will end up with more educational debt.

Courtney McAnuff, Vice President for Enrollment Services, Eastern Michigan University

Iowa

Iowa College Student Aid Commission
200 10th Street, Fourth Floor
Des Moines, IA 50309
Phone: 515-725-3400
Toll-free: 1-800-383-4222
Fax: 515-725-3401
E-mail: info@iowacollegeaid.org
Website: www.iowacollegeaid.gov

Kansas

Kansas Board of Regents
Curtis State Office Building
1000 SW Jackson Street, Suite 520
Topeka, KS 66612-1368
Phone: 785-296-3421
Fax: 785-296-0983
Website: www.kansasregents.org

Kentucky

Kentucky Higher Education Assistance Authority
P.O. Box 798
Frankfort, KY 40602-0798
Phone: 502-696-7200
Toll-free: 1-800-928-8926
Fax: 502-696-7496
TTY: 1-800-855-2880
E-mail: inquiries@kheaa.com
Website: www.kheaa.com

Louisiana

Louisiana Office of Student Financial Assistance
P.O. Box 91202
Baton Rouge, LA 70821-9202
Phone: 225-922-1012
Toll-free: 1-800-259-5626 x1012
Fax: 225-922-0790
E-mail: custserv@osfa.state.la.us
Website: www.osfa.state.la.us

Maine

Finance Authority of Maine (FAME)
P.O. Box 949
Augusta, ME 04332-0949
Phone: 207-623-3263
Toll-free: 1-800-228-3734
Fax: 207-623-0095
TTY: 207-626-2717
E-mail: education@famemaine.com
Website: www.famemaine.com

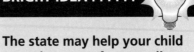

BRIGHT IDEA . . . . . .

The state may help your child attend an out-of-state college. While some state aid programs require that your child attend college within the state, others are willing to help students who decide to go beyond their borders. Don't assume that state aid is based on geography.

Maryland

Maryland Higher Education Commission
839 Bestgate Road Suite 400
Annapolis, MD 21401-3013
Phone: 410-260-4500
In-state toll-free: 1-800-974-0203
Fax: 410-260-3200
TTY: 1-800-735-2258
Website: www.mhec.state.md.us

Massachusetts

Massachusetts Board of Higher Education
One Ashburton Place, Room 1401
Boston, MA 02108
Phone: 617-994-6950
Fax: 617-727-6397
E-mail: bhe@bhe.mass.edu
Website: www.mass.edu

Michigan

Michigan Student Financial Services Bureau
P.O. Box 30047
Lansing, MI 48909-7547
Toll-free: 1-800-642-5626 x37054
Fax: 517-241-0155

E-mail: sfs@michigan.gov
Website: www.michigan.gov/studentaid

Minnesota

Minnesota Office of Higher Education
1450 Energy Park Drive, Suite 350
Saint Paul, MN 55108-5227
Phone: 651-259-3901
Toll-free: 1-800-657-3866
Fax: 651-642-0675
TTY: 1-800-642-0597
E-mail: ohe@state.mn.us
Website: www.ohe.state.mn.us

Mississippi

Mississippi Institutions of Higher Learning
3825 Ridgewood Road
Jackson, MS 39211-6453
Phone: 601-432-6647
In-state toll-free: 1-800-327-2980
Fax: 601-432-6527
E-mail: commissioner@ihl.state.ms.us
Website: www.ihl.state.ms.us

Missouri

Missouri Department of Higher Education
3515 Amazonas Drive
Jefferson City, MO 65109-5717
Phone: 573-751-2361
Toll-free: 1-800-473-6757
Fax: 573-751-6635
TTY: 1-800-735-2966
E-mail: info@dhe.mo.gov
Website: www.dhe.mo.gov

Montana

Montana University System
46 North Last Chance Gulch
P.O. Box 203201
Helena, MT 59620-3201
Phone: 406-444-6570
Fax: 406-444-1469
Website: www.mus.edu

Nebraska

Nebraska Coordinating Commission for Postsecondary Education
140 North Eighth Street, Suite 300
P.O. Box 95005
Lincoln, NE 68509-5005
Phone: 402-471-2847
Fax: 402-471-2886
Website: www.ccpe.state.ne.us

Nevada

Nevada Department of Education
700 East Fifth Street
Carson City, NV 89701
Phone: 775-687-9200
Fax: 775-687-9101
Website: www.doe.nv.gov

New Hampshire

New Hampshire Postsecondary Education Commission
3 Barrell Court, Suite 300
Concord, NH 03301-8543
Phone: 603-271-2555
Fax: 603-271-2696
TTY: 1-800-735-2964
Website: www.state.nh.us/postsecondary

New Jersey

Commission on Higher Education
20 West State Street
P.O. Box 542
Trenton, NJ 08625-0542
Phone: 609-292-4310
Fax: 609-292-7225
E-mail: nj_che@che.state.nj.us
Website: www.state.nj.us/highereducation/

New Mexico

New Mexico Higher Education Department
1068 Cerrillos Road
Santa Fe, NM 87505
Phone: 505-476-6500
Toll-free: 1-800-279-9777
Fax: 505-476-6511
TTY: 1-800-659-8331
E-mail: highered@state.nm.us
Website: http://hed.state.nm.us

New York

New York State Higher Education Services Corporation
99 Washington Avenue
Albany, NY 12255

Straight Talk with a Financial Aid Administrator ▶ **Receiving state aid may be automatic**

In our state, the Ohio Board of Regents administers state financial aid programs. When a student fills out the Free Application for Federal Student Aid (FAFSA) a copy is automatically sent to the Board of Regents. There are grants the Board of Regents provides including part-time and full-time instructional grants. These awards can only be used to cover tuition. Ohio students who complete the FAFSA are automatically considered for these awards.

Veronica J. Leech, Director of Financial Aid, Central State University

Phone: 518-473-1574
Toll-free: 1-888-697-4372
Fax: 518-474-2839
TTY: 1-800-445-5234
E-mail: webmail@hesc.org
Website: www.hesc.org

North Carolina

North Carolina State Education Assistance Authority
P.O. Box 13663
Research Triangle Park, NC 27709-3663
Phone: 919-549-8614
In-state toll-free: 1-866-866-2362
Fax: 919-549-8481
E-mail: programinformation@cfnc.org
Website: www.cfnc.org

North Dakota

North Dakota University System
North Dakota Student Financial Assistance Program
Department 215
600 East Boulevard Avenue
Bismarck, ND 58505-0230
Phone: 701-328-4114
Fax: 701-328-2961
E-mail: ndus.office@ndus.nodak.edu
Website: www.ndus.edu

Ohio

Ohio Board of Regents
State Grants and Scholarships Department
P.O. Box 182452
Columbus, OH 43218-2452
Phone: 614-466-7420
Toll-free: 1-888-833-1133
Fax: 614-752-5903
Website: http://regents.ohio.gov

Oklahoma

Oklahoma State Regents for Higher Education
655 Research Parkway, Suite 200
Oklahoma City, OK 73104
Phone: 405-225-9100
Toll-free: 1-800-858-1840
Fax: 405-225-9230
E-mail: studentinfo@osrhe.edu
Website: www.okhighered.org

Oregon

Oregon Student Assistance Commission
1500 Valley River Drive, Suite 100
Eugene, OR 97401
Phone: 541-687-7400
Toll-free: 1-800-452-8807
Fax: 541-687-7414
E-mail: public_information@mercury.osac.state.or.us
Website: www.osac.state.or.us

Pennsylvania

Office of Postsecondary and Higher Education
Department of Education
333 Market Street, 12th Floor
Harrisburg, PA 17126
Phone: 717-787-5041
Fax: 717-772-3622
TTY: 717-783-8445
Website: www.pdehighered.state.pa.us/higher/

Rhode Island

Rhode Island Higher Education Assistance Authority
560 Jefferson Boulevard, Suite 100
Warwick, RI 02886
Phone: 401-736-1100
Toll-free: 1-800-922-9855
Fax: 401-732-3541
TTY: 401-734-9481
Website: www.riheaa.org

South Carolina

South Carolina Commission on Higher Education
1333 Main Street, Suite 200
Columbia, SC 29201
Phone: 803-737-2260
Toll-free: 1-877-349-7183
Fax: 803-737-2297
Website: www.che.sc.gov

South Dakota

South Dakota Board of Regents
306 East Capitol Avenue, Suite 200
Pierre, SD 57501
Phone: 605-773-3455
Fax: 605-773-5320
E-mail: info@sdbor.edu
Website: www.sdbor.edu

Tennessee

Tennessee Higher Education Commission
Parkway Towers
404 James Robertson Parkway, Suite 1900
Nashville, TN 37243-0830
Phone: 615-741-3605
Fax: 615-741-6230
Website: www.state.tn.us/thec/

Texas

Texas Higher Education Coordinating
Board
P.O. Box 12788
Austin, TX 78711
Phone: 512-427-6101
Toll-free: 1-800-242-3062
Fax: 512-427-6127
Website: www.thecb.state.tx.us

MONEY SAVER . . . .

Don't overlook automatic scholarships from your state. In some states, if your child has a certain GPA or test scores, he or she is eligible for a scholarship— all you have to do is claim it. Contact your state higher education agency (listed in this chapter) to make sure you know about all the programs that are offered, so you don't leave money on the table.

Utah

Utah State Board of Regents
Gateway Center
60 South 400 West
Salt Lake City, UT 84101-1284
Phone: 801-321-7103
Fax: 801-321-7156
Website: www.utahsbr.edu

Vermont

Vermont Student Assistance Corporation
10 East Allen Street
P.O. Box 2000
Winooski, VT 05404-2601
Phone: 802-655-9602
Toll-free: 1-800-642-3177
Fax: 802-654-3765
TTY: 1-800-281-3341
E-mail: info@vsac.org
Website: www.vsac.org

Virginia

State Council of Higher Education for Virginia
James Monroe Building
101 North 14th Street, Ninth Floor
Richmond, VA 23219
Phone: 804-225-2600
Fax: 804-225-2604
TTY: 804-371-8017
Website: www.schev.edu

Washington

Washington State Higher Education Coordinating Board
P.O. Box 43430
917 Lakeridge Way
Olympia, WA 98504-3430
Phone: 360-753-7800

Fax: 360-753-7808
E-mail: info@hecb.wa.gov
Website: www.hecb.wa.gov

West Virginia

West Virginia Higher Education Policy Commission
1018 Kanawha Boulevard, East, Suite 700
Charleston, WV 25301
Phone: 304-558-0699
Fax: 304-558-1011
Website: http://wvhepcnew.wvnet.edu

Wisconsin

Wisconsin Higher Educational Aids Board
131 West Wilson Street, Suite 902
Madison, WI 53703
Phone: 608-267-2206
Fax: 608-267-2808
E-mail: heabmail@wisconsin.gov
Website: www.heab.state.wi.us

Wyoming

Wyoming Community College Commission
2020 Carey Avenue, Eighth Floor
Cheyenne, WY 82002
Phone: 307-777-7763
Fax: 307-777-6567
Website: www.commission.wcc.edu

U.S. Territories

American Samoa
American Samoa Community College
Board of Higher Education
P.O. Box 2609
Pago Pago, AS 96799-2609
Phone: 684-699-9155
Website: www.amsamoa.edu

Commonwealth of the Northern Mariana Islands
Northern Marianas College
Office of the President
P.O. Box 501250
Saipan, MP 96950-1250
Phone: 670-234-5498 x1000
Fax: 670-234-0759
Website: www.nmcnet.edu

Puerto Rico
Puerto Rico Council on Higher Education
P.O. Box 19900
San Juan, PR 00910-1900
Phone: 787-641-7100
Fax: 787-641-2573
Website: www.ces.gobierno.pr

Republic of the Marshall Islands
RMI Scholarship Grant and Loan Board
P.O. Box 1436
3 Lagoon Road
Majuro, MH 96960
Phone: 692-625-7325
Website: www.rmischolarship.net

Virgin Islands
Virgin Islands Department of Education
Charlotte Amalie
1834 Kongens Gade
St. Thomas, VI 00801
Phone: 340-774-0100
Fax: 340-779-7153
Website: www.doe.vi

CHAPTER 10

What's the Best Way to Save for College?

What you'll learn:

- Why it's never too late to save
- A savings strategy that doesn't require counting pennies
- How to maximize 529 savings plans and Coverdell ESAs
- How Individual Development Accounts can double your savings
- What to do if you have less than a year to save

The joyous day arrives: Your baby boy or girl is born. On the way home from the hospital, you stop at the bank to open a college savings account. Every month you sock away money, and when your child is ready for college, the money is there.

Sounds great, doesn't it? Unfortunately, in the real world, most parents either don't or can't do this. Even with the best intentions, parents don't save enough because of daily living expenses and unexpected emergencies.

Does this mean it's too late to open a college savings account? No! Regardless of how few years remain until your child starts college—even if it is next year—you can jump-start your savings. If you are one of the families that missed the stop at the bank on the way home from the hospital, don't despair. It's never too late to start saving.

Never Too Late to Save

Although financial aid and scholarships may help you fund your child's college education, you can't rely on them to pay for everything. This is why, whether you have a toddler or a teenager, it is important to start saving today. Consider the following advantages of having strong college savings:

Financial aid and scholarships are not guaranteed. There is no certainty that your child will win enough scholarships or your family will receive enough financial aid to cover all college expenses. Also, what you receive one year may not be what you will receive the next. The only sure thing is your own savings, and that may be just enough to fill a critical gap.

Each dollar you save is one less dollar you'll have to borrow. The less you have to borrow, the less you have to repay. In fact, the dollar you save today may actually be worth more if it helps you borrow less tomorrow.

Your savings belong to you. Unlike financial aid or scholarships, the money in a savings account is under your control. You are not relying on financial aid calculations or the decisions of scholarship judges; instead, you are banking on the power of your own pocketbook. Nothing puts you in control like your own money.

Colleges expect you to contribute. No matter what your financial situation, colleges expect you to contribute to your child's education. For most people, the only way to do this is to save.

Saving trains your family to live on less. Instituting an aggressive savings plan will help your family learn to forgo unnecessary spending. Parents who are supporting a child in college can attest to the personal sacrifices that must be made. If you learn to live on less now, these sacrifices won't seem as difficult.

This chapter will show you how to implement a ruthless saving strategy that makes every penny work harder. You will learn about savings plans that allow your money to grow tax-free and discover some little-known programs that can double or even triple your savings. But remember, these strategies aren't worth anything unless you resolve to start saving today!

Smart Saving Strategies: 1 - 2 - 3

Some parents envision saving for college as endlessly clipping coupons and dining on rice and beans. Even more unappealing is the dreaded b-word: budget. The prospect of saving every receipt and keeping track of every penny can be enough to make parents give up before they start.

While there are many ways to establish a saving strategy, the following method does not involve keeping a log of every expenditure or clipping coupons (unless you want to). This strategy will produce maximum results in a limited time.

In part, this system works because saving for college, unlike saving money in general, involves achieving a specific goal in a certain amount of time. You know approximately how much college will cost and exactly how long until your child starts school. And you know that your saving strategy is temporary—it is only needed until your last child graduates from college.

Smart Saving Step 1: Set Your Goal

You probably wouldn't embark on a road trip without a destination, so why would you start saving without knowing how much you need? Determining that amount

KEY CONCEPT . . . .

It's never too late to save for college. Think about it this way: If your child is a high school senior, you still have four years before you receive the last college tuition bill. Regardless of how soon you'll receive the first tuition bill, if you start saving now you'll be in a better position to pay the last one.

is often more art than science. Some parts of the equation are easy. You know what college costs today, and you know which direction costs are heading (up). How much they will rise is less certain, especially if your child will not enroll for many years; but it is safe to assume that college prices will increase between 5 percent and 7 percent a year.

You may not know whether your child will attend a public or private college. If your child is a high school junior or senior, you can just ask; if he or she is in kindergarten, you'll have to guess.

Finally, because few families pay the full sticker price for college, you need to take into account the financial aid and scholarships your child might receive. Chapter 3 describes how financial aid is determined. Your child might also receive grants and/or scholarships, but it is almost impossible to determine how much this could be.

The best way to set a goal is to look at the worst-case scenario. Assume that you will receive zero help from college grants and private scholarships. In other words, assume that you will have to pay the entire cost of your child's education.

Start by going to the Sallie Mae website (www.salliemae.com) and selecting "Long-Term Planning Calculator" under "Assessing Your Needs." This calculator estimates the monthly savings required to support up to three children in college. The calculator asks for the current cost of attending a college and how much you have already saved. You can enter values for the rate at which college prices are expected to increase, the rate of return you expect to earn on your savings and the number of years before each child starts college. When you press the "calculate" button, you'll see an estimate of how much you need to save each month to pay the total cost of your children's education. But before you push that button, sit down. It can be overwhelming.

Here's an example:

You have two children. Your daughter will attend college in two years and your son in eight. The older child wants to attend a state university; the younger child has no idea. Taking the national average, you enter into the Long-Term Planning Calculator the cost of one year at a public university, which is $13,589. Since you want to see the worst-case scenario, you assume that your son will attend a more expensive private college. Enter the current national average for one year, which is $32,307. Remember, these averages are the total cost for one year, including tuition, fees and room and board.

On the basis of these numbers, the calculator shows that your daughter will need $69,077 for four years at a public university and your son will need $246,459 for four years at a private college. (He won't be starting college for eight years—the $32,307 a year figure will be history by then.) Take a deep breath and remember that these are sticker prices. They do not take into account financial aid, scholarships or grants. This is a worst-case scenario, in which you receive no outside assistance.

Next, the calculator asks how much you have already saved and how much you are putting away each month for college. Let's assume that you have managed to save $8,000 for your daughter and $5,000 for your son. Each month you put $100 into each child's college savings accounts. Assuming a 5 percent return, the calculator shows that you will have a total of $11,358 in your

---

Straight Talk with a Financial Aid Administrator ▶ **A college savings means having a choice**

Many parents believe the federal or state government should cover the entire cost of the student's education and they do not have to save money for college. That is not the case. It is the parent's and student's responsibility to plan ahead for educational costs. Financial aid is intended to supplement, not replace, the family's contribution. It is important to plan early and save for a student's education. It really is never too early to save. The fact is the more money a family saves, the more options will be available to them to attend the colleges of their choice.

Peggy Loewy-Wellisch, Associate Vice President for Student Financial Services, Nova Southeastern University

daughter's account and $19,227 in your son's account when each is ready for college.

Finally, the calculator reveals the shortfall. For your daughter, you will need an additional $57,719; for your son, an additional $227,232. To accumulate this amount, you'd have to save $4,222 a month.

Let's try to relieve that feeling in the pit of your stomach.

The 60/40 Rule

You can't save more than you bring home each week, so you need to work with what you have. An aggressive target is the "60/40 rule." Look at your total monthly income and take 40 percent as your savings goal, using the remaining 60 percent to pay for everything else. Obviously, this is not easy. The rule is designed to push you to save, which will involve cutting expenses. Here is an example.

If you and your spouse earn a combined income of $65,000 a year, your monthly take-home pay after withholding for taxes is in the neighborhood of $4,100. Applying the 60/40 rule, you should save $1,640 for college each month. The remaining $2,460 has to cover everything else.

Going back to our original example of the family with two children, imagine that instead of saving $100 a month for each child, you save $1,640, so that each child's account gets $820. If you enter this new amount into the Long-Term Savings Calculator, you'll see that your daughter's account will have $29,492 in it when she goes to college in two years (including the $8,000 you started with). When your son goes to college in eight years, his account will have $104,000 in it (including the $5,000 you started with). While this does not cover the entire cost of either college, it covers at least 40 percent. That's a huge accomplishment!

In addition to federal financial aid, your children may win scholarships, receive additional aid from the state and college, work while they're in school, and/or contribute money from their own savings. If you save 40 percent of your children's total college costs (remember, these numbers include tuition, fees and room and board), it's likely that you will be able to afford to send your child to any college in the country.

So, set your savings goal at 40 percent of your take-home pay. Once you implement the 60/40 rule, you won't have to count pennies or track expenses. You simply put away the 40 percent and live on the rest.

Smart Saving Step 2: Reduce Expenses

For most families, saving 40 percent of take-home pay is not possible without reducing expenses, and the best way to do this is with a written budget. (Once you get on the 60/40 plan, you may not need to keep the budget—unless you find yourself slipping back into old spending habits.) Review a typical month and list how you spend your money. Divide your expenses into two columns: necessary and discretionary. Necessary expenses include:

- Mortgage or rent payments
- Groceries
- Gasoline
- County, state and federal taxes
- Health, life, home and car insurance
- School expenses
- Utilities (water, electricity, telephone, sewer and heat)
- Vehicle maintenance and repair
- Medical expenses/prescriptions
- House maintenance (if you own your home)
- Necessary clothing for work and school

Discretionary expenses are everything else:

- Entertainment (rental movies, theater movies, dining out, etc.)
- Purchases (clothes, books, CDs, etc. that you don't absolutely need)
- Home electronics
- Car payments (remember, you can always sell a car and purchase a cheaper one)
- Cable television

Your lists may be somewhat different from these. For example, you may need an Internet connection for work; however, if it is just used for fun, it is discretionary. Clothing can fall into either category: A dress shirt for the office is necessary; an Italian leather jacket is not.

Take your time and figure out how much money you spend on each of these categories in an average month. Compare your expenses to your monthly income. Then focus on eliminating every nonessential expense you possibly can. Do you really need those $3 cappuccinos when you could make a cup of coffee at home instead? Does your family need to eat out that often? Can you use the library instead of buying books?

See what you can do to reduce necessary expenses as well. Can you reset the thermostat so the heating bill goes down? Are you getting the best rates on all your

Straight Talk with a Financial Aid Administrator ▶ **Common misconceptions about financial aid packages**

A common misconception about financial aid packages is there are some factors such as credit card debt, saving for retirement or the purchase of a second home parents may assume have a significant impact on the award package. In most cases, these types of expenses have far less impact than parents might assume.

The financial aid process does allow for special circumstances to be taken into consideration and adjustments to be made in what a family is expected to contribute. However, institutions have different policies of how they respond to various levels of consumer indebtedness and past spending and saving patterns. In general the policy exhibited by most institutions (and the federal government) indicates that the parents must assume the primary responsibility for funding college and educational expenses. For practical purposes what this means is significant credit card debt, purchase of a second home and saving for retirement far beyond what might be reasonably expected will have very little impact on financial aid offers. Each institution will have slightly different policies for a wide range of circumstances, but in general remember consumer debt, particularly debt due to luxury or convenience items, will need to take second place to funding educational expenses. Families with high levels of consumer debt are often surprised financial aid calculations do not take this debt into account when determining what they are expected to pay for college.

Dr. Lawrence Burt, Associate VP for Student Affairs & Director of Student Financial Services, University of Texas at Austin

---

insurance? Could you refinance your home mortgage and lower your interest rate? Can you drive a little less or use public transportation to curb fuel and car repair costs? Small savings can make a big difference at the end of the month.

One family realized that they were spending nearly $300 a month eating at restaurants and fast-food chains. They switched to eating at home and having a barbecue when they wanted something special. They added more than $3,000 a year to their college savings account through this one simple step.

If it helps when you're cutting expenses, remember that you won't have to live like this forever—only until your last child graduates from college. After that you'll suddenly free up 40 percent of your income for other goodies like increased retirement savings and, yes, even some luxuries.

Get Rid of Consumer Debt

If you have large credit card or other consumer debt that is eating away a huge portion of your monthly income, you may need to create a special plan. First and foremost, cut up those credit cards so you don't keep charging. Consumer debt hurts in two ways: The obvious one is you have to make payments each month to service the debt; less obvious is that federal financial aid does not take consumer debt into account. From the federal government's point of view, this debt does not exist in determining how much money your child needs for college. If you need help controlling spending or paying off your debts, find a qualified financial planner, consumer credit counselor or other competent financial service. Depending on the size of your debts, you may need to address this issue before you can even begin to save for college.

While there are no quick and easy solutions, the following are some steps to get debt under control.

Shred the cards. By cutting them up, you will ensure that once you get out of debt, you won't fall back in. If you must have a card, get a debit card that takes money directly out of a bank account.

Straight Talk with a Financial Aid Administrator ▶ **Saving for college is a team sport**

Families should view this period in their life not as a "financial aid" experience but rather as a "paying for college" experience. Look at the big picture, which means you need to start saving as soon as possible. Even if you only have six months before your child starts college, it's not too late. If you can save $1,000 during this time, that's still $1,000 you didn't have before. From experience I can tell you any amount saved will make a positive difference. A good savings plan is part of the family's overall approach to paying for college.

Families should view paying for college as a team sport, a family commitment. Some parents forget this means including the child. Sit down and have a serious conversation about what you expect your child to contribute. Maybe it means saving a certain amount or just enough to pay for books. The key is to work together and make saving a family project. I feel so strongly about this aspect that I co-authored a book for families called *How to Save for College* (Random House, 2004). My co-author (Joe Russo of Notre Dame) and I stress the importance of getting everyone on board and having a solid plan.

Jim Belvin, Director of Financial Aid, Duke University

Budget your payments. Just as you created a plan to save for college, you need a plan to pay off your credit card debt. Determine how much you can afford to pay each month and figure out how long it will take to pay off the entire balance. Make this a priority.

Sell stuff. If you have assets such as cars, boats or collectible coins, consider selling them to pay off your debts. You can always replace them when you're on sounder financial footing.

Consolidate debt. If you are paying high interest rates on credit card debt, you may be able to get a consolidation loan at a lower interest rate. A common tactic is to use a home equity loan. As long as the interest rate and costs are lower than the rates you are paying on the credit card, this can be a good idea.

Cautiously explore a credit counselor service. Local nonprofit credit counseling organizations may be able to help you. However, be very careful, as there have been complaints about services that do not deliver on their promises. Also, there may be major consequences such as negative impact on your credit report and/or difficulty getting loan approval if you use a service to negotiate with your creditors. If you decide to use a service, carefully follow up on references and check it out with the Better Business Bureau.

Teach your child to avoid falling into debt. While this won't lower your own debt, it can help your child. Use your experience with debt to educate your child on how to use credit responsibly. As a college student, he or she will be inundated with credit card offers. Make sure your child understands the consequences of over-spending.

For more information on credit card debt, go to the Federal Trade Commission's website (www.ftc.gov) and read the free publication "Knee Deep in Debt." Once your credit card debt is under control, you can move forward with your college savings plan.

Delay Big Purchases

The hard work of even the most frugal and dedicated savers can be wiped out by a few big-ticket purchases. While some large expenses, such as medical bills, are unavoidable, others can be delayed. Instead of buying a new car, push the old one a few more years. A new kitchen would be wonderful, but so would paying for your child's education without having to take out a second mortgage.

Big purchases usually have long-term consequences. The new car will saddle you with higher insurance payments. Remodeling the kitchen may force you to take out a home equity loan. As long as the purchases are not essential (do spend the money to fix a leaking roof), consider putting them off until after your child graduates from college.

Protect Your Savings from the Enemy: You

Once you've set a goal, guarantee that you achieve it. How? Don't let yourself get your hands on any of the money earmarked for college. Set up automatic withdrawal from your bank account each month to transfer the money to a separate savings account, or write a check on payday for the amount to be saved. Where should this money go? Good options include a dedicated college savings account at a bank, a Coverdell ESA or a 529 savings plan (more on these later in the chapter). Wherever you put the money, make sure it is separate from the normal checking account used to pay bills. That way you won't be tempted to spend it.

Expect to Make Sacrifices

You won't see many parents of college students eating at fancy restaurants or sailing in the Caribbean. Luxuries take a back seat to tuition, so expect to make major sacrifices in your lifestyle to boost your savings for college.

Straight Talk with a Financial Aid Administrator ▶ **Why should parents save for college?**

Parents are expected to contribute to their child's education. As the cost of college rises, it's becoming more important to set aside money to help meet the cost of education in the future. Parents should look into various means of saving funds that can be tax-free or have other benefits. These include the Coverdell Education Savings Accounts and the tax-free 529 plans. Additional information is available by checking with local savings associations, the IRS website or a tax accountant or financial manager. It's also important for parents to realize it's never too late to save for college. Check with lending institutions regarding IRAs and other savings plans to assist your child. You can even have grandparents contribute to savings for the student. The key is to be proactive by defining saving goals. Set aside a specific amount of funds that can be saved without causing undue financial stress on the family.

Peggy Loewy-Wellisch, Associate Vice President for Student Financial Services, Nova Southeastern University

---

As you are saving, think about the gift you are giving your child: a college education that will prepare him or her for future success. Also, repeat several times a day, "We will not always have to live this way." Once your children graduate from college, you can loosen up on your finances. Until then, be prepared to live frugally.

Smart Saving Step 3: Grow Your Money

Saving for college doesn't mean just putting money in the bank. While a savings account pays interest, there are other ways to build your money with some added benefits—such as having it grow tax-free. Your choices include

KEY CONCEPT . . . .

Colleges expect all families to save. One of the basic philosophies behind financial aid is that it is primarily the family's responsibility to pay for college. Every family is expected to save as much as possible to meet this responsibility. If a family conscientiously saves and still does not have enough, financial aid is available to help fill the gap. But financial aid will not help families that could have—but chose not to—save at all.

- Coverdell Education Savings Accounts (ESAs)
- 529 savings plans
- Independent 529 plans
- Prepaid tuition plans
- Government savings bonds
- Individual development accounts (IDAs)
- UTMA/UGMA accounts
- Trust funds
- Equities, such as stocks and mutual funds
- Retirement accounts

With any investment strategy, it's crucial to understand the risk. If you have a number of years before your child goes to college, you might want to be more aggressive and take more risks to get a higher return, since you have time to ride out downturns. However, if your child is near college age, you must be more conservative. You don't want all your money in volatile high-tech stocks that sour right before you need to write the tuition check. You can't expect your child to delay going to college while you try to earn back lost investments.

To understand the risk of each type of investment, ask questions before opening any kind of account. Never rely on only one source of information, be it a broker or a book, regarding how to invest your money. The consequences are too important not to seek second and third opinions.

BRIGHT IDEA . . . . . .

Don't assume that your state's 529 savings plan is the best.
You are not obligated to use your own state's 529 savings plan. Another state may offer higher limits, lower fees or more flexibility. When you compare 529 savings plans, however, factor in the possible tax benefits of using your own state's program.

Coverdell Education Savings Account (ESA)

Saving money is a good thing, but it's even better when your money grows without being taxed. This is the key benefit of the Coverdell Education Savings Account (ESA). Once you set up the account and name a beneficiary (who must be under the age of 18), you may start contributing up to $2,000 a year in the account to invest in any combination of stocks, bonds, mutual funds, certificates of deposit, money market funds and cash.

As your money grows, you defer paying federal income tax on any gains. In many states, you will not have to pay state taxes either. When you are ready to use the money to pay for the beneficiary's educational expenses (which may include tuition, room and board, books and supplies, computers and transportation), you may withdraw the money tax-free.

The definition of "educational expenses" is quite broad for the Coverdell. In fact, your Coverdell savings are not limited to paying for college but may be used for educational expenses for elementary and high school. In other words, you may use the Coverdell to pay private school tuition.

The Coverdell's disadvantages are the income limits and how much you may sock away each year. For each child you may contribute a maximum of $2,000 a year. If you only have a year or two before your child goes to college, you're not going to be able to realize a lot of tax-free gains.

Also, to be able to contribute the $2,000 per year maximum, you must have a modified adjusted gross income (MAGI) of $95,000 or less if you are a single tax filer and $190,000 or less if you are married and file jointly. If you make more, the amounts of your contributions are gradually reduced. If you earned more than $110,000 as a single filer or $220,000 as a joint filer, you may not contribute to a Coverdell account.

The Coverdell requires some knowledge of investing, as you must decide how your money is allocated. You'll actually choose the individual stocks and mutual funds. This is not so good if you are uncomfortable making investment decisions.

Like all special savings plans with tax benefits, if you don't use the money for qualified educational expenses, you will have to pay the taxes that you would otherwise owe along with a stiff 10 percent penalty. However, if for some reason the beneficiary of a Coverdell account does not use the money for qualified educational expenses by age 30, he or she may transfer it to a relative to avoid the penalty.

You can open a Coverdell account at banks, brokerage houses, securities firms and mutual fund companies. When you're researching where to open a Coverdell, be sure to note any minimums on the account. Some institutions require that you invest a minimum amount each year to avoid paying an account maintenance fee. Also, be sure to understand the fees and commissions of each institution.

For most families, the Coverdell ESA will be the first dedicated college savings account they open, because it is flexible in the options for both investing and spending.

529 Savings Plan

Given the buzz about the 529 savings plan, you'd think it was the best thing since compound interest. While there are some real advantages to 529 savings plans, they are not magical solutions.

Like any investment, a 529 savings plan rises and falls with the stock market and does not guarantee specific returns. And the tax-free status (the major benefit of the plan) applies only to the earnings that are generated. If you only have a year until

---

Straight Talk with a Financial Aid Administrator ▶ **All families can save something for college**

Not everyone is in a position to save $500 a month for college. But even parents who can't afford to save much need to realize any amount they can put away is important. Plan early so your money has time to grow.

We see many low-income families who put a little away here and there over the years so by the time their child is ready for college they have accumulated a sizable savings. These families often have planned ahead since they knew they could not save a lot each year. By using time to their advantage they were able to overcome the lack of a lot of spare resources. While these parents no doubt made a lot of sacrifices, they knew the reason for doing so was for their children to have a better life.

Veronica J. Leech, Director of Financial Aid, Central State University

your child enters college, you probably won't see much benefit from a 529 plan; but for long-term savings, the right one can help you build a college fund faster.

The 529 plans are popular not because they have had phenomenal rates of return (many plans lost value in the down markets of the past five years), but because of the tax-free aspect and because contribution limits are much higher than for the Coverdell—most plans cap the contribution at $200,000 a student. In addition, any family member may contribute, including your rich Uncle Leo.

These plans are offered by every state and the District of Columbia, and many states offer more than one. You don't have to participate in your own state's plan; you are free to sign up for any 529 plan. However, you should check your state's tax regulations, because some states allow you to take a state tax deduction on the money you put into a 529 plan. If you live in one of these states, you'll probably find that your own state plan will offer the best deal.

All the money you put into a 529 plan grows free from federal income tax. Depending on your state, it may also be free from state tax, as long as you use the money for qualified college educational expenses.

Unlike the Coverdell, all the money in a 529 plan must be used for college-related expenses or you not only pay the taxes that would have been owed on any gains but also a 10 percent penalty. On the other hand, 529 plans are very flexible when it comes to changing the beneficiary: Even if you originally opened a 529 plan for one child, you don't have to use that money for him or her. You may use the money for any member of your family, including yourself.

TIME SAVER . . . .

Use online calculators to tweak your savings plan. On the Sallie Mae website (www.salliemae.com), you'll find several useful calculators to help fine-tune your savings plan. The Future Savings Calculator estimates the amount of money you will have saved by the time your child enters college. The Monthly Savings Calculator, on the other hand, estimates the amount you'll need to save each month to meet your savings goal. These tools will help you develop an overall savings strategy.

Downside of the 529 Plan

The disadvantage of the 529 plan is that you don't choose your investments; they are determined by the plan. Like mutual fund families, most 529 plans have various investment tracks, such as conservative, moderate and aggressive. Most also offer an age-based track that is more aggressive when your child is younger and becomes increasingly conservative as your child gets closer to college age. Typically, you may only make changes in tracks or between different 529 plans once a year.

The 529 savings plan is not a quick fix for your college money needs. To make a 529 plan work, you have to be a consistent saver over a long period. You also need good returns on your money, as the primary benefit is not having to pay taxes on gains. It's important to take your time and choose the right plan for your family.

MONEY SAVER . . . .

Don't sign up until you know the fees charged for a 529 savings plan. There's no free lunch with 529 savings plans. Every plan charges a fee, and these can significantly affect how much your savings will grow. Take fees into account when you project how much your money will grow, and compare different plans.

How to Choose a 529 Plan

Because you may participate in any state's 529 savings plan, regardless of where you live, you have a lot of options—maybe too many. As you consider the merits of various plans, focus on these areas.

Low expense ratio and other fees. Understand all the fees before you sign up. Pay particular attention to annual account maintenance fees, transfer fees and commissions. The account maintenance fee is a percentage and is also known as the expense ratio. Try to find a plan with an expense ratio of less than 1.5 percent a year.

Investment track options. More options usually mean a better plan. Look for a plan that provides a good mix of investment tracks. (Remember, you probably will be able to make changes only once a year.) You want as much flexibility in the plan as possible.

Ease of changing account beneficiary. Make sure you can change the beneficiary in case your child does not need all the money for college.

State benefits. You don't have to use your state's 529 savings plan, but you should know what benefits, if any, it offers. Some states allow you to write off contributions to or earnings from the 529 plan on your state taxes. This can be a huge benefit over investing in another state's plan. A few states even offer matching contributions.

Other considerations are the minimum amount you need to open the account, conveniences such as online transactions and whether the plan accepts contributions at any time during the year.

Jump-Start a 529 Plan with a Super Gift

If you or a relative has a large sum of cash to give your child to pay for college, you are limited by the current $12,000 annual gift exclusion. If you give more than $12,000, you will be subject to a gift tax. However, with a 529 plan, you may make five years' worth of gifts in one year. That means that you or a relative could give your child up to $60,000 as a single person or $120,000 as a couple. The giver does not incur any gift taxes, and your child will have access to a significant sum of money for college. This is an excellent way for grandparents to transfer money from their estate without incurring taxes.

529 Savings Plans Are Not Yet Fully Mature

A danger of 529 savings plans is that because they are relatively new, the rules are still changing. Be aware of the following trend before you invest.

A few states have begun to tax the earnings of 529 plans sponsored by other states. If you live in one of these states, this tax will make out-of-state 529 plans very unattractive. As state budgets shrink, it is likely that more states will tax out-of-state 529 plans as a way of generating revenue.

Research Your State's Plan

You will find a detailed description of each state's 529 savings plan on the Sallie Mae website (www.salliemae.com). Don't rush your decision. It's better to invest the time now to pick the right plan than to regret a hasty decision years from now.

Independent 529 Plan for Private Colleges

The Independent 529 plan is sponsored by a consortium of more than 240 private universities and colleges. This plan offers the same federal tax benefits as state-sponsored 529 plans and, in addition, locks in tuition rates where they are when you start the plan. You get the tax and estate planning benefits of traditional 529 plans and the ability to freeze tuition at today's rate characteristic of a prepaid plan. Your rate of return is based on the increase in college costs; thus, if college tuition increases 7 percent a year, your effective rate of return with the Independent 529 plan will be approximately 7 percent.

The catch, of course, is that the plan is good only at the schools that participate, but it offers an interesting alternative for families whose child plans to attend one of the member colleges and who want to lock in tuition at today's prices. You can learn more about this innovative approach at www.independent529plan.com.

Pre-paid College Tuition Plans

Pre-paid college tuition plans are like the first cousins of 529 plans—while not technically 529 plans, they are often mentioned in the same context. Prepaid tuition plans are run by the state treasurer's office. They allow families to contribute a fixed amount of money on a monthly or yearly basis to buy a fixed number of tuition credits at a public college or university at today's prices. In this manner, families essentially prepay their children's tuition.

If prices have gone up by the time your child is ready to enter college (and you can be sure they will), the state will pay for the increase. Most prepaid tuition plans require that your child be a high school freshman or younger when you start the plan. These plans are good if you are fairly certain that your child will attend your state's college or university. If the child decides to attend a private or out-of-state school, the state will usually refund the amount you put into the plan, along with some interest.

BRIGHT IDEA . . . . . .

Read exciting Coverdell examples in IRS Publication 970. You can learn the nitty-gritty details of the Coverdell (as well as 529 plans and other tax breaks) by downloading the latest version of IRS Publication 970. Visit the IRS website (www.irs.gov) and search for Publication 970. It even applies real-life examples.

It is important to understand what you are buying with a prepaid plan. Some states' plans cover tuition but not room and board, which can be a hefty expense. Also, be sure you understand what will happen if your child decides not to go to that school and whether you are permitted to change beneficiaries.

Please note that many states in recent years have decided to cancel prepaid tuition plans, so it is critical to determine if your state offers these types of plans.

Comparison of Prepaid Tuition, Coverdell and 529 Plans

The following is a quick summary of the pros and cons of the three kinds of savings plans to help you decide which one is best for your family. Remember, you don't have to limit yourself to one plan. Depending on your situation, you may want to use more than one.

Coverdell ESA

- All distributions are tax-free as long as they are used for qualified educational expenses.
- You have total control over how your money is invested. You may choose among stocks, bonds, mutual funds and cash.
- You may use the money to pay for primary and secondary educational costs, including tuition, room, board, uniforms, tutoring and even computer equipment and software.
- The money must be used by the beneficiary or designated to another relative before the beneficiary turns 30.

- The annual contribution limit is $2,000 per beneficiary, which means you have to start early to make the Coverdell effective.
- There are income limits on who can contribute to a Coverdell.

529 Savings Plans

- All distributions are tax-free as long as they are used for qualified college expenses.
- The funds in the plan are controlled by the contributor. This means that you can ensure that the money is used for college and you may transfer it to another beneficiary if necessary.
- The contribution limits are very high.
- There is no income limit for contributing to a 529 savings plan.
- Certain states offer significant state tax savings for using the in-state plan.
- Investments in a 529 plan are managed by a fund manager—you don't pick your own stocks.
- The money may only be used for college or graduate school expenses.
- 529 plans are not very flexible—there are restrictions on how often you can switch investment tracks and plans.

Pre-Paid Tuition Plans

- These are low-risk plans: Your child's tuition is guaranteed as long as you meet the schedule of payments.
- Some states do not offer prepaid plans.
- The plan locks you into a specific college system. If you are saving for a young child, there is a chance that he or she may not want to go to the state college, or you may move to another state and not be able to transfer the fund.
- Depending on your plan, it may cover only tuition and not room and board, which is often a significant portion of the cost of attendance.

Use Both Coverdell and 529 Savings Plans

There is no reason you can't use both a Coverdell and a 529 savings plan. With the Coverdell you control the investments, so you could ensure their diversification. Also, you may use the Coverdell for primary and secondary expenses; for example, your child's attendance at a private high school.

The 529 savings plan will allow you to save significantly more than the Coverdell, and other family members may contribute. Depending on the tax laws, you might enjoy significant state tax deductions for using your state's own 529 savings plan.

Government Savings Bonds

For a child, no birthday gift is more disappointing than a savings bond. While the face value may be impressive, the wait to redeem it can seem like an eternity. As a parent, however, buying bonds for your child's education is a good idea. You may be able to exclude the interest earned from taxes if you use the proceeds to pay for qualified educational expenses.

HEAD START . . . .

Ensure consistent investing by going on autopilot. Once you start investing, consider doing it automatically. For example, mutual funds let you set up automatic withdrawals to purchase a certain number of shares each month. If you have a tendency to be haphazard with your investments, the automatic approach will ensure that you buy on a regular basis.

Eligible bonds are series EE bonds issued on January 1990 and later and all Series I bonds. To cash in the bonds tax-free, you must have been at least 24 years old when you purchased them, and the bonds must be registered in your name or your spouse's name. Your child may be listed as a beneficiary but not as a co-owner. You must meet specific income limits. For the 2007 tax year, your modified adjusted gross income must be less than $65,600 if you are filing single and less than $98,400 if you file jointly. If you make more than this amount, your tax benefits will be reduced. If you earn more than $80,600 as a single filer or $128,400 as a joint filer, you may not deduct any interest.

Unfortunately, savings bonds given to your child as a gift aren't eligible for tax-free treatment. In fact, any bonds not purchased by you are ineligible. For more information, go to www.savingsbonds.gov.

Under the Education Bond Program, you may cash in your bonds and use the proceeds to fund a 529 savings plan tax-free. The limitations are the same as those described in the previous two paragraphs.

Individual Development Account Program

You may be able to double or triple your savings with an Individual Development Account (IDA). IDAs are designed to help low-income workers quickly save money for school by matching their savings. The idea is that if you are working but have a low income, the best way to improve your financial status is to build your savings, which can then be used to purchase an asset such as a house, business or education for a member of your family.

The IDA was created to help speed this process; it is managed by a network of nonprofit organizations. If you qualify for the IDA program, you set a goal, such as saving $2,000 for college. When you reach that goal, the IDA network matches what

you have saved by a ratio of anywhere from two to seven. Matched funds come from financial institutions, foundations, religious congregations and state and local governments.

IDA programs usually set their own specific participation requirements. In general, you must be within 200 percent of the poverty level. This works out to an income of less than $20,800 for an individual or $42,400 for a family of four.

The hardest part of participating in an IDA program is finding one. IDAs are offered by a hodgepodge of agencies, so you'll have to do some digging. Go to the IDA Network website (www.idanetwork.org) and click on "IDA Directory" to find contact information for IDA programs in your state. This is not an official or comprehensive list of organizations, but it will give you an idea of where to start looking. Also contact foundations and nonprofits in your area, as well as local bank managers.

Once you find an IDA in your area, make sure you understand the participation guidelines. If you qualify, an IDA can shorten the time it takes to meet your educational savings goal.

Gifting Money for College

Before 529 savings plans were established, the Uniform Transfers to Minors Act (UTMA) and the Uniform Gifts to Minors Act (UGMA) were the best ways to transfer money from you or a relative to your child and pay the least amount of tax. Under UTMA/UGMA, children under age 14 do not pay tax on the first $850 in earnings each year; the next $850 is taxed at their tax bracket. After age 19, all earnings are taxed at the child's tax bracket, which is usually the lowest.

Coverdell ESAs and 529 savings plans offer an alternative for transferring money to children tax-free. Most 529 plans accept funds from a custodial account, although they usually may accept only cash, which means that any investments in the custodial account must be liquidated and taxes paid on the gains before they can be transferred. Be sure to estimate the taxes you might owe if you cash out a custodial account.

One advantage of transferring money using a 529 plan is that the money stays under your control. With a custodial account or a Coverdell ESA, the money becomes the property of the child at age 18 or 21, depending on your state's laws. And once that happens, you cannot control how the money is spent. It is not unheard of for UTMA/UGMA money to go toward buying a new sports car instead of paying tuition. If this is a possibility with your child, you'll have more control with a 529 plan.

The major limitation of a 529 savings plan is that the money must be used to pay for educational expenses. If you want to help your child save for a down payment on a house or any other non-education-related use, the UTMA/UGMA may be the best option.

Bulls and Bears: Tips for Investing

If you choose to use a 529 plan, most of your investment decisions will be made for you. Once you pick the investment track you want to follow within your plan, the fund manager will make the day-to-day decisions. As with a mutual fund, you just keep adding money. If you open a Coverdell or simply invest on your own, keep in mind that investing for college is different from investing for other goals (such as retirement) because you don't have much flexibility over when you'll need the money. In an emergency, you could defer retirement for a few years; not so with a college education. Regardless of the vehicle you use to invest, it would be wise to incorporate the following tips:

Minimize risk and maximize return with dollar cost averaging. If you want to be conservative in your investment approach, consider dollar cost averaging. This method is based on two principles: (1) in the long term, the market always rises, and (2) in the short term, it is next to impossible to "time" the market. Therefore, it is best to invest a fixed amount or percentage each month. Some months the market will be up and you'll be buying high; other months the market will be down and you'll be buying at a bargain price. Over time, this will average out. Combined with an automatic investment option, this is a low-maintenance way to invest.

Diversify. Part of being conservative with your investments is diversifying your portfolio. Don't keep all your money in one stock or even one market sector; spread it around so a big leak in one part of your portfolio won't sink your whole investment boat.

Play conservatively. You don't want to gamble with your child's future. There is risk in any kind of investment, but don't speculate on "sure bets" or "hot tips," and make sure you are not being too aggressive when you are nearing the time you'll need the money.

Take a lesson from age-based 529 savings plans. Most 529 plans employ a conservative, age-based approach. When your child is young, the fund invests more aggressively in stocks and mutual funds. As your child gets older, more money is shifted into fixed-income investments, such as bonds. When your child is a few years from college, most of the money is kept in money market funds. You don't want a disaster in the stock market to affect your child's chances of getting an education. If you're controlling the investments yourself, move them into more conservative areas as you near the time when you'll need the money.

Don't Forget IRAs

With college bills racing toward you like a locomotive, it may be tempting to divert all your funds away from retirement and into college. While this may be an appropriate choice for some families, don't stop saving for retirement without considering the long-term consequences.

In general, retirement accounts are not the ideal investment in which to save for college. However, there are some special rules that make dipping into them a viable option. That's because the government makes an exception to the 10 percent early withdrawal penalty (for funds withdrawn before age 59 ½), **as long as the money is used for eligible college expenses**, for both traditional and ROTH IRAs. After that, though, income taxes may be due, as follows:

- For a traditional IRA, taxes may be due on the amount withdrawn, depending on whether the funds are from pre-taxed dollars or from money previously taxed.

- For a Roth IRA, there are no taxes or penalties for withdrawing the contribution portion, since it was taxed at the time that it was contributed into the account. However, when withdrawn, the earnings portion of a Roth IRA is taxed.

If the amount withdrawn exceeds the eligible expenses, the excess funds are subject to the early withdrawal penalty.

The downside to tapping retirement accounts to fund college expenses is that you are taking money away from your future. It's helpful to know, though, that in an emergency you can dip into some of your retirement money without being subjected to the penalty.

Before moving all of your savings away from retirement to college, consider a less drastic option. Keep saving for retirement so you can still take advantage of the tax incentives and benefits of long-term savings.

For additional guidance, please see a financial advisor.

Zero Coupon Bonds

Zero coupon bonds are issued at a discount from their face value. After a specified maturity date, you can redeem the bond for the full face value. Make sure the maturity date is before you will need the money for college expenses; if you plan correctly, you can have bonds mature each year when tuition bills will be due. Zero coupon bonds are relatively safe investments; they are available through the U.S. Treasury and brokerage firms.

Impact of Savings on Financial Aid

As you read in Chapter 3, your assets and your child's may be taken into account by the financial aid calculation. In general, assets owned by parents are assessed at a lower rate (up to 5.65 percent) than assets in the child's name (35 percent). The following chart shows how each savings vehicle is treated in the financial aid calculation.

Impact on Federal Financial Aid Calculation

Type	Parent Asset	Student Asset
Coverdell ESA	X	
529 savings plan	X	
Independent 529 plan	X	
Prepaid tuition plan	X	
Government savings bond*	X	
Individual development account	X	
UTMA/UGMA account		X
Trust fund		X
Equities such as stocks and mutual funds*	X	
Retirement account	*Not considered in federal financial aid calculation*	

* Assumes that bonds or equities are purchased by the parent and held in the parent's name. Any bonds or equities purchased by the student or held in the student's name are considered an asset of the student.

Don't use impact on financial aid as your primary guide in creating a saving strategy. Some parents neglect saving because they believe it is better to try to qualify for more financial aid than to save their own money. But financial aid rarely covers 100 percent of a college education, nor is it always free money. The aid often has a large student loan component, which will need to be repaid. You would not want a smaller than expected financial aid package to keep your child from attending his or her first-choice college. Having sufficient personal savings is the only way to ensure that your child will have a choice.

If You're in a Time Crunch

Ideally, you begin saving for college when your child is a toddler. But what if your child is a teenager and you have less than a year until he or she starts college?

Most of the savings vehicles described in this chapter work through reinvesting tax-free gains, which requires time. If your child is heading off to college in the next few months, you don't have this luxury. But even without the advantage of time, remember the golden rule: It's never too late to save.

If your child starts college tomorrow, you still have a year to save for sophomore year, two years before junior year and three before senior year. If you start putting away money on the first day your child starts school, you will still have four years before you pay the last tuition bill.

Don't let lack of time be an excuse for not saving. You can still implement the first two Smart Saving Steps. First, you can set a goal for how much to save. Remember to use the Monthly Savings Calculator on the Sallie Mae website (www.salliemae. com). This will help create a road map for how much you need. Second, you can start cutting expenses. It's amazing how much a family can save once it resolves to tighten its collective belt. While you may have to rely on loans and financial aid to pay for the first year, by cutting expenses and boosting savings you will improve your ability to pay future bills.

The Big Picture

For many parents, saving for college is a challenge. Saving money means learning about investment options and how to forgo spending and delay purchases. It helps to remember the reason for your sacrifice. If you are able to save, your child will have the freedom to attend the school that best matches his or her goals, regardless of cost. Your child will be on the way to a college degree, the launch pad for future success. And you will be secure in knowing that you have the means to pay for it.

CHAPTER 11

Can a Parent Catch a Tax Break?

What you'll learn:

- Which tax credits save you the most money
- How to comply with the "no double dipping" rule
- Which college-related expenses you can deduct
- Where to get more help with tax issues

The statesman Benjamin Franklin declared, "In this world, nothing can be said to be certain, except death and taxes." As the parent of a college-bound student, you can count one more certainty in life: tuition bills. Fortunately, Uncle Sam understands how hard it can be to pay both the tax and tuition collectors. To provide relief, the federal government offers educational tax credits and deductions, both of which allow you to send less money to the tax collector so you have more to put toward tuition and other college expenses. If you use them correctly, these tax breaks will put money back in your pocket.

Uncle Sam Wants You—To Have More Money

If you were stranded on a desert island with only one book to read, you would not want it to be the *Internal Revenue Code of the United States of America*. Nothing is more incomprehensible than the laws that govern our taxes. However, buried in the Code are a few golden rules that can save you money.

In this chapter, you will learn about credits and deductions you may be eligible to claim, and how to choose among tax breaks to pick the one that gives you the biggest benefit. The last thing you want during these financially tight college years is to pay more taxes than you should.

The fine print: *The information in this chapter is not designed to be tax advice. Neither the authors nor the publisher is engaged in providing such advice. It is important* *that you seek the services of a competent tax professional. In addition, this chapter makes use of the latest tax information at the time of publication; however, by the time you read the book, rules and interpretations may have changed. Again, be sure to consult a tax professional.*

General Precautions before You Claim a Tax Break

Before you claim any tax credit or deduction, make sure you qualify. Most tax benefits have income requirements. If your income is over the limit, it may trigger a phase-out, which means that the amount you can claim will need to be reduced. At a certain level, your income may prevent you from taking advantage of a tax break altogether.

But don't despair if you are close to an income limit. You may be able to lower your taxable income by boosting contributions to certain retirement plans or flexible spending accounts. If at first glance it seems you are over the limit for any of the following tax breaks, check with your accountant or tax professional to see if you can lower your taxable income to grab a bigger slice of the tax break pie.

When Judy Collins sang "I've looked at love from both sides now," she was not referring to income taxes, but this is a good approach for dealing with tax issues. Whenever you are contemplating a tax strategy, take the time to view it from all perspectives. Some strategies that save you money on taxes may end up costing you more elsewhere. In addition, tax codes and their complex interpretations change frequently, and every family's financial situation is unique. It is worth repeating here: *Seek the advice of a competent accountant or tax professional before you make any decisions.*

Tax Credits Versus Deductions

The two types of tax benefits are *credits* and *deductions*. Both are helpful, but credits usually have more of an effect on your taxes. A tax credit reduces the amount of tax you owe dollar-for-dollar. For example, if you qualify for a $1,650 tax credit, you will pay $1,650 less on April 15. A tax deduction reduces the income on which your tax is calculated. If you are in the 25 percent tax bracket, a $1,650 tax deduction translates into a $412.50 savings.

The two major tax credits available for college expenses are the Hope and Lifetime Learning tax credits.

Behind Door #1: The $1,650 Hope Tax Credit

The Hope tax credit reduces your taxes dollar-for-dollar. You may receive up to $1,650 in Hope credits per student. There are some restrictions: The credit may be claimed only for students who are college freshmen or sophomores as of the beginning of the year for which the credit will be claimed, and it may be claimed only twice per student. The following explanation will help you figure out your Hope tax credit(s).

BRIGHT IDEA . . . . . .

If you're in a bind, get help from the source. If you have a question about your eligibility for a tax break or about which form to use, get answers from the people who wrote the rules: the IRS. Visit the IRS website (www.irs.gov) or schedule a phone or personal appointment. Call toll-free at 1-800-829-1040, or try the Everyday Tax Solutions service by calling your local IRS office to set up an appointment.

First, look at the total you have paid out of your own pocket for tuition. Do not count money that came from the tax-free earnings portion of Coverdell ESAs or 529 savings plans or from other tax-free sources such as veterans educational assistance, Pell grants or scholarships. (Claiming a credit for money that is already tax-free is considered "double dipping" and is a big no-no to the IRS.) However, you may use the contribution portion of Coverdell ESAs and 529 savings plans, since only the earnings, not what you contribute, are tax-free. Remember that the Hope credit applies only to money spent on tuition and related fees, not on room and board or other expenses such as nonacademic fees like optional student activity fees, athletic fees, insurance and similar items. So, if you are drawing on 529 or Coverdell savings, try to use these savings to pay for room and board and pay tuition out of your pocket.

Calculate your maximum credit. You may claim 100 percent of the first $1,100 and 50 percent of the next $1,100 that you pay for tuition and related fees. In other words, to claim the full $1,650 per student, you must pay at least $2,200 in qualified education expenses for that student.

Make sure you meet the income requirements. Single taxpayers qualify for the full credit if their modified adjusted gross income (MAGI) does not exceed $47,000; they may claim a partial credit if their MAGI is between $47,000 and $57,000. Married couples filing jointly get the full credit if their income does not exceed $94,000; a partial credit if it is between $94,000 and $114,000.

If you fall into the partial-credit category, you may claim a percentage of the Hope credit according to the percentage by which your income exceeds the first limit. Here's an example:

Jody Connors is a single filer who earns $50,000. This is $3,000 over the first limit for the Hope credit. She divides the $3,000 by the phase-out range or $10,000 (the difference between $47,000 and $57,000, the two limits for the Hope credit for single filers). This tells her that she is 0.3 or 30 percent over the first limit. Thus, Jody may claim 70 percent of the credit or $1,155 ($1,650 x 0.7 = $1,155). The process is the same for joint filers, except that the phase-out range is $20,000 (the difference between $94,000 and $114,000).

Additional restrictions. Students must be enrolled at least half time in a program that leads to a degree, certificate or other recognized educational credential and must not have a felony conviction for possessing or distributing a controlled substance.

If you meet these requirements, you may claim the Hope tax credit. To do so, file your taxes using Form 1040 or 1040A and attach Form 8863 Education Credits.

IRS Pop Quiz

The IRS has provided the following self-test to help you determine whether you can claim the Hope tax credit for your child. This test assumes that you have paid some money out of your own pocket for tuition and that you are within the income limits.

Q: Did the student complete the first two years of postsecondary education before the beginning of the tax year?

A: YES — Sorry, the student is not eligible.
A: NO — Go to next question.

Q: Was the credit claimed for this student in two previous tax years?

A: YES — Sorry, the student is not eligible.
A: NO — Go to next question.

Q: Was the student enrolled at least half time in a program leading to a degree, certificate or other recognized educational credential for at least one academic period beginning during the tax year?

A: NO — Sorry, the student is not eligible.
A: YES — Go to next question.

Q: Is the student free of any federal or state felony conviction for possessing or distributing a controlled substance as of the end of the tax year?

A: NO — Sorry, the student is not eligible.

A: YES — The student is eligible.

Behind Door #2: The $2,000 Lifetime Learning Credit

The Lifetime Learning credit is similar to the Hope credit in that it reduces the tax you owe dollar-for-dollar. Unlike the Hope, the Lifetime Learning credit may be used for any student for any year of college, graduate school or even continuing education and is available per return only. For example, a joint filing couple with two children could claim no more than a $2,000 credit even if there was more than one family member incurring qualifying expenses. You may not claim both a Hope and a Lifetime Learning credit for the same student in the same tax year. As a result, it is usually to your advantage to claim the Hope credit for the first two years and the Lifetime Learning credit for the subsequent years.

The following are the rules that determine whether you may claim the Lifetime Learning credit.

Calculate your maximum credit. The maximum amount of the Lifetime Learning credit is $2,000 per tax return. This credit is determined by taking 20 percent of what you pay for tuition (not room and board or other expenses) up to $10,000. Thus, to claim the full $2,000 credit, you must spend at least $10,000 from your

---

Straight Talk with a Financial Aid Administrator ▶ **Where to learn about educational tax credits**

Parents should take advantage of every tax credit and deduction available. IRS Publication 970 (which can be found on their website at www.irs.gov) provides more information regarding various tax credits, such as the Hope Scholarship and Lifetime Learning tax credit, tax-free employer education reimbursements and tax breaks on student loan interest. Other good sources of information include speaking with financial specialists, reading articles in magazines and books, viewing information on the Web and attending financial workshops.

Peggy Loewy-Wellisch, Associate Vice President for Student Financial Services, Nova Southeastern University

own pocket on tuition. Remember, money that is already tax-free, such as the earnings from Coverdell ESAs and 529 savings plans, as well as expenses for a student for whom you are claiming a Hope credit, do not qualify.

Make sure you meet the income requirements. The income limits for the Lifetime Learning credit are the same as those for the Hope credit (see above). In addition, the fees you have paid must be for a student whom you claim as an exemption on your tax return.

Fewer restrictions. The restriction against felony drug convictions that may prevent a student from getting a Hope credit does not apply to the Lifetime Learning credit. Also, the student does not have to study toward a degree. This credit may be used for eligible courses that are not part of a postsecondary degree program or to acquire or improve job skills at any educational institution that participates in a student aid program administered by the Department of Education. This includes virtually all accredited, private or public, nonprofit and proprietary (privately owned, profit-making) postsecondary institutions.

The Lifetime Learning credit is a great alternative to the Hope credit, especially once your child is past the first two years of college. If you meet all the requirements, file your taxes using Form 1040 or 1040A and attach Form 8863 Education Credits.

No Double Dipping!

Both the Hope and Lifetime Learning credits are based on the amount of money you pay for tuition and related fees. To avoid running afoul of the double-dipping rule, do not count money that comes from tax-free earnings such as Coverdell ESAs and 529 savings plans, scholarships, veterans educational assistance or Pell grants. You may have to do some financial juggling to make sure that you pay tuition bills from the right source of money.

Imagine that you have a Coverdell ESA with a balance of $6,000 when your child starts the second year of college. Assume that you spent the contribution portion of your Coverdell during the first year; the remaining $6,000 is tax-free earnings, which will remain tax-free as long as you use it for educational expenses. If this year's tuition is $6,000 and you use the entire amount to pay the tuition bill, you will not be able to claim the Hope credit. However, if you withdraw only $3,800 from the Coverdell and pay the remaining $2,200 with money from your savings account (or a student loan), you will be able to claim the full $1,650 Hope tax credit. Plus, you will still have $2,200 in the Coverdell ESA for next year's tuition.

As you can see, you need to plan how you will take advantage of tax breaks before you start paying for college. With a little advance planning, you can make the most of these tax breaks.

Choose Your Tax Credit Wisely

You may claim only one credit per student per year, so make sure you pick the right one each time. The following comparison of Hope and Lifetime Learning credits will help you make that decision.

Hope Credit

- Up to $1,650 credit per eligible student. To get the maximum amount, you must have spent at least $2,200 on qualified tuition expenses.

- The Hope credit is available only in the first two years of postsecondary education.

- Your child must be pursuing an undergraduate degree or other recognized educational credential and must be enrolled at least half time for at least one academic period.

- Your child may not have any felony drug convictions.

Lifetime Learning Credit

- Up to $2,000 credit per tax return if you spent $10,000 or more of your own money on qualified tuition expenses. You may claim less if you spent less. To figure the credit, take 20 percent of what you spent on qualified expenses up to the maximum of $10,000. Expenses for a student for whom you are claiming a Hope credit do not qualify.

- The Lifetime Learning credit is available for all years of postsecondary education and for courses to acquire or improve job skills.

- Your child does not need to be pursuing a degree or other recognized educational credential.

- The felony drug conviction rule does not apply for the Lifetime Learning credit.

If you qualify for both credits, you probably will want to use the Hope credit in the first two years and the Lifetime Learning credit after that.

Education Tax Deductions

Although tax deductions are not as lucrative as tax credits, they still reduce your taxable income. Depending on your tax bracket, this could save you hundreds or even thousands of dollars.

Educational Expense Deduction

One of the most common education deductions is for money you pay for tuition and fees. You may deduct up to $4,000 of tuition expenses (not room and board or other expenses) and related fees that you paid for each student as long as you are not also claiming a Hope or Lifetime Learning credit on the student. Again, you may not count scholarships or the tax-free earnings portion of Coverdell or 529 savings plans as part of the money you paid toward tuition.

You must meet income requirements for this deduction, although they are more generous than those for the tax credits. The full deduction is available to a single taxpayer with a modified adjusted gross income (MAGI) of $65,000 or less, or a couple filing jointly with an MAGI of $130,000 or less. If the MAGI is between $65,000 and $80,000 ($130,000 and $160,000 married filing jointly), the maximum deduction is $2,000.

Because of the higher income limits, some taxpayers who do not qualify for the Hope or Lifetime Learning tax credits are able to take a deduction on tuition costs.

Student Loan Interest Deduction

In addition to any tax credits or deductions you may claim, student loan interest is tax deductible up to $2,500 a year. The loan must have been used for qualified higher education expenses, including tuition, fees, room and board, supplies and other related expenses. The maximum allowable deduction is gradually reduced for single taxpayers whose MAGI exceeds $55,000 but is below $70,000. For married taxpayers filing jointly, the MAGI may exceed $110,000 but must be below $140,000.

Usually, loan-origination fees (other than fees for services), capitalized interest, interest on revolving lines of credit, voluntary interest payments and interest on refinanced student loans (both consolidated loans and collapsed loans) are deductible. If you paid any individual lender or loan servicer $600 or more in interest during the taxable year, that lender or loan servicer should send you a Form 1098-E with the amount of interest paid during the year. You may receive multiple Forms 1098-E if you have loans with different lenders or servicers. If you do not receive a Form 1098-E, the qualifying interest paid is still deductible.

Remember Those Bonds?

If you cashed in a government savings bond to pay for qualified educational expenses, you may be able to exclude the interest earned from your federal income tax. The bond must be a Series EE bond issued after 1990 or a Series I bond, and must be issued in your name or the name of both you and your spouse. You must have been at least 24 years old when you purchased it, and it may not be a gift to or be in the name of your child. You may, however, designate your child as a beneficiary of the bond in the event of the holder's death.

USEFUL TERM . . . . .

Tax credit. A credit reduces the amount of tax you owe dollar-for-dollar. A credit of $1,000 means you pay $1,000 less in taxes.

Tax deduction. A deduction reduces the amount of money on which your tax is calculated. A deduction of $1,000 would translate into paying $250 less in taxes if you are in the 25 percent federal tax bracket.

If you meet these requirements and your MAGI is less than $65,600 (single filers) or $98,400 (joint filers), you may deduct interest on the bond that you used to pay tuition. If your MAGI is higher than these amounts but below $80,600 (single filers) and $128,400 (joint filers), you will still be able to exclude a portion of the interest. Refer to IRS Form 8815 to figure out the interest exclusion. Note that a married individual must file a joint return to qualify for the exclusion.

Tax-Free Scholarships and Grants

In addition to providing free cash for college, scholarships and grants have another benefit: Academic scholarships or grants used for qualified tuition, fees, supplies for coursework and books are generally not taxable. For a scholarship or grant to be nontaxable, the following conditions apply:

- Your child is a candidate for a degree at an educational institution.

- The amounts received as a scholarship or fellowship are used for tuition and fees required for enrollment or attendance at the educational institution, or for books, supplies and equipment required for courses of instruction.

- The amounts received are not a payment for services.

Unfortunately, you may not exclude from taxable income any scholarships or grants that are used to pay for room and board.

Staying Current with Tax Changes

Tax questions are never easy, in part because tax codes are constantly changing and being reinterpreted. In general, income and other limits are usually adjusted upward each year, so make sure you know the current limits when you're looking for tax breaks. You may be above the limit now, but you may qualify in the future. It is best to talk to a professional regarding your specific tax situation; but if you're the do-it-yourself type, you can get information from the IRS website (www.irs. gov) or schedule a phone or personal appointment. Call 1-800-829-1040 or your local IRS office to set up an appointment. If you use TTY/TDD equipment, call 1-800-829-4059.

Sorting through tax codes may not be your idea of a good time, but it is definitely worth it to learn how Uncle Sam can put some tuition money back into your pocket.

CHAPTER 12

How Can We Make College Cheaper?

What you'll learn:

- How to cut college costs
- Why community college is a smart bargain
- When to pay in-state tuition even if you're not a resident
- How to earn college credits to graduate early

Under the motto "Pork: The Other Tuition Payment," Lindenwood University in Missouri allows students to trade 25 hogs for one year of tuition. Not everyone is lucky enough to own a pig farm, but this unique bartering arrangement underscores the fact that paying for college can, at times, require creative solutions.

If you've explored the traditional ways of getting money for college and still find yourself short, consider working the other side of the equation: reducing the cost of college. There are plenty of ways to do this, from finding colleges that charge less to considering military or public service programs that defray tuition expenses. Your child can also take tests to receive college credits while in high school, which can shorten the amount of time he or she spends in college and, thus, the expense.

A little creativity goes a long way in cutting costs. Has your child considered combining an undergraduate and graduate program? How about taking an accelerated program or using summer school to earn college credits? Has your child explored getting state residency to qualify for lower tuition rates or looked at reciprocity agreements with neighboring states? While it's important to maximize the money you have, it can be just as valuable to explore ways to minimize costs.

With a little effort, you can stretch the money you have for college.

Straight Talk with a Financial Aid Administrator ▶ **Community colleges offer a quality education at an affordable price**

One misconception about community college is low price equals a lower-quality education. This is absolutely untrue. We can charge less because we don't need to support a lot of the "extras" that drive up the costs of a typical four-year college. We don't have to pay for high-priced athletic programs or maintain expensive dorms. Some community colleges do provide dorms for students who can't commute, but generally we don't need as extensive a residential program.

These savings are invested in education. Contrary to popular belief, community college professors have the same qualifications as those at four-year colleges. Plus, we tend to attract professors who truly enjoy teaching and working with students. We also have average class sizes that are smaller than our four-year counterparts, which means students get more personal attention.

Community colleges have active campus communities complete with student activities, clubs and sports programs. In fact, an athlete at a community college can get far more game time and recognition than at a four-year school. And if an athlete wants to compete at a Division I level, it's always possible to transfer after receiving an associate's degree at a community college.

Dawnia Smith, Director of Financial Aid,
Cincinnati State Technical and Community College

Hidden Gems: America's Community Colleges

Take a hard look at your local community colleges. Many students ignore these colleges, but they are a great way to complete two years of education for less than one-third the price of a four-year college. Many four-year colleges offer automatic admission and scholarships to community college students who transfer into their schools. When it comes time to get a job, potential employers are interested in the school a student graduated from, not the path he or she took to get to that school.

In choosing a community college, make sure that all credits will transfer smoothly. Ask to see the school's "articulation agreements"—special agreements colleges set up with one another that specify which classes are equivalent and what credits will transfer. If you know which four-year school your child will want to transfer to, make sure that school will count all (or at least enough) of his or her credits to allow the student to graduate on time. If the credits don't count and your child has to repeat courses, it may take longer to graduate, which reduces the cost savings.

For all the latest information on attending community colleges, visit Sallie Mae's website at www.salliemae.com.

Get In-State Tuition

In the past, a student could live in a state for a year, claim residency and then pay in-state tuition. Most states have cracked down on the practice of claiming residency only to get a discounted education. States now make a distinction between being a resident for taxation purposes and for tuition purposes. In fact, many states allow the public university system to set the rules governing who can pay in-state tuition.

In general, most states require that a student meet the following criteria to claim residency for in-state tuition:

- Duration. Most states require that a student live in the state for at least 12 months before claiming residency.
- Intention. Most states require that the student show the intention of remaining in the state after graduating from college.
- Independence. Most states require that the student be financially independent from out-of-state parents before claiming residency.

Exceptions to residency requirements may include the following:

- The student is from a military family.
- The student's family recently moved.
- The student lives near the state border.

If your child can qualify as a state resident, it will certainly cut the cost of attending a public university.

Save Money with a Reciprocity Agreement

Your child may be able to get in-state tuition without being a resident. Some state university systems have buddied up with neighboring state systems to grant in-state tuition at each other's schools. These reciprocity agreements can save you a ton of money. If your child wants to go to school in a neighboring state, contact the office of admissions at the college to see if there are any discounts, including reciprocal in-state tuition rates.

Get Help from Your College

In addition to in-state tuition, your child may qualify for a two-for-one tuition deal. If you have twins or children who are attending the same college at the same time, you may be able to get two educations for the price of one. Another possibility for help is that virtually all colleges provide scholarships to the children of employees, and some support the children of alumni. See Chapter 8 for more information on these programs.

Spend Less Time in School

The early bird gets the worm, and the student who graduates early saves money. The cost of a college education largely depends on the amount of time a student spends there; if your child can earn a degree in less time, you will pay less. The following are some ways to graduate faster.

Straight Talk with a Financial Aid Administrator ▶	**Community college: more choices, less pressure**

For teens who are not 100 percent sure what they want to study, the price of attending a four-year university often puts a tremendous amount of pressure to pick a major quickly. After all, each semester and each class is costing their families a bundle. And if students choose majors that are not the right fit or if they change their minds, it can easily lead to spending more time and money in college. It's scary and stressful for both parents and students to fork out the kind of money that they do today to pay for a four-year college. In the worst-case scenario a student may become so frustrated with the time and expense of being unable to finish the degree that they drop out of college entirely.

This is much less of a problem at a community college, where tuition and cost per course are much more affordable. This encourages students to explore different academic majors or career fields before making a final decision. Part of a community college education is to also find out what you are truly passionate about, and we provide various tests that help students figure out which academic and career areas fit them. At a community college even if students take an extra semester, they are still saving a tremendous amount of money over a four-year school. Making a wrong academic choice at a community college does not carry a stiff financial penalty.

Dawnia Smith, Director of Financial Aid,
Cincinnati State Technical and Community College

Use AP or IB Tests to Gain Advanced Standing

If your child takes the Advanced Placement (AP) or International Baccalaureate (IB) exam, he or she may enter college with college credits, which can shorten the amount of time in school. With enough credits from AP or IB tests, your child may be eligible to enter college as a sophomore instead of a freshman (advanced standing). The rules that govern advanced standing vary by college; contact the admissions office to get the details. For information about AP tests, go to www.collegeboard. com; for information about IB tests, go to www.ibo.org.

HEAD START . . . .

Don't wait until your child gets accepted to contact the college. College financial aid offices are more than happy to speak with parents of potential applicants. Counselors can help you plan how to meet college costs and give tips on what you should be doing now to get ready.

Use CLEP to Skip Classes

In addition to the AP and IB exams, some colleges may let your child take the College Level Examination Program (CLEP) exams to receive college credit. Currently, 2,900 colleges give credit or advanced standing to students who pass CLEP exams. There is usually a fee to take the test, but the results could save you thousands of dollars in tuition.

There are two kinds of CLEP exams. One covers general subjects such as math, English, humanities, natural science, social science and history. The other is a subject exam that covers a particular course, such as a foreign language course. For example, if your child has taken French in high school and tests at the equivalent of one year of college French classes, he or she may receive credit for a year of French. There are currently 30 subject exams. To learn more about CLEP, go to the College Board website (www.collegeboard.com).

Graduate Early with Summer School

Summer school may sound like a death sentence to your child, but it offers a number of advantages, including these:

- Getting a head start on a difficult class
- Making up for low grades
- Building credits toward early graduation
- Taking less expensive courses

Graduating early or attending an accelerated program can save money, but there are some important considerations. Often an accelerated program means taking more classes at one time, which may be difficult for some students. If it affects their grades or causes other stress in their lives, this may not be a benefit. However, for some students who can meet the program goals, graduating early or enrolling in an accelerated program will not only allow them to begin their professions earlier, but it will also save money by reducing the amount of time in school, saving room and board, transportation and other educational expenses, as well as reducing the amount of loans they would have to repay.

Peggy Loewy-Wellisch, Associate Vice President for Student Financial Services, Nova Southeastern University

- Taking shorter courses (because they may meet more often than regular classes or for more hours at a time)
- Taking classes that are close to home
- Scheduling classes around a summer job

Check with the college to make sure summer course credits will transfer without any problems.

Max Out on Credits

If the college charges a set price for a semester, your child may be able to take more courses than normal, earning additional credits and graduating early without additional expense. Naturally, the student must be able to handle the extra work and maintain his or her grades. If this is feasible for your child, one or two extra classes each semester could enable him or her to graduate a semester or even a year early.

Do a Joint Degree Program

Your child may already know that he or she will need an advanced or professional degree. Fields such as law, medicine and even business require—or, at the very least, reward—advanced degrees. In many other fields, a master's degree is a decided advantage for career advancement. If your child plans to get a degree beyond a bachelor's, find out if the college offers a joint degree program.

Some colleges allow students to combine an undergraduate degree (BA or BS) with a graduate degree (MA or MS) in one year less than it would normally take to receive both degrees. For certain majors at the University at Buffalo, for example, students can earn a bachelor's and master's degree in five years. This shaves time (and money) from an undergraduate/graduate education.

Choose a Major Wisely—and Early

"What are you going to major in?" High school seniors hear that question over and over as the talk about college escalates. In fact, most college freshmen have not yet chosen a major, or they end up switching. Changing majors is the number-one cause of students taking extra time to graduate, because they may have to catch up on required courses. Encourage your child to start thinking about a major even before college. During the first year, suggest that he or she explore a number of different majors and classes. You don't want your child to get locked into something too early, but you do want him or her to explore the options and declare a major that will stick.

Work and Learn Together

How does this sound? Your child gains valuable work experience and college is less expensive. Cooperative education programs (co-ops) allow students to work and

Straight Talk with a Financial Aid Administrator ▶ **Why co-op education works**

Cincinnati State is the fourth-largest co-op college in the country. One reason is we have an excellent partnership with Disney World in Orlando, which employs many of our students. A typical co-op student will attend class for one semester and then work for one semester. During the work semester, the student will be enrolled in two college credit hours and could potentially continue to receive financial aid. But even if a student doesn't take classes and only works during that semester, the financial aid package will not be lost. It is waiting for the student upon returning to school the next semester. Co-op is a great way to pay for college. Plus, the work is directly related to the student's education so it can help with the job search after graduation. It's not unusual for some of our co-op students to be hired directly after graduation by their co-op employers.

Dawnia Smith, Director of Financial Aid,
Cincinnati State Technical and Community College

attend school at the same time. They offer the benefits of work experience and a paycheck without causing the student to miss out on the college experience.

Co-ops work because companies, governments and nonprofit organizations offer real jobs to students. Job assignments are managed by the college, and students are matched with jobs that fit their major or are in career areas they wish to explore. Each year, more than 50,000 employers hire college co-op students in nearly every field.

To find out how to be a part of a co-op, speak to the cooperative education office and check the website of the National Commission for Cooperative Education (www.co-op.edu). You can also look through the *Directory of College Cooperative Education Programs* at your local library. This book lists more than 460 colleges that offer co-op programs. These programs can help your child work while attending college and graduate with a bona fide resume.

Bottom Line, Be Creative

If you've maxed out financial aid, scholarships and savings, the next step is to look at reducing costs. As you look at ways to cut costs, think creatively and openly. Don't get stuck thinking that the only way to pay for college is to find more money. The solution may lie in reducing the costs.

CHAPTER 13

What About the Military or Public Service?

What you'll learn:

- How to make the most of military education benefits
- Programs that allow you to go to college first and serve later
- How public service can help pay for college

What would you trade for a college education? While most students exchange money, some are willing to use another valuable commodity: their time. Both the military and public service organizations have discovered that providing education benefits is a strong incentive for students to join.

Is this a fair trade? It depends on the student. If the student values the experience and knowledge to be gained from the military or public service, it can be a very good deal. If the student's time is worth more than the benefit provided or if the time spent in service could be better spent elsewhere, the trade is not so attractive.

For some students, exchanging service is well worth the lifelong rewards of a college education.

Soldiering Your Way to an Education

The military has long provided opportunities to get an education. Not only does it run its own academies, but all service members are eligible to receive a variety of educational benefits. The military needs highly educated soldiers. To meet this need, it offers to pay for students' higher education before they enter the military through the extensive Reserve Officers Training Corps (ROTC) program, which is established at most colleges.

BRIGHT IDEA . . . . . .

Take advantage of VEAP.
While in the military, your child may elect to participate in the Veterans Educational Assistance Program (VEAP), which deducts money from military pay. Uncle Sam matches contributions on a $2 for $1 basis. Funds may be used for degree, certificate, correspondence or apprenticeship/on-the-job training programs, and for vocational flight training programs.

The requirement for taking advantage of these educational opportunities is obvious: service in the military. But it doesn't necessarily have to be active, full-time duty. Some benefits are directed to those who serve part-time in the Reserves and National Guard. Some are designed for spouses and children, and a few scholarships are available for grandchildren.

The following is a rundown of the most common military benefits.

The G.I. Bill

The Montgomery G.I. Bill was signed into law June 22, 1944, by President Franklin D. Roosevelt. Originally known as the "G.I. Bill of Rights," it provided educational benefits for veterans returning from World War II. The bill has been amended several times in the intervening years, and the benefits have been expanded not only to help veterans return to civilian life but also as an incentive for enlistment in today's all-volunteer military.

The G.I. Bill helps three types of students affiliated with the military: active duty veterans, Reserve veterans and the survivors and dependents of veterans.

Active duty service members: The G.I. Bill provides up to three years of educational benefits for veterans for degree and certificate programs, flight training, apprenticeship, on-the-job training and correspondence courses. Recipients must take advantage of the benefits within 10 years of being discharged.

Selected Reserve veterans: The G.I. Bill for Selected Reserve covers the Army Reserve, Navy Reserve, Air Force Reserve, Marine Corps Reserve and Coast Guard Reserve, as well as the Army National Guard and the Air National Guard. Students must continue to serve in the Reserves while they take advantage of the benefits.

Survivors and dependents of veterans: The Survivors' and Dependents' Educational Assistance (DEA) program provides up to 45 months of education benefits for eligible dependents of veterans who are permanently and totally disabled, who died while on active duty or as a result of a service-related condition or who is hospitalized or receiving outpatient treatment for a service connected permanent and total disability.

For more information on these G.I. Bill programs, go to www.gibill.va.gov.

State-Sponsored National Guard Benefits

If your child joins the National Guard, he or she qualifies for the G.I. Bill for Selected Reserve. Some states offer additional benefits to supplement the G.I. Bill. For example, the Wisconsin Army National Guard Tuition Grant provides up to eight semesters of full tuition benefits, and students may use the benefits at Wisconsin colleges or select schools outside of Wisconsin. Get more information about your state's National Guard benefits at www.ang.af.mil or www.arng.army.mil.

States also provide military benefits to active duty service members, veterans and even dependents. Check with your state's Department of Veterans Affairs. Texas offers tuition waivers for veterans: If your child is a Texas resident when he or she joins the military, he or she may be exempt from having to pay tuition at public colleges and universities after being discharged. A good resource is www.military.com, which offers a summary of many state benefits.

Going to College First and Serving Later

Some students prefer to attend college with their classmates and then serve in the military. The ROTC program and military academies let students do this by paying for their educations and requiring that they serve a designated number of years after graduation.

The Reserve Officers Training Corps Program (ROTC)

Each branch of the military runs its own ROTC program, which pays for most or all of tuition and related expenses at almost any college. In exchange, students must attend training during the school year and, often, for part of the summer. There are two ways to enter ROTC: (1) high school students may compete for a four-year, full-tuition ROTC scholarship; (2) college students may take ROTC courses as electives and then compete for ROTC scholarships that cover the remaining years in college.

ROTC scholarship recipients must serve in the military for a specific number of years after graduating, usually based on the number of years the student received the scholarship. If Army ROTC paid for four years of education, your child owes the Army four years of service. Students may fulfill this obligation either through active duty or by serving in the Reserves or the National Guard. (Active duty usually means a shorter time commitment.)

In addition to receiving generous scholarships, ROTC students enter the military after graduation as officers. In fact, most officers in the military come through the ROTC program. Each service branch runs its ROTC program slightly differently. You can learn more by visiting the appropriate service's website or recruiting center.

Navy and Marine ROTC program:

- Provides tuition support
- Prepares students for service as commissioned officers in the Navy or Marine Corps
- Offers both four-year and two-year scholarships
- Scholarships cover tuition expenses, books, fees and a living allowance
- Offers the Navy Nurse Corps NROTC Program for students pursuing the bachelor's degree in nursing (BSN)
- Graduates are commissioned as ensigns in the Naval Reserve or second lieutenants in the Marine Corps Reserve
- Members typically must serve for eight years, with at least three to four years in active duty status

The applicant must be a U.S. citizen between the ages of 17 and 26 years, have a high school diploma or GED and have minimum Scholastic Aptitude Test (SAT) or American College Test (ACT) scores. More information and applications are available at https://www.nrotc.navy.mil or from a Navy recruiting center.

Army ROTC program:

- Is available at 700 schools
- Offers four-, three- and two-year scholarships of full tuition, fees and monthly stipend
- Awards are based on merit, including academic achievements, extracurricular activities and interviews
- Offers the Army ROTC Nurse Program, which has four-, three- and two-year scholarships
- Graduates are commissioned as second lieutenants and must serve either part time in the Army National Guard or Army Reserve or full time on active duty

Applications are available on the Army ROTC website at www.goarmy.com/rotc or from an Army recruiting center.

Air Force ROTC program:

- Offers scholarships for entering college freshmen and students who are already in college
- Pays up to full tuition, fees, books and a monthly stipend
- Allows students to study any major, but the majority of scholarships are for students pursuing technical majors in: architecture, chemistry, computer science, mathematics, physics, operations research,

aeronautical engineering, aerospace engineering, astronautical engineering, architectural engineering, civil engineering, computer engineering, environmental engineering, meteorology/atmospheric sciences, electrical engineering and mechanical engineering. Only a small number of scholarships will be awarded for students pursuing non-technical majors.

The applicant must be a U.S. citizen, have a high school diploma or GED certificate, be between the ages of 17 and 30 years, complete a physical exam and have minimum SAT or ACT scores. Applications are available on the Air Force ROTC website at www.afrotc.com or from an Air Force recruiting center.

Military Academies

The services run their own higher education academies that provide a general college education with specialized military training. Students receive a full four-year scholarship that covers tuition, room and board, books, a monthly stipend and a computer.

To be accepted at a military academy, a student must be an unmarried U.S. citizen between the ages of 17 and 22 years. Selection is based on academic performance, skills, talents and achievements. Some academies require nomination by a member of Congress. Graduates are commissioned as officers and must serve for a specific number of years. Generally, military academy students intend to make the military a career. For more information on the academies, call, write or go online:

U.S. Military Academy at West Point
West Point, NY 10996
(845) 938-4011
www.usma.edu

U.S. Naval Academy
Candidate Guidance Office
117 Decatur Road
Annapolis, MD 21402-5000
(410) 293-4361
www.usna.edu

U.S. Air Force Academy
HQ USAFA/RRS
2304 Cadet Drive, Suite 200
USAF Academy, CO 80840
(800) 443-9266
www.usafa.af.mil

BRIGHT IDEA . . . . . .

Earn credit for military training. Many colleges automatically give course credit for military service. Additional credit may be given for specialized training and education received in the military. For example, any College Level General or Subject Matter Tests taken at the United States Armed Forces Institute (USAFI) may count for credit. To get credit for military training, your child will need to provide documentation.

U.S. Coast Guard Academy
31 Mohegan Avenue
New London, CT 06320-8103
(800) 883-USCG
www.cga.edu

U.S. Merchant Marine Academy
300 Steamboat Road
Kings Point, NY 11024
(516) 773-5000
www.usmma.edu

Military and Veteran Scholarships

Even without serving, your child may be able to win a military-related scholarship. Many veterans organizations provide awards to veterans, their spouses and dependents. Contact these organizations to see if they offer any scholarships for which your child might be eligible. Also, get in touch with local and state military and veterans organizations. You can find a list of veterans associations, many of which offer scholarships, at the Department of Veterans Affairs website (http://www1.va.gov/vso/).

Earning Education Money for Community Service

Getting college cash for service is not limited to the military—public service programs have adopted the same strategy to attract volunteers. As with the military, your child will have to serve to receive the education benefits. However, if your child is drawn to volunteerism, the following groups may offer a good deal.

AmeriCorps. If they serve full time, usually for 10 to 12 months, students may be eligible for an educational award of up to $4,725. After successfully completing a term of service, AmeriCorps members who are enrolled are eligible to receive an education award. The education award can be used to pay education costs at qualified institutions of higher education or training, or to repay qualified student loans. Part-time service means eligibility for a partial award. For details, go to the AmeriCorps website at www.americorps.org.

Peace Corps. Currently, more than 7,533 Peace Corps volunteers are serving in 72 countries, working to bring clean water to communities, teach children, help start new small businesses and stop the spread of AIDS. Volunteers receive intensive language and cross-cultural training to become part of the communities where they serve. They speak the local language and adapt to the cultures and customs of the people with whom they work. Participants may have their student loans deferred, receive $6,000 after completing the program and receive fellowships or academic credit for master's degrees. For more information, go to www.peacecorps.gov.

Trade Your Time for College Dollars

The idea of trading service in the military or in public service for college financing is not new; but as the price and importance of a college education go up, this type of exchange gains in value to the student. Such a decision should not be made casually. Your child will pay for an education with one of the most valuable commodities: time. But if this approach fits into your child's overall goals, it could be one of the best trades he or she ever makes.

CHAPTER 14

Financial Aid Scams

What you will learn:

- The most common financial aid and scholarship scams
- How to spot a scam

The offer looks tempting: For a small fee, this company will cure your tuition headaches. They will find hidden scholarships, apply for grants and even fill out your child's financial aid form. The promise that attracts your attention is that every single client will win a scholarship—guaranteed! Ignoring the warning voice inside, you send a check. After all, what's a few hundred dollars compared with tuition bills in the tens of thousands?

You just got scammed.

In return for your hard-earned money, you will get nothing more than publicly available information and lists of scholarships, from books and websites that you could easily have found yourself. As for the guaranteed scholarship, if the company makes good on this promise at all (unlikely) the "scholarship" your child wins will be worth just a fraction of the amount you paid for the service. Ouch.

Keeping Your Money Safe

Finding money to pay for college can be extremely stressful for families, and this makes you vulnerable. Watch out for dubious and deceptive offers, which come in many forms. Some arrive in the mail from official-sounding organizations. Others offer free seminars, where they will hard-sell you on a paid service. Most make promises they can't keep. A few are downright criminal and just take your money and run.

While many financial aid and scholarship services have honest and philanthropic intentions, there are always some that do not. According to the Federal Trade Commission, in one year alone there were more than 175,000 reported cases of scholarship scams, costing consumers $22 million. And many people don't report these scams. Some estimates are as high as $100 million lost every year.

In this chapter, you will learn how to identify the warning signs of a scam, so you can protect your money and avoid offers that are "too good to be true."

How to Spot a Scam

The first step in spotting a scam is to understand precisely why they work so well. Most parents are worried about paying for college, and their anxiety makes them more likely to believe a false promise. Also, because parents don't have extensive experience with financial aid, they are likely to rely on alleged experts for information. If you fall into this category, recognize that you are at risk of becoming a victim. Awareness of your vulnerability will help you disarm the most powerful weapon of financial aid scammers: your fear and lack of knowledge.

Straight Talk with a Financial Aid Administrator ▸ **Don't be the victim of a scam**

The most critical feature in identifying a scam is whether there is a charge that is applied for a service. It's common for needy families to pay $1,000 or more for assistance in obtaining financial aid. Such costs are inappropriate and a scam. If there is a promise of an improved amount or type of financial aid award the family can expect, the offer is most likely a scam. It's just not possible to guarantee an improved level of grant or scholarship support.

There are some legitimate companies that can assist in filling out forms and provide a legitimate level of assistance. Such costs should be relevant and appropriate for the level of service provided.

Even better, virtually every financial aid office has professionals that provide assistance free of charge to families. Families can go to a local college or university and sit down with a financial aid professional at no charge for help completing the required documents. Parents should always contact the financial aid office of the college their child is interested in attending directly. Frequently the only tangible thing a family gets when they pay for help in obtaining financial aid is a cancelled check.

Dr. Lawrence Burt, Associate VP for Student Affairs & Director of Student Financial Services, University of Texas at Austin

---

The good news is that by reading this book, you have become much more knowledgeable about how the process works. For example, you know that applying for federal financial aid is free, so you won't fall for paying a fee. You also know that, with few exceptions, there is no such thing as a "guaranteed" scholarship. This knowledge will be tremendously useful in helping you spot a potential scam.

Common Financial Aid and Scholarship Scams

Most scams make the same basic promise: Pay us, and you won't have to worry about how to pay for tuition. The following are examples of common offers:

KEY CONCEPT . . . .

Check the references of any service or adviser. Legitimate services and advisers can help you with college planning; however, it's not always easy to separate the good from the bad. Be sure to request the names of former clients you can contact. Also, do a search at the Better Business Bureau website (www.bbb.org) to see if any complaints have been lodged against the company. Take a proactive approach to keeping your money safe.

For a fee, our company will help you fill out the very complicated FAFSA. With our assistance, you will save hours or even days of time and you are guaranteed to get more in financial aid than you would have otherwise.

It may be tempting to get help with the FAFSA, but you already have line-by-line help right here in this book. Also, you can contact your child's high school or the financial aid office at a local college for help. Most schools host financial aid nights to walk parents through the form. The Department of Education has a toll-free number (1-800-4-FED-AID) if you have any questions. All of this assistance is *free*.

For a fee, we'll fill out your FAFSA, and we guarantee that you will get more grants than if you filled out the form yourself.

This offer can get you in big trouble. It doesn't matter who fills out the application; if the numbers are accurate, the results will be the same. Most "services" that make this offer will simply lie on the application, but because *you* sign the form attesting to its accuracy, *you* are liable for all the numbers. Parents can and do get arrested and fined if they knowingly or unknowingly let someone fill out their FAFSA using fraudulent information.

Pay us and we will create a personalized financial aid plan for your child. We have a library of hundreds of resources that we will use to create an individualized financial aid plan for you.

What they don't mention is that these resources can easily be found on the Internet or in the library. Save hundreds of dollars and find the scholarships yourself. You'll do a more thorough job and are more likely to find scholarships that fit your child's situation.

> *Pay us and we will research and identify the 20 scholarships that fit you best. Why spend weeks researching scholarships when our specialized researchers can do it for you? We have scholarship sources that no one else does. Plus, you are guaranteed to win at least one.*

Once again, you will receive information (in this case, a list of scholarships) that you could have found on your own. Scholarship offers are not kept secret; in fact, they're well publicized. Think about it: If you were offering a scholarship, wouldn't you want the information to reach the largest number of students? Of course!

> *Each year, millions of dollars in scholarships go unawarded. Pay us and we will locate unclaimed scholarship dollars that your son or daughter can win.*

The reality is that there are very few "unclaimed" scholarships. Scholarships that are not awarded usually have very specific eligibility requirements, such as living in a particular city or working for a certain employer. These scholarships aren't helpful if your child is not eligible. As you learned in Chapter 7, you can find thousands of scholarships on your own in books and on the Internet without paying a search fee.

> *You are a finalist for our scholarship. Pay the registration fee, and you're guaranteed to win!*

Straight Talk with a Financial Aid Administrator ▶ **Financial aid information is free**

Unfortunately, there are some charlatans who promise families they can "beat the system." Usually this involves practices that are illegal and can land a parent into serious trouble including time in jail. We also see families who spend money on scholarship search services that are totally worthless. You don't need to spend money to find scholarships. You can get everything you need for free. You can find websites that offer free searches. And, of course, libraries and financial aid offices offer a wealth of free information. The services that charge a fee offer nothing more than you can get for free with a little bit of effort.

Jim Belvin, Director of Financial Aid, Duke University

Straight Talk with a Financial Aid Administrator ▶ **First-generation families are the most likely to be scammed**

Many students at Central State University are the first in their family to attend college. These first-generation families are often targeted by unscrupulous businesses that end up taking their money without providing much in return. For example, the term "guaranteed scholarship" hooks a lot of these families. After paying, what they receive is a list of available awards they could have gotten for free on their own. None of the scholarships turn out to be guaranteed; they still need to apply to receive them. But, since these families don't have any experience with the financial aid process, some assume you have to pay for these types of services and it is a normal part of the process. The advice I give to these families is to research available scholarships on their own through the various websites that are available for free. If parents have questions about an offer for a service they should contact the financial aid office immediately. We can answer their questions and help them avoid being taken.

Veronica J. Leech, Director of Financial Aid, Central State University

---

If you didn't submit an application for this scholarship, how can you have won? The truth is that you are not guaranteed to win or, if you do win, the prize will be less than the registration fee. With very few exceptions, applying for a scholarship does not involve fees. (Some music, art and performance scholarships require a nominal fee, because the judges need to review portfolios or tapes.)

> *You've won our scholarship, guaranteed! All we need is your credit card number to verify your eligibility.*

Instead of winning a scholarship, you will see some surprise charges on your next credit card statement.

> *You qualify for our exclusive, incredibly low-interest loan program. All you need to do is pay us to lock in the rate.*

You could pay the fee but not get the loan. Or you may get the loan, but the interest rate (or hidden fees) may be far higher than if you shopped around. Whenever you are exploring loan options, be sure you understand all the terms and fees. Check with your college's financial aid office if you have any questions.

> *Come to our informative financial aid seminar, where you'll learn our secret strategies for financial aid found nowhere else in the world.*

Not all seminars are scams or rip-offs. However, if the seminar sounds like a sales pitch or includes promises that are too good to be true, don't go. If you're already there, walk out.

In general, the common trait of dubious offers is that you are asked to pay a significant amount of money. Particularly if you are applying for a scholarship, don't pay for the privilege. Scholarships are meant to give you money, not the other way around.

Red Flags of a Scam

While each scam is different and scammers are constantly developing new pitches, the following are common red flags:

- **Registration, entry or administrative fee.** Legitimate scholarship programs do not require an upfront fee. Do not pay anything more than the cost of postage.

Straight Talk with a Financial Aid Administrator ▶ **How to avoid unscrupulous services and scams**

Unscrupulous companies do take advantage of students and parents by telling them they can get more financial aid dollars. They offer "money-back guarantees" of more money for college but attach conditions that make it impossible to receive a refund. Some companies tell students they have been selected as a finalist but require an up-front fee or will debit the student's checking account for a length of time to cover the fee. Additionally, some companies assist students with the financial aid process and in completing the FAFSA and charge them for the service.

Parents and students can avoid these scams by checking with their financial aid offices and by contacting the Federal Trade Commission if they have a question about such a company. Some common traits or red flags include companies that guarantee your money back, state that scholarships will cost some money and use lines such as "You are a finalist" or "We will do all the work." Parents and students should not have to pay a fee to receive information. All the information a family needs can be had for free, and many venues offer this information.

Peggy Loewy-Wellisch, Associate Vice President for Student Financial Services, Nova Southeastern University

---

- **Requiring payment in cash.** With cash there is no paper trail in case you get in trouble or want a refund.

- **Soliciting your credit card or bank account number.** Never give out this kind of financial information to anyone who contacts you if you have not requested them to do so.

- **Refusal to reveal name, address or phone number.** Something is wrong when the person on the telephone won't reveal his or her name or contact information.

- **Guarantee.** Remember, there is no such thing as a guaranteed scholarship in exchange for a fee. Legitimate scholarships are based on merit or need, not on your willingness to pay a registration fee.

If you discover that you have been the victim of one of these scams, don't be embarrassed. It happens to thousands of parents and students every year. Report your experience to the Better Business Bureau and the Federal Trade Commission (www.ftc.gov) to help prevent it from happening to others.

The old adage applies to scholarships and financial aid: *If an offer sounds too good to be true, it probably is.*

CHAPTER 15

Conclusion: The Start of a New Journey

Fast-forward four years. It's a warm, sunny day, and you're sitting outside on a folding chair, surrounded by other proud parents. A name is announced and you jump out of your chair, clapping and whistling. Your child turns toward you, flashes a radiant smile and holds the prize aloft.

A college diploma.

Years of saving and sacrifice have made this moment possible. And as proud as you are of your child, you also deserve a high-five. You navigated the difficult waters of paying for college without drowning in loans, hocking all your possessions or living on beans and rice.

Take a bow. You deserve it.

A Happy Ending

Right now, though, graduation day seems far, far away. You are just beginning the process of applying for financial aid.

It's a tough journey, no doubt about it. Yet it's one that you as a parent can complete, no matter what your circumstances. Think of how far you've already come. In just the time it's taken you to read this book, you now

- Understand how to complete financial aid applications and how the government and colleges determine how much financial aid you deserve.

- Are able to evaluate and compare financial aid packages to select the best one.

- Know under what circumstances you may ask for a financial aid reassessment and how to do so.

- Are familiar with the advantages and disadvantages of federal, private and alternative sources of student and parent loans.

- Have learned strategies to help your child find and win scholarships.

- Are familiar with the resources available from colleges and the state.

- Know how to save for college and how to take advantage of tax credits and deductions.

- Can spot a financial aid scam.

Most of all, you probably feel more confident and optimistic about paying for college. You have a reliable, up-to-date and logical arsenal of resources and techniques to make your child's college education affordable.

The only thing left to do is to put these strategies into action. As you turn your knowledge into college dollars, here are a few final tips to keep in mind:

Start as early as possible. Whether your child is a toddler or a teenager, it's never too early to start planning for college. If your child is young, you can use tax-advantaged savings programs, contribute to prepaid tuition plans and develop long-term investment strategies.

It's never too late. Even if your child is headed off to college in the fall or is already in college, don't despair. College lasts at least four years—saving now can help in later years of school. Plus, colleges, states and private scholarship organizations offer many resources. Your child should apply for scholarships throughout college.

Get your child involved. Don't tackle financial aid alone. Paying for college is a family responsibility. Hold a family meeting to make sure your child understands his or her responsibilities before, during and after college, and what kind of sacrifices the family is making to enable him or her to go to school. A child who grasps the importance of a college degree will be more serious about studies and about contributing to college costs.

BRIGHT IDEA . . . . . .

Stay informed. Sign up for the free Sallie Mae (www.salliemae.com) monthly e-mail newsletter. It is jam-packed with useful information and tips.

Never stop learning. While this book is a great source of information, it never hurts to learn more. One of the best ways to stay current is to visit the

Sallie Mae website (www.salliemae.com), where you'll find useful tools such as a free scholarship database that is continually updated, calculators and tip-filled articles.

Don't be afraid to ask for help. The financial aid process can be confusing, with its own jargon and acronyms. If you get stuck, seek help. Contact your high school guidance counselor, college financial aid administrator, state higher education agency or the Federal Student Aid Information Center at 1-800-4-FED-AID. A lot of experts are available to help you through this process.

Take action. It's not enough to know how the financial aid process works. You need to take the next step and put that knowledge to use. Take an honest look at your finances, how much college will cost and how you plan to meet those costs. Then go for it! The sooner you start, the more you'll have when the tuition bills come due.

If doubt creeps in along the way and you question the sacrifice, picture your child on graduation day.

The dream is worth the time and effort, don't you think?

We wish you the best of luck!

Resources from Sallie Mae

Sallie Mae offers an abundance of resources to guide you and your child on the "planning and paying for college" process, many of which are referenced in this book. Please visit www.salliemae.com to find these tools and more.

Searches

■ **Free Scholarship Search.** Registered Sallie Mae website users have access to an award database of more than 2.9 million scholarships worth in excess of $16 billion. Every time you log on or update your profile, a new search matches you with the latest scholarship opportunities.

■ **School Search Tool.** Search for schools by name, state or characteristics from a database of nearly 4,000. Once you've selected the schools that interest you, view detailed information on campus life, student demographics, housing and academic requirements, expenses and student financial aid. The Online College Application Search gives you access to hundreds of online college applications.

■ **Research Online Degree Programs.** Powerful search engine of online, accredited undergraduate and graduate course offerings as well as extensive educational resources.

"Best of the Web" by *Forbes* Magazine

Sallie Mae's website was recently recognized as one of the best Internet sites for college planning by *Forbes* magazine.

Calculators

■ **Long Term Planning Calculator.** Estimate the monthly savings that will be required to support up to three children who are planning to attend college. The calculator asks for the present cost of attending a college, the number of years before each student enters school, current savings and the anticipated annual return on their savings.

■ **College Cost Calculator.** Estimate the future cost of a college education. Costs are based on average annual increases and the number of anticipated years spent in school.

■ **Future Savings Calculator.** Estimate the dollar amount that will be saved when the student enters school. The calculator asks for monthly saving amounts, the saving's average return and the number of years until the student enters school.

■ **Monthly Savings Calculator.** Estimate the dollar amount families will need to save on a monthly basis to meet their college savings goal. The calculator asks for the target savings goal, currently available savings, number of years until the student enters school and the average return.

■ **Repayment Calculator.** Designed to help students and parents borrow responsibly. The tool will estimate the monthly loan payments based on the principal balance, interest rate and loan term.

■ **Expected Family Contribution (EFC) Estimator.** Helps families estimate their potential financial responsibility well before submitting the FAFSA and receiving the official EFC from the Student Aid Report (SAR).

Tools

■ **School Affordability Analyzer.** Enables students to determine the average cost of attending their choice schools, the average financial aid offered and how much out-of-pocket expenses a family might incur. Once students have a general idea of their financial need, various payment options can be evaluated to show how students and their families can best contribute to the cost of a higher education.

■ **School Search Tool.** Helps students evaluate which schools are right for them by allowing side-by-side school comparisons. Students can search for schools by name within each state and view information on admissions, campus environment, enrollment, freshman admissions profiles, school expense and financial aid. Students can view up to three schools at once, side-by-side, from a database of nearly 4,000 schools.

■ **College Application Tool.** Offers students access to hundreds of online college applications.

■ **Online Award Analyzer.** Enables students to compare their financial aid award packages from each school. Determine if the financial aid award and savings are enough to cover the cost of attendance. Analyze options for borrowing additional money when savings are not enough. View an estimate of the monthly payments associated with borrowing different loan amounts.

■ **Online Student Loan Applications.** Students (undergraduate and graduate) and their parents can apply online for a variety of loans—federal and private loans for students and PLUS loans for parents.

Get the Sallie Mae FREE E-Newsletters

Let Sallie Mae's free monthly e-Newsletters help you find your way through the college maze. Drawing upon a network of experts, our newsletters provide you with valuable information on planning and paying for college. These newsletters will help you navigate the college selection, application and financing process. You'll find information on deadlines, tuition trends and financial aid. To subscribe, visit www.salliemae.com.

Loans Available from Sallie Mae's Partner Lenders

Federal Loans:

Federal Stafford Loan

Federal PLUS Loan

Federal Perkins Loan

Private Loans:

Signature Student Loan®

Tuition Answer Loan℠

Community College Loan℠

Continuing Education Loan℠

The Career Training Loan℠

The K-12 Family Education Loan℠

MEDLOANS®

LAWLOANS®

MBA LOANS®

StudentEXCEL®

GradEXCEL®

Learn more at www.salliemae.com

Checklists

You can find useful checklists on the Sallie Mae website. Please note that online registration is required to access checklists.

❏ **"Go-to-College" Calendar.** A checklist that describes what you should be doing and when during the college planning process. Contains helpful reminders for tasks you may need to complete and dates to have them done.

❏ **College Nights and Fairs.** A checklist to help you select questions to ask at college fairs and nights. Also, designed to keep track of the responses and business cards you receive.

❏ **School Interview.** A checklist to help you prepare for your admissions interview—questions you should be prepared to answer and interview tips.

❏ **Campus Visit.** A checklist to help you prepare for your visit to a school—how to plan the visit, what to do and look for while there.

❏ **School Application.** A checklist to help you through the school application process. Use it to keep track of deadlines, essays, recommendations and transcripts.

❏ **Applying for Financial Aid.** A checklist to help you make sure your paperwork is in order.

❏ **FAFSA: Finding Tax Information Worksheet.** A worksheet to help you find and organize the necessary financial information to complete the FAFSA.

❏ **Recommended Reading List.** A checklist of reading materials to help you prepare for college. The list is comprised of the classics—from The Bible to The Swiss Family Robinson.

❏ **Packing for College.** A checklist to help you pack for college—from quarters and laundry detergent to your mouse pad. Packing for college just got easier—you'll remember items most students forget!

Six Great Reasons to Register at Salliemae.com

- ■ Win a $1,000 scholarship
- ■ Receive newsletters
- ■ Run a free scholarship search
- ■ Save research from the site
- ■ Apply for student loans
- ■ Download checklists

Find More at www.salliemae.com

FAFSA and CSS/PROFILE

- ■ **Six steps to completing the FAFSA**
- ■ **Pre-application worksheet**
- ■ **Get answers to frequently asked questions about the FAFSA**
- ■ **Learn about FAFSA-on-the-Web**
- ■ **Deadlines for the FAFSA by state**
- ■ **Learn more about the CSS/ PROFILE®**

General Loan Information

- ■ **Chart comparing federal loan programs**
- ■ **Interest rates and APRs**

Learn About Loans and Apply Online

- **Learn about loans for students**
- **Learn about loans for parents (PLUS and Tuition Answer)**
- **Apply for Stafford, PLUS or private loans**

Additional Information

- **Department of Education (FAFSA)**
www.fafsa.ed.gov

- **Internal Revenue Service (Pub 970; Tax Benefits of Education)**
www.irs.gov/publications/p970/index.html

Attention Parents

Sign up for Sallie Mae's free e-Newsletters. These newsletters will help you navigate the college selection, application and financing process. You'll find information on deadlines, tuition trends and financial aid. Plus, you'll be entered to win $10,000 in the Parent Answer Sweepstakes!

Scholarships from Sallie Mae

Sallie Mae offers a variety of scholarships to help you and your child pay for college. Apply for some free cash for college today!

Sallie Mae

Sallie Mae
12061 Bluemont Way
Reston, VA 20190
Website: www.salliemae.com

Sallie Mae Student Scholarship

Purpose: To help students pay for college.
Eligibility: Applicants may be high school, undergraduate or graduate students and must register on the Sallie Mae website. Each month one registered user is selected in a random drawing to receive the scholarship.
Deadline: Varies.
Amount: $1,000.
Number of Awards: 1 per month.
How to Apply: Register at www.salliemae.com.

Parent Answer

Parent Answer Sweepstakes

Purpose: To help parents pay for their children's college education.
Eligibility: The sweepstakes is open to all U.S. residents who are parents of undergraduate college students.
Deadline: May 31.
Amount: $10,000.
Number of Awards: 1.
How to Apply: Register to receive the Sallie Mae email newsletter at www.salliemae.com.

Sallie Mae Fund

Scholarship Management Services
Scholarship America
One Scholarship Way, P.O. Box 297
Saint Peter, MN 56082
Website: www.thesalliemaefund.org

The Sallie Mae Fund Unmet Need Scholarship Program

Purpose: For many students, the unmet need—the gap between the college cost and the financial aid package—is too big to manage. The Sallie Mae Fund will provide $1 million this year to help meet last dollar needs of low-income students.

Eligibility: Applicants must be U.S. citizens or permanent residents, have a family adjusted gross income of $30,000 or less, demonstrate unmet financial need of at least $1,000 after the financial aid award package has been determined, be a high school senior or graduate planning to enroll or a student already enrolled in a full-time undergraduate course of study at a postsecondary institution and have a minimum 2.5 GPA (on a 4.0 scale) or a minimum GED score of 42.

Deadline: May 31.

Amount: $1,000-$3,800.

How to Apply: Applications are available online.

The Sallie Mae Fund First in Family® Scholarship Program

Purpose: Geared to raise awareness among the Hispanic-American community of higher education opportunities, this award was developed in partnership with the Hispanic College Fund.

Eligibility: Applicants must be a U.S. citizen or permanent resident, be of Hispanic descent, be the first in their family to attend college, be a high school senior or graduate planning to enroll or a student already enrolled in a full-time undergraduate course of study at a postsecondary institution and have a minimum GPA of 3.0 (on a 4.0 scale).

Deadline: April 15.

Amount: $500-$5,000.

How to Apply: Applications are available at the Hispanic College Fund website at www.hispanicfund.org.

The Sallie Mae Fund American Dream Scholarship Program

Purpose: To increase the number of African-American students attending college.

Eligibility: Applicants must be U.S. citizens or permanent residents, be of African-American descent, demonstrate financial need, be a high school senior or graduate planning to enroll or a student already enrolled in a full-time undergraduate course of study at an accredited postsecondary institution and have a minimum cumulative GPA of 2.5 (on a 4.0 scale).

Deadline: April 15.

Amount: $500-$5,000.

How to Apply: Applications are available at the UNCF website at www.uncf.org.

The Sallie Mae 911 Education Fund Scholarship Program

Purpose: The Sallie Mae 911 Education Fund was created in response to the terrorist attacks that occurred on September 11.

Eligibility: The scholarship program is open to children of those who were killed or permanently disabled as a result of the terrorist attacks who are enrolled as full-time undergraduate students at approved accredited institutions.

Deadline: Open.

Amount: Up to $2,500 per school year and may be renewed on an annual academic basis subject to satisfactory academic progress.

How to Apply: Applications are available online.

The Premier "Going-To-College" Website
www.salliemae.com

Sallie Mae provides superior content and functionality, and a wide array of solutions for planning and paying for college. The site guides users through the entire process—from early planning and estimating, to applying for federal and private loans online. Reflecting Sallie Mae's unique position as a trusted institution in the student loan industry, the website is designed to be the reliable, objective resource for anyone interested in a higher education.

Sallie Mae has the tools necessary for students and parents to plan for all aspects of higher education, and we are committed to being the most comprehensive paying for college site on the Internet.

 Sallie Mae's website has been named Forbes.com's **Best of the Web** multiple times in the college-planning category.

You Have Questions. We Have Answers.
www.parentanswer.com

If you have questions about paying for college, Sallie Mae's Parent Answer website can help. This valuable resource is dedicated to helping parents plan and pay for their child's college education.

At Parent Answer you can:

- Learn about ways to pay for college
- Evaluate award letters
- Research different loan options
- Apply for a student or parent loan electronically

Don't forget to sign up for Parent Answer's free e-newsletters with tips, reminders and timely information to guide you through the process of sending your child to college.

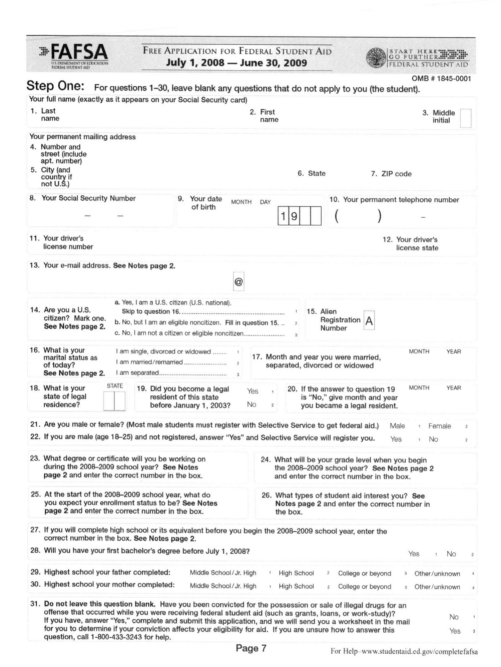

Step Two: Answer questions 32–55 about yourself (the student). If you are married as of today, include information about your spouse (your husband or wife). If you are single, separated, divorced or widowed, answer only about yourself.

32. For 2007, have you (the student) completed your IRS income tax return or another tax return listed in question 33?
   a. I have already completed my return. ¹
   b. I will file, but I have not yet completed my return. ²
   c. I'm not going to file. (Skip to question 38.) ³

33. What income tax return did you file or will you file for 2007?
   a. IRS 1040 .... ¹
   b. IRS 1040A or 1040EZ .... ²
   c. A foreign tax return. **See Notes page 2.** .... ³
   d. A tax return with Puerto Rico, another U.S. territory or freely associated state. **See Notes page 2.** .... ⁴

34. If you have filed or will file a 1040, were you eligible to file a 1040A or 1040EZ? **See Notes page 2.**
   Yes ¹   No ²   Don't Know ³

For questions 35–47, if the answer is zero or the question does not apply to you, enter 0.

35. What was your (and spouse's) adjusted gross income for 2007? Adjusted gross income is on IRS Form 1040—line 37; 1040A—line 21; or 1040EZ—line 4. $

36. Enter your (and spouse's) income tax for 2007. Income tax amount is on IRS Form 1040—line 57; 1040A—line 35; or 1040EZ—line 10. $

37. Enter your (and spouse's) exemptions for 2007. Exemptions are on IRS Form 1040—line 6d or on Form 1040A—line 6d. For Form 1040EZ, see Notes page 3.

38. How much did you earn from working in 2007? **See Notes page 3.**   You $

39. How much did your spouse earn from working in 2007? **See Notes page 3.**   Your Spouse $

Student (and Spouse) Worksheets (40–42)

40-42. **Go to Page 5** and complete the columns on the left of Worksheets A, B and C. Enter the student (and spouse) totals in questions 40, 41 and 42, respectively. Even though you may have few of the Worksheet items, check each line carefully.
   Worksheet A (40) $
   Worksheet B (41) $
   Worksheet C (42) $

43. As of today, what is your (and spouse's) total current balance of cash, savings and checking accounts? Do not include student financial aid. $

44. As of today, what is the net worth of your (and spouse's) investments, including real estate (not your home)? Net worth means current value minus debt. **See Notes page 3.** $

45. As of today, what is the net worth of your (and spouse's) current businesses and/or investment farms? For a family farm or family business, **see Notes page 3.** $

46-47. If you receive veterans education benefits, for how many months from July 1, 2008, through June 30, 2009, will you receive these benefits, and what amount will you receive per month? Do not include your spouse's veterans education benefits.
   Months (46)
   Monthly Amount (47) $

Step Three: Answer all eight questions (48-55) in this step.

48. Were you born before January 1, 1985? ....   Yes ¹   No ²

49. At the beginning of the 2008–2009 school year, will you be working on a master's or doctorate program (such as an MA, MBA, MD, JD, PhD, EdD, or graduate certificate, etc.)? ....   Yes ¹   No ²

50. As of today, are you married? (Answer "Yes" if you are separated but not divorced.) ....   Yes ¹   No ²

51. Do you have children who receive more than half of their support from you? ....   Yes ¹   No ²

52. Do you have dependents (other than your children or spouse) who live with you and who receive more than half of their support from you, now and through June 30, 2009? ....   Yes ¹   No ²

53. Are (a) both of your parents deceased, or (b) are you (or were you until age 18) a ward/dependent of the court? ....   Yes ¹   No ²

54. Are you currently serving on active duty in the U.S. Armed Forces for purposes other than training? **See Notes page 3.** ....   Yes ¹   No ²

55. Are you a veteran of the U.S. Armed Forces? **See Notes page 3.** ....   Yes ¹   No ²

If you (the student) answered "No" to every question in Step Three, go to Step Four.
If you answered "Yes" to any question in Step Three, skip Step Four and go to Step Five on page 10.
(Health Profession Students: Your college may require you to complete Step Four even if you answered "Yes" to any Step Three question.)

For Help — 1-800-433-3243

Sample - Do Not Submit

Step Four: Complete this step if you (the student) answered "No" to all questions in Step Three. Go to **Notes** page 3 to determine who is a parent for this step.

56. What is your parents' marital status as of today?

Married/Remarried 1   Divorced/Separated 3

Single 2   Widowed 4

57. Month and year they were married, separated, divorced or widowed   MONTH   YEAR

What are the Social Security Numbers, names and dates of birth of the parents reporting information on this form? If your parent does not have a Social Security Number, you must enter 000-00-0000. Enter two digits for each day and month (e.g., for May 31, enter 05 31).

58. FATHER'S/STEPFATHER'S SOCIAL SECURITY NUMBER   59. FATHER'S/STEPFATHER'S LAST NAME, AND   60. FIRST INITIAL   61. FATHER'S/STEPFATHER'S DATE OF BIRTH   1 9

62. MOTHER'S/STEPMOTHER'S SOCIAL SECURITY NUMBER   63. MOTHER'S/STEPMOTHER'S LAST NAME, AND   64. FIRST INITIAL   65. MOTHER'S/STEPMOTHER'S DATE OF BIRTH   1 9

66. Go to **Notes** page 3 to determine how many people are in your parents' household. Enter that number here.

67. Go to **Notes** page 4 to determine how many in question 66 (exclude your parents) will be college students between July 1, 2008, and June 30, 2009. Enter that number here.

68. What is your parents' state of legal residence?   STATE

69. Did your parents become legal residents of this state before January 1, 2003?   Yes 1   No 2

70. If the answer to question 69 is "No," give month and year legal residency began for the parent who has lived in the state the longest.   MONTH   YEAR

In 2007, did you, your parents or anyone in your parents' household (from question 66) receive benefits from any of the federal benefit programs listed? Mark all the programs that apply. See **Notes** page 4.

71. Supplemental Security Income   72. Food Stamps   73. Free or Reduced Price Lunch   74. TANF   75. WIC

76. For 2007, have your parents completed their IRS income tax return or another tax return listed in question 77?

a. My parents have already completed their return. 1

b. My parents will file, but they have not yet completed their return. 2

c. My parents are not going to file. **(Skip to question 82.)** 3

77. What income tax return did your parents file or will they file for 2007?

a. IRS 1040 1

b. IRS 1040A or 1040EZ...................................... 2

c. A foreign tax return. See **Notes** page 2. 3

d. A tax return with Puerto Rico, another U.S. territory or freely associated state. See **Notes** page 2. 4

78. If your parents have filed or will file a 1040, were they eligible to file a 1040A or 1040EZ? See **Notes** page 2.   Yes 1   No 2   Don't Know 3

For questions 79–89, if the answer is zero or the question does not apply, enter 0.

79. What was your parents' adjusted gross income for 2007? Adjusted gross income is on IRS Form 1040—line 37; 1040A—line 21; or 1040EZ—line 4. $

80. Enter your parents' income tax for 2007. Income tax amount is on IRS Form 1040—line 57; 1040A—line 35; or 1040EZ—line 10. $

81. Enter your parents' exemptions for 2007. Exemptions are on IRS Form 1040—line 6d or on Form 1040A—line 6d. For Form 1040EZ, see **Notes** page 3.

82. How much did your father/stepfather earn from working in 2007? See **Notes** page 3.   Father/Stepfather $

83. How much did your mother/stepmother earn from working in 2007? See **Notes** page 3.   Mother/Stepmother $

Parent Worksheets (84–86)

84-86. Go to page 5 and complete the columns on the right of Worksheets A, B and C. Enter the parents' totals in questions 84, 85 and 86, respectively. Even though your parents may have few of the Worksheet items, check each line carefully.

Worksheet A (84) $

Worksheet B (85) $

Worksheet C (86) $

Step Four CONTINUED on page 10

Page 9

For Help–www.studentaid.ed.gov/completefafsa

Sample - Do Not Submit

286

Step Four CONTINUED from page 9

87. As of today, what is your parents' total current balance of cash, savings and checking accounts? $

88. As of today, what is the net worth of your parents' investments, including real estate (not your parents' home)? Net worth means current value minus debt. **See Notes page 3.** $

89. As of today, what is the net worth of your parents' current businesses and/or investment farms? For a family farm or family business, **see Notes page 3.** $

Step Five: Complete this step only if you (the student) answered "Yes" to any Step Three question.

90. **Go to Notes page 4** to determine how many people are in your (and your spouse's) household. Enter that number here.

91. **Go to Notes page 4** to determine how many people in question 90 will be college students, attending at least half-time between July 1, 2008, and June 30, 2009. Enter that number here.

In 2007, did you (or your spouse) or anyone in your household (from question 90) receive benefits from any of the federal benefit programs listed? Mark all that apply. **See Notes page 4.**

92. Supplemental Security Income
93. Food Stamps
94. Free or Reduced Price Lunch
95. TANF
96. WIC

Step Six: Indicate which colleges you want to receive your FAFSA information.

Enter the six-digit federal school code and your housing plans. Look for the federal school codes at **www.fafsa.ed.gov**, at your college financial aid office, at your public library or by asking your high school guidance counselor. If you cannot get the federal school code, write in the complete name, address, city and state of the college. For state aid, you may wish to list your preferred college first. To have more colleges receive your FAFSA information, read *What is the FAFSA?* on page 6.

1ST FEDERAL SCHOOL CODE	NAME OF COLLEGE	STATE	HOUSING PLANS
97.a OR	ADDRESS AND CITY		97.b on campus 1 / off campus 2 / with parent 3
2ND FEDERAL SCHOOL CODE 97.c OR	NAME OF COLLEGE / ADDRESS AND CITY	STATE	97.d on campus 1 / off campus 2 / with parent 3
3RD FEDERAL SCHOOL CODE 97.e OR	NAME OF COLLEGE / ADDRESS AND CITY	STATE	97.f on campus 1 / off campus 2 / with parent 3
4TH FEDERAL SCHOOL CODE 97.g OR	NAME OF COLLEGE / ADDRESS AND CITY	STATE	97.h on campus 1 / off campus 2 / with parent 3

Step Seven: Read, sign and date.

If you are the student, by signing this application you certify that you (1) will use federal and/or state student financial aid only to pay the cost of attending an institution of higher education, (2) are not in default on a federal student loan or have made satisfactory arrangements to repay it, (3) do not owe money back on a federal student grant or have made satisfactory arrangements to repay it, (4) will notify your college if you default on a federal student loan and (5) will not receive a Federal Pell Grant from more than one college for the same period of time.

If you are the parent or the student, by signing this application you agree, if asked, to provide information that will verify the accuracy of your completed form. This information may include U.S. or state income tax forms that you filed or are required to file. Also, you certify that you understand that the Secretary of Education has the authority to verify information reported on this application with the Internal Revenue Service and other federal agencies. If you sign any document related to the federal student aid programs electronically using a Personal Identification Number (PIN), you certify that you are the person identified by the PIN and have not disclosed that PIN to anyone else. If you purposely give false or misleading information, you may be fined up to $20,000, sent to prison, or both.

98. Date this form was completed.

MONTH DAY 2008 or 2009

99. Student (Sign below)

Parent (A parent from Step Four sign below)

If this form was filled out by someone other than you, your spouse or your parents, that person must complete this part.

Preparer's name, firm and address.

100. Preparer's Social Security Number (or 101)

101. Employer ID number (or 100)

102. Preparer's signature and date

COLLEGE USE ONLY:

D/O ○ 1

FAA Signature

DATA ENTRY USE ONLY: ○ P   ○ •   ○ L   ○ E

Federal School Code

For Help—1-800-433-3243

Sample - Do Not Submit

Contributors

Throughout this book you have met Financial Aid Administrators from some of America's best colleges who have shared their insights and advice on how to make college affordable. Without the contributions from these financial aid professionals this book would not have been possible.

James M. Bauer
University of Miami

James Bauer is the Assistant Dean of Enrollment Management and Director of Financial Assistance Services at the University of Miami (www.miami.edu) in Coral Gables, Florida. Mr. Bauer began his career in financial aid as a volunteer in the financial aid office at Miami University where he was earning his master's in student personnel administration and counseling. After receiving his degree, Mr. Bauer entered the financial aid profession and has served at various colleges in Ohio and Indiana including Ball State University, The College of Wooster and Marietta College. Prior to coming to the University of Miami, Mr. Bauer was the Director of Financial Aid at Illinois State University.

The oldest of seven children, Mr. Bauer spent four years at Divine Heart Seminary in northern Indiana with the intention of becoming a Catholic priest. Those plans changed, however, once Mr. Bauer was an undergraduate at John Carroll University.

Married and with three daughters, Mr. Bauer was an avid soccer player and licensed FIFA referee until an injury forced him to cut back. Not content to remain still, Mr. Bauer still walks three miles daily and is currently the faculty advisor to the University of Miami Rowing Club. In addition, he is a serious science fiction reader, currently rereading Isaac Asimov's *Foundation Series*.

To combat the stress of his job, Mr. Bauer enjoys periodic retreats with his family to his parent's farm located on Pumpkin Ridge in Nonesuch, KY, where he rejuvenates himself with time spent mowing fields on a 1964 Ford 801 tractor.

Jim Belvin
Duke University

Jim Belvin has spent much of his professional career at Duke University (www.duke.edu), where he has served as the Director of Financial Aid for almost 30 years. While Mr. Belvin can count many accomplishments during his tenure, he is most proud of his involvements with the 568 Group which created a new need-analysis methodology known as the "Consensus Approach to Determining Family Ability to Pay for College."

In addition to assisting Duke students, Mr. Belvin is a member of the Sallie Mae Advisory Board, Princeton Review Advisory Board, College Board Trustee Finance Committee and USA GROUP Advisory Board.

Throughout his long career, Mr. Belvin has seen the benefits to families who plan for college early and is a strong proponent of saving for college. This has led him to co-author *How to Save for College* (Random House), a book that walks parents through the process of creating a realistic long-term plan for accumulating money for college.

Outside of work, Mr. Belvin enjoys spending time with his family, playing golf, reading history books and, of course, following Duke basketball.

Dr. Lawrence Burt
University of Texas at Austin

Dr. Lawrence Burt is Associate Vice President-Student Affairs and Director-Office of Student Financial Services at the University of Texas at Austin (www.utexas.edu). Dr. Burt began his career in financial aid at Southern Illinois University-Edwardsville in 1974. He worked his way up the ranks to Associate Director at Northern Illinois University. In 1984 Dr. Burt became Associate Director at UCLA and was promoted to Director three years later. He began his career at UT in 1994 as Director and became Associate Vice President-Student Affairs in 2003. During his time at UT Austin, Dr. Burt has helped to develop a number of unique scholarship programs, and as a result the university was recognized as a *Scholarship Provider of the Year* by the National Scholarship Providers Association.

In addition to his duties at the university, Dr. Burt has served on a number of commissions, councils and advisory boards and currently serves on the U.S. Department of Education's National Advisory Committee on Institutional Quality and Integrity (NACIQI). Dr. Burt is also the chair of the Texas Student Services Efficiency Committee and a member of the Council for the Management of Educational Finance.

When not in the office or working with students, Dr. Burt enjoys golf, gardening, swimming and spending time with his family: especially his granddaughter, Milla.

Jevita R. de Freitas
George Mason University

Jevita de Freitas began her career at George Mason University (www.gmu.edu) as a financial aid counselor and worked her way up through the department to become Director of the Office of Student Financial Aid four years ago. With 16 years of experience in the financial aid field, she is now responsible for awarding approximately $90 million in financial aid funds to more than 11,000 students. For her service to Mason students she has received the university's Margaret C. Howell Award for promoting civility, respect and diversity throughout the university and the community it serves.

Ms. de Freitas earned her bachelor's degree in psychology and history at New England College and prior to working at GMU she was the Director of Financial Aid at ATI Career Institute.

Ms. de Freitas now serves on the State Council for Higher Education in Virginia (SCHEV) and the Financial Aid Advisory Board for the Virginia Association of Student Financial Aid Administrators (VASFAA) and is the chairperson of the Student Welfare Subcommittee for the Mason Athletic Council. Each year she conducts approximately 35 financial aid workshops at local high schools and student and civic organizations.

When not working, her hobbies include playing with and spoiling her goddaughter Cecilia and Cecilia's brother Patrick, watching baseball, soccer and hockey, reading mystery novels and attempting to complete the Sunday *New York Times* crossword puzzle without help from the Internet.

Veronica Leech
Central State University

With more than 20 years of experience in financial aid, Ms. Leech is the Director of Financial Aid at Central State University (www.centralstate. edu), an HBCU in Wilberforce, Ohio, and is responsible for administering more than $12 million in federal and state financial aid programs. Although her job can be stressful at times, Ms. Leech finds that her ability to help meet the needs of all students—especially those from multi-cultural and disadvantaged backgrounds—to be immensely rewarding.

Ms. Leech received her bachelor's degree in sociology from Wright State University and has worked previously as the Director of Financial Aid at Clark State Community College and in financial aid administration at Sinclair Community College and Wilberforce University.

As part of her commitment to the profession, Ms. Leech is an active member of the National Association of Student Financial Aid Administrators, Midwest Association of Student Financial Aid Administrators, Ohio Association of Student Financial Aid Administrators and the National Institute for Leadership Development.

Outside of work, Ms. Leech enjoys spending time with her family while putting her son through college and is active in leadership positions in her church.

Peggy Loewy-Wellisch
Nova Southeastern University

As the Associate Vice President of Student Financial Services and Registration at Nova Southeastern University (www.nova.edu) in Fort Lauderdale-Davie, Florida, Ms. Wellisch oversees the Office of Student Financial Assistance, Bursar's Office, Registrar's Office, One-Stop Center, Enrollment Processing Services and University Call Center. During her tenure at NSU, Ms. Wellisch has made it a priority to promote excellent customer service and implement technology that has led Student Financial Services and Registration into the 21st Century.

Prior to coming to NSU, Ms. Wellisch was a Marketing Manager at the Florida Education Loan Marketing Corporation and spent over 24 years at Miami-Dade Community College, where she was the District Director of Financial Aid and Scholarships.

Throughout her career in financial aid, Ms. Wellisch has become a leader in her profession. She sits on several advisory boards including Sallie Mae, SAGE, USA Funds National and State Advisory Councils and the NelNet Advisory Council. She has worked for the U.S. Department of Education as a consultant to Project EASI (Easy Access for Students & Institutions) to redesign the financial aid delivery system. Ms. Wellisch is also the author of a publication entitled, *College Money for the Asking in Florida.*

Working in financial aid for over 30 years, Ms. Wellisch has developed a deep commitment to serving students and their families. Despite the various responsibilities of her job, she always remembers that priority number one is the students she serves.

Courtney McAnuff
Eastern Michigan University

Courtney McAnuff is the Vice President for Enrollment Services at Eastern Michigan University (www.emich.edu) in Ypsilanti, Michigan. Mr. McAnuff earned a bachelor's degree from the City College of New York, a master's from Hofstra University and is completing his doctorate at Wayne State University. Mr. McAnuff began his career in higher education as an instructor at SUNY Farmingdale before accepting an administrative position as a financial aid counselor. There he advanced to the position of Director of Financial Aid and was the recipient of the Chancellor's Award for Most Outstanding Administrator before joining Eastern Michigan University in 1980.

During his career at EMU, Mr. McAnuff has served as Director of Financial Aid, Director and Dean of Admissions and Financial Aid, Assistant and Associate Vice President for Marketing and Student Affairs and, since 1996, Vice President for Enrollment Services. Mr. McAnuff has also served as a consultant at 15 colleges and universities, as well as the College Board, where he served on the National Hispanic Scholars Committee.

During his service at Eastern Michigan University, Mr. McAnuff has been awarded the Gold Medallion Award and the Progress and Commitment Award. He has also been honored as A Boss of the Year by the Ypsilanti Area Jaycees. His commitment to the community has been reflected in his membership on the Board of Directors of the Cope O'Brien Center, Ypsilanti Meals on Wheels, the Ann Arbor Public Library, St. Joseph Mercy Hospital Community Health and Glacier Hills Retirement Complex. Mr. McAnuff also serves on the Executive Board of the First Presbyterian Church in Ann Arbor.

Mr. McAnuff lives in Ann Arbor with his wife Sharon. They have three children, a son Brandon, in his final year of college and two daughters, Stacey and Lisa, both of whom have completed college and have begun their own careers in business.

Dawnia Smith
Cincinnati State Technical and Community College

 Dawnia Smith is the Director of Financial Aid at Cincinnati State Technical and Community College (www.cincinnatistate.edu) in Cincinnati, Ohio. During her tenure at Cincinnati State, Ms. Smith has implemented numerous electronic processes that have successfully streamlined the financial aid process for students, one of which includes Sallie Mae's Your Electronic Award (YEA). She is also a member of her state, regional and national financial aid associations.

Before coming to Cincinnati State, Ms. Smith was the Director of Financial Aid at three different southern colleges including South Arkansas Community College in El Dorado, Arkansas, Bainbridge College in Bainbridge, Georgia and Trident Technical College in Charleston, South Carolina. A native southerner, Ms. Smith received her bachelor's degree and MBA from Henderson State University in Arkadelphia, Arkansas.

When not working, Ms. Smith enjoys playing tennis, watching the Reds and Bengals play ball and going to Kings Island Amusement Park and other outings with her two daughters, one of whom currently attends Cincinnati State.

Glossary of Terms

AA—An associate of arts degree. Can be earned at most two-year colleges.

Academic period—A measured term of enrollment (such as a semester, quarter, trimester or clock or credit hour).

Academic year—A period of time schools use to measure a quantity of study. For example, a school's academic year may consist of a fall and spring semester, during which a student must complete 24 semester hours. Academic years vary from school to school, and even from educational program to educational program at the same school.

Accrued interest—Interest that accumulates on the unpaid principal balance of a loan.

ACT®—A test to measure a student's ability in math, verbal comprehension and problem solving. Usually students take this test during their junior or senior year of high school.

Adjusted gross income (AGI)—All taxable income less IRS allowable adjustments to income. This figure is from U.S. IRS tax forms.

Advanced Placement Test—Test used to earn credit for college subjects studied in high school and scored on a scale from 1 to 5 (the best possible score). They are offered by the Educational Testing Service (ETS) in May. Also known as AP tests.

Aid package—A combination of financial aid (scholarships, grants, loans and/or work study) determined by the financial aid office of a college or university. See also award letter.

Amortization—The process of gradually repaying a loan over an extended period of time through periodic installments of principal and interest.

Annual Percentage Rate (APR)—The total annual cost of a loan, including all fees and interest. Usually expressed as a percentage. Also known as APR.

Anticipated graduation date (AGD)—The date the lender (or servicer) expects the student to graduate. Also known as AGD.

ASVAB—Armed Services Vocational Aptitude Battery. It is a test designed to measure aptitude in 10 different career-related skills or activities and at a particular stage—namely individuals between the ages of 16 and 24—in life.

Average daily balance (ADB)—The sum of unpaid principal balance outstanding on all qualifying loans at each actual interest rate for each day of the quarter, divided by the sum of the number of days in the quarter. Also known as ADB.

Award letter—An official document issued by a financial aid office listing all the financial aid awarded to the student. The award letter will include information about the cost of attendance and terms and conditions for the financial aid. See also aid package.

BA or BS—BA stands for bachelor of arts, and BS stands for bachelor of science. Both degrees can be earned at four-year colleges. The type of degree awarded depends on the kinds of courses offered at the particular school.

Bankruptcy—A person is declared bankrupt, when found to be legally insolvent and the person's property is distributed among creditors or otherwise administered to satisfy the interests of creditors. Generally, federal student loans cannot be discharged through bankruptcy.

Base year—The tax year prior to the academic year (award year) for which financial aid is requested. Financial information from this year is used to determine eligibility for financial aid. For example, if a student is submitting a FAFSA in March 2009 for academic year 2009-2010, the base year to be used is 2008.

Borrower—The person who applies for a loan and receives the proceeds (or money) of the loan.

Budget—The total cost of attending a postsecondary institution for one academic year. The student's budget usually includes tuition, fees, room, board, books, supplies, travel and personal expenses. Each institution develops its own student budget.

Bursar's Office—The university office that is responsible for the billing and collection of university charges.

Campus-based aid—Financial aid programs administered by the university. The federal government provides the university with a fixed annual allocation which is awarded by the financial aid administrator to deserving students. The Perkins Loan Program, Federal Supplemental Educational Opportunity Grant (FSEOG) and Federal Work-Study are examples of campus-based aid.

Cancellation—The release of a borrower from the obligation to repay his or her loan. There are three different cancellation periods within the loan life cycle: before disbursement is made, after disbursement is made but before repayment begins and once repayment begins. Before disbursement is made, the borrower may cancel (or un-apply for) the loan by telling the lender that the loan is not wanted. After first disbursement and before repayment, the borrower has the right to return the loan proceeds in full within 120 days (afterwards the borrower owes fees and any accrued interest) and thereby cancel the loan. In this same cancellation period, the borrower may also effect a "partial" cancellation by returning individual (but not all) disbursements. After repayment begins, the borrower must meet certain requirements or conditions to be eligible for discharge from federal student loans. A loan cannot be discharged or cancelled because the borrower didn't complete the program of study at the school (unless the borrower was unable to complete the program because of school closure), didn't like the school or the program of study or didn't obtain employment after completing the program of study. See also discharge and cancellation options.

Cancellation options—The conditions for federal loan cancellation or discharge are based on the loan program (i.e., FFELP, FDLP, Perkins). The total and permanent disability or death of a borrower are the only conditions that justify 100 percent cancellation of a loan in any of the programs. Conditions such as being a full-time teacher (in designated studies or demographic areas), nurse or medical technician, Vista or Peace Corp volunteer or a member of the U.S. Armed Forces may qualify the borrower for 50 percent to 100 percent discharge on Perkins Loans only. Bankruptcy may be a valid condition for discharge. However, this may only occur if repaying the loans would cause the borrower or his/her family "undue hardship."

Capitalization—Addition of unpaid interest to the principal balance of a loan which increases the total outstanding balance due. See also interest capitalization.

Certification—A process by which the college, university, trade school or vocation school verifies that a student is enrolled on at least a half-time basis, is making satisfactory academic process and therefore eligible for federal and private loans. Certification must be made prior to disbursement of funds.

Citizen/eligible noncitizen—To be eligible for federal student aid, the borrower must be a: 1) U.S. citizen; 2) U.S. national (including natives of American Samoa or Swain's Island); or, 3) U.S. permanent resident who has an I-151, I-551 or I-551C (Alien Registration Card). If not in one of these categories, the borrower must have an Arrival-Departure Record (I-94) from U.S. Immigration and Naturalization Service showing one of the following designations in order to be eligible: "Refugee," "Asylum Granted," "Indefinite Parole" and/or "Humanitarian Parole" or "Cuban-Haitian Entrant, Status Pending." If the borrower has only a Notice of Approval to Apply for Permanent Residence (I-171 or I-464), the borrower is not eligible for federal student aid. If the borrower is in the U.S. on an F1 or F2 student visa only, or on a J1 or J2 exchange visitor visa only or with a G series visa, then the borrower is not eligible for federal student aid.

Claim—An application made to a guarantor for payment of an insured student loan for loss of payment due to borrower death, total and permanent disability, bankruptcy, default or school closure.

Co-borrower—A person who signs the promissory note in addition to the borrower and is responsible for the obligation if the borrower does not pay. A co-borrower must be able to pass a credit review and must live in the United States.

Collateral—Property of a borrower that is pledged by the borrower to protect the interests of a lender. In other words, it may become property of the lender if the borrower fails to repay the associated loan. Collateral is the lender's security for loans made.

Collection—The activities and/or actions associated with getting payment on unpaid loan principal and interest from a borrower after that borrower defaults on the loan. The players in the loan process that could be taking these actions include lenders, guarantors, servicers and collection agencies.

Comaker—One of two individuals who are joint borrowers on a federal parent (PLUS) loan or on a consolidation loan, and who are jointly liable for the repayment of the loan.

Combined billing—Lenders (or servicers) generally offer a combined bill for all of a borrower's loans serviced by that lender/servicer so that the borrower only needs to make one payment per month for all of the loans.

Consolidation—Combining several federal (and possibly private) loans from multiple lenders into a single loan to reduce the monthly payment amount and/or increase the repayment period.

Cooperative work-study education (Co-op)—A program in which the student alternates between full-time college study and full-time paid employment related to the student's area of study. Under this plan, a bachelor's degree often requires five years to complete.

Cosigner—A person who signs the promissory note in addition to the borrower and is responsible for the obligation if the borrower does not pay. A cosigner must be able to pass a credit review and must live in the United States.

Cost of attendance (COA)—The total cost of attending a postsecondary institution for one academic year. The student's budget usually includes tuition, fees, room, board, supplies, transportation and personal expenses. Also known as COA.

Coupon book—A loan repayment tool. Generally, coupon books are provided by lenders (or servicers) to borrowers rather than monthly bills to remind borrowers of their obligation to pay and to associate the borrower's payment with his/her account (once received via mail). Coupon books are mailed to the borrower periodically and contain all of the periodic coupons required by the borrower until the next coupon book is scheduled for printing and mailing or until the loan is paid in full.

Credit bureau—A credit bureau is an agency that gathers and stores credit information on individuals. When a credit report is needed for a loan application, a credit bureau produces a report to the lender based on the gathered data. The lender also reports back to credit bureaus how much an individual borrowed and whether the individual makes payments when due. This information is then available to potential employers and creditors in the future.

Credit report—A report that contains details about your borrowing habits and money-management skills. Lenders use credit reports to determine if they should approve a loan and to set the terms (interest rate, fees and length) of the loan.

Credit score—A number, generally between 330 and 830, that reflects the credit history shown in a borrower's credit report and that is part of the process of setting interest rates and terms for loans. To arrive at a single score, a credit bureau assigns numerical values to specific pieces of a borrower's personal financial information, such as outstanding debt, the number of inquiries on your credit history, the number of open accounts, etc. These values are put through a series of mathematical calculations to produce the single number, the credit score. A borrower's credit score is considered predictive of the borrower's future credit performance.

Credit-ready—A credit-ready borrower is one who has no credit history OR a credit history with no excessive number of delinquencies on consumer loans or revolving charge accounts; no prior education loan defaults; no derogatory credit items such as charge offs, foreclosures, open judgments, bankruptcy, etc.

Credit-worthy—An individual with no negative credit history per the criteria established by the lender.

CSS/Financial Aid PROFILE®—The financial aid application service of the College Board that collects additional information used by colleges, universities and scholarship programs in awarding private financial aid funds. Also known as the PROFILE.

Custodial account—In a custodial account, a minor is the owner of the account, however, an adult controls the investment until the minor is 18 (i.e., reaches majority). The interest and dividends on the account are then taxed based on the minor's lower income bracket. If the minor has little other income, these earnings may escape tax altogether. Custodial accounts include those governed by the Uniform Gifts to Minors Act and/or the Uniform Transfer to Minors Act.

Data release number (DRN)—Piece of information on the Student Aid Report (SAR) in the upper right hand corner of the first page (next to the printed EFC). This number is needed to identify the appropriate FAFSA data for release to additional schools (beyond the six schools possibly listed by the student in the original FAFSA submission). Also known as DRN.

Default—Failure to repay a loan according to the terms agreed to when the borrower signed a promissory note for the loan. Default occurs at 180 days when the delinquency date is prior to 10/7/98, and 270 days when the delinquency date is on or after 10/7/98.

Deferment—A period during which a borrower, who meets certain criteria, may suspend loan payments. For some loans the federal government pays the interest during a deferment. On others, the interest accrues and is capitalized, and the borrower is responsible for paying it.

Delinquency—Failure to make monthly loan payments when due. Delinquency begins with the first missed payment.

Demographics—Information pertaining to the vital data for a borrower (e.g., name, address, school, birthdate, SSN). Also known as demographic information.

Dependent student—An undergraduate student whose parents provide more than half of their financial support. A dependent student is not married, is under 24 years of age, has no legal dependents, is not an orphan or ward of the court, nor a veteran of the U.S. Armed Forces. Parents of a dependent student must submit parental information on the FAFSA for their son or daughter to be considered for financial aid. (See also Independent student.)

Direct Lending—The William D. Ford Federal Direct Loan Program. Stafford and PLUS loans are available directly from the federal government rather than through commercial lenders. Selected colleges and universities participate in this program. Once known as FDSLP for Federal Direct Student Loan Program. Also known as FDLP.

Disbursement—The release of loan funds to the school for delivery to the borrower. Disbursements are usually made in equal multiple installments co-payable to the borrower and the school.

Discharge—The release of a borrower from the obligation to repay his or her loan. There are three different cancellation periods within the loan life cycle: before disbursement is made, after disbursement is made but before repayment begins and once repayment begins. Before disbursement is made, the borrower may cancel (or un-apply for) the loan by telling the lender that the loan is not wanted. After first disbursement and before repayment, the borrower has the right to return the loan proceeds in full within 120 days (afterwards the borrower owes fees and any accrued interest) and thereby cancel the loan. In this same cancellation period, the borrower may also effect a "partial" cancellation by returning individual (but not all) disbursements. After repayment begins, the borrower must meet certain requirements or conditions to be eligible for discharge from federal student loans. A loan cannot be discharged or cancelled because the borrower didn't complete the program of study at the school (unless the borrower was unable to complete the program because of school closure), didn't like the school or the program of study or didn't obtain employment after completing the program of study. See also cancellation and cancellation options.

Disclosure statement—Statement of the total cost and amount of a loan, including the interest rate and any additional finance charges.

Due diligence—The federal government requires that a lender, holder or servicer exercise reasonable care and diligence in the making, servicing and collection of insured federal student loans in order to retain the insurance (against default claims) of the loans.

Early Action—A college admissions program that consists of earlier deadlines and notification dates than the regular admissions process, but that does not require a binding commitment of the student if admission is offered. The student applying under this program may apply to many schools.

Early Decision—A college admissions program that consists of earlier deadlines and notification dates than the regular admissions process, and that requires a binding commitment of the student if admission is offered. The student applying under this program should apply to only one school. The student will not know what financial aid will be awarded prior to commiting.

ED—U.S. Department of Education. Government agency that administers several federal student financial aid programs, including the Federal Pell Grant, the Federal Work-Study Program, the Federal Perkins Loan, the FFELP and the FDLP.

Educational Testing Service—Company that produces and administers the SAT and other educational achievement tests. Also known as ETS.

Electronic funds transfer (EFT)—Any transfer of funds that is initiated through electronic means, such as data transmission by computer rather than a paper based transaction, such as a check. Also known as EFT.

Endorser—An individual who endorses the promissory note and is responsible for payment of the loan if the borrower does not pay. Sometimes referred to as the cosigner.

Endowment—Funds owned by an institution and invested to produce income to support the operation of the institution. Many educational institutions use a portion of their endowment income for financial aid.

Enrollment status—An indication of whether you are a full-time or part-time student. Generally you must be enrolled at least half-time (and in some cases full-time) to qualify for financial aid.

Entitlement—Entitlement programs award funds to all qualified applicants. The Pell Grant is an example of such a program.

Entrance counseling—Students with federal educational loans are required to receive counseling before they receive their first loan disbursement, during which the borrower's rights and responsibilities and loan terms and conditions are reviewed with the student. This session may be conducted online, by video, in person with the FAA or FAO or in group meeting.

Exit counseling—Students with federal educational loans are required to receive counseling before they graduate or withdraw (i.e., leave school), during which the borrower's rights and responsibilities and loan terms and conditions are reviewed with the student. This session may be conducted online, by video, in person with the FAA or FAO or in group meeting.

Expected Family Contribution (EFC)—Amount a family is expected to contribute to a student's education, based on family earnings, net assets, savings, size of family and number of students in college. Also known as EFC.

Extended repayment plan—A recent addition to repayment options for the federal loan programs is the extended repayment plan. If a borrower has more than $30,000 in federal loans to repay, he or she may qualify to extend the repayment period to 25 years.

FAFSA—Free Application for Federal Student Aid. The form that must be completed by students and parents applying for Federal Title IV student aid.

FAT—Financial Aid Transcript. A record of all federal aid received by students at each school attended.

FDLP—The William D. Ford Federal Direct Loan Program. Stafford and PLUS loans are available directly from the federal government rather than through commercial lenders. Selected colleges and universities participate in this program. Once known as FDSLP for Federal Direct Student Loan Program. Also known as Direct Lending.

Federal methodology—The need analysis formula mandated by federal law to determine a family's Expected Family Contribution (EFC).

Federal Processor—The organization that processes the information submitted on the Free Application for Federal Student Aid (FAFSA) and uses it to compute eligibility for federal student aid.

Federal Student Aid Information Center—Office associated with the Department of Education that is available to assist students and families on applying for financial aid from the federal government. Also known as FSAIC.

Federal Supplemental Educational Opportunity Grant (FSEOG)—A federal grant for undergraduate students with exceptional financial need. FSEOG amounts range from $100 to $4,000 per year.

Federal Work-Study Program—This federal program provides part-time jobs for undergraduate and graduate students with financial need, allowing them to earn money to help pay education expenses. Also known as FWS.

Fellowship—A form of aid given to graduate students to help support their education. Some fellowships include tuition waivers or payments to universities in lieu of tuition. Most fellowships include a stipend to cover reasonable living expenses (e.g., just above the poverty line). Fellowships are a form of gift aid and do not have to be repaid.

FFELP—The Federal Family Education Loan Program. Stafford and PLUS loans are financed by private lenders and guaranteed by the federal government.

Financial aid—Financial assistance in the form of scholarships, grants, work-study and loans for education.

Financial Aid Administrator (FAA)—A college or university employee who is involved in the administration of financial aid. Also known as Financial Aid Advisors, Officers or Counselors.

Financial aid award letter—The total amount of financial aid (federal and nonfederal) such as scholarships, grants, loans, and/or work-study for which a student is eligible.

Financial Aid Officer (FAO)—A college or university employee who is involved in the administration of financial aid. Also known as Financial Aid Advisors, Administrators or Counselors.

Financial aid package—The total amount of financial aid (federal and nonfederal) such as scholarships, grants, loans and/or work-study for which a student is eligible.

Financial aid transcript—A record of all federal aid received by students at each school attended. Also known as FAT.

Financial need—The difference between the cost of attendance at a college and the Expected Family Contribution. Also known as financial aid eligibility.

Fixed interest—On a fixed interest loan, the interest rate remains the same for the life of the loan.

Forbearance—Temporary cessation of regularly scheduled payments or temporarily permitting smaller payments than were originally scheduled.

Free Application for Federal Student Aid—The form that must be completed by students and parents applying for Federal Title IV student aid. Also known as FAFSA.

FWS—Federal Work-Study. (*See Federal Work-Study Program.*)

GED—General Education Development Certificate. A certificate students receive if they've passed a specific, approved high school equivalency test. Students who don't have a high school diploma but who have a GED may still qualify for federal student aid. A school that admits students without a high school diploma must make a GED program in the vicinity of the school available to these students and must inform them about the program.

Gift aid—Financial aid, such as grants and scholarships, which does not need to be repaid.

GPA—Grade point average. An average of a student's grades, where the grades have been converted to a 4.0 scale—with 4.0 being an A, 3.0 being a B and 2.0 being a C.

Grace period—Specified period of time between the date a student graduates or drops below half-time status and the date loan repayment begins. There is only one grace period per federal student loan.

Graduate student—A student in a postsecondary institution who is enrolled in a master's or higher level degree program.

Graduated repayment—A repayment schedule where the monthly payments are smaller at the start of the repayment period and become larger later on.

Grants—Financial aid awards that do not have to be repaid. Grants are available through the federal government, state agencies and colleges.

Gross income—Income before taxes, deductions and allowances have been subtracted.

Guarantor—State agency or private non-profit institution that insures student loans for lenders and helps administer the FFELP. See also guaranty agency.

Guaranty agency—State agency or private non-profit institution that insures student loans for lenders and helps administer the FFELP. See also guarantor.

Half-time—At schools measuring progress by credit hours and semesters, trimesters or quarters, half-time enrollment is at least six semester hours or quarter hours per term. At schools measuring progress by credit hours but not using semesters, trimesters or quarters, half-time enrollment is at least 12 semester hours or 18 quarter hours per year. At schools measuring progress by clock hours, half-time enrollment is at least 12 hours per week. Note that schools may choose to set higher minimums than these. A student must attend school at least half time to be eligible to receive FDLP or FFELP loans. Half-time enrollment is not a requirement to receive aid from the Federal Pell Grant, Federal Supplemental Educational Opportunity Grant (FSEOG), Federal Work-Study and Federal Perkins Loan programs.

Holder—The institution that owns a loan.

Home equity—The portion of a home's value that the homeowner owns outright; it is the difference between the fair market value of the home and the sum of the principal balances remaining on mortgage loans held by the homeowner for that home.

Home equity line of credit—A variation of the home equity loan that allows a home-owner to draw money against (i.e., write checks) the home's equity on an ongoing basis. Generally, a home equity line of credit features a variable interest rate, a specific time period during which money may be withdrawn and a repayment period following any withdrawal. The credit also revolves on a home equity line of credit: as soon as principal is repaid, it may be borrowed again. Also abbreviated as HELOC.

Home equity loan—A loan based on a homeowner's equity in the home. The home equity loan features a fixed rate, payment and term.

HOPE Scholarship—The HOPE Scholarship provides a family up to a $1,650 maximum tax credit per year per dependent student.

In-school—The status of a borrower which is defined as beginning on the date on which the borrower is enrolled on at least a half-time basis and continuing until the borrower terminates enrollment on at least a half-time basis at a participating school.

Income—The amount of money received from employment (salary, wages, tips), profit from financial instruments (interest, dividends, capital gains) or other sources (welfare, disability, child support, Social Security and pensions).

Income-based repayment—(Income Sensitive/Income Contingent) Repayment schedule where the amount of the monthly payments is based on the income earned by the borrower.

Independent student—A student who is either married, 24 years of age or older, enrolled in a graduate or professional education program, has legal dependents other than a spouse, is an orphan or ward of the court or a veteran of the U.S. Armed Forces.

Individual Retirement Account (IRA)—An individual tax-deferred savings and investment account meant to accumulate funds for retirement. Also known as IRA. Currently, the maximum yearly contribution to all retirement IRAs is $5,000 or if you are 50 or older $6,000. Before 1997, there was only one type of IRA, now often referred to as a traditional IRA.

Information Review Form—A document associated with the Student Aid Report (SAR) on which the borrower can correct any incorrect information on the SAR. Document is returned to the Department of Education.

Institutional loan—Loans specific to a college, university or other postsecondary educational institution. Eligibility and loan characteristics will vary among institutions.

Institutional Methodology—When a college or university uses its own formula to determine financial need for allocation of the school's own financial aid funds, the formula is referred to as the Institutional Methodology.

Institutional Student Information Record (ISIR)—The Department of Education forwards information electronically about a student who has applied for federal student aid via the FAFSA to the schools indicated by the student on that application. Also known as ISIR.

Insurance—The agreement between the guaranty agency and the lender for the lender to receive reimbursement from the guaranty agency for its losses on claims.

Insurance fee—A fee charged by guaranty agencies, which is deducted from loan proceeds and used to insure against defaulted loans.

Interest—An amount, calculated as a percent of the principal loan amount, that is charged for borrowed money. See fixed interest and variable interest.

Interest capitalization—Addition of unpaid interest to the principal balance of a loan which increases the total outstanding balance due. See also capitalization.

Interest-only payment—A payment that covers only accrued interest owed on a loan and none of the principal balance. Interest-only payments do not prohibit borrowers from making additional or larger payments at any time if the borrower desires.

Interest subsidy—Interest the federal government pays on certain loans while borrowers are in school, during authorized deferment or during grace periods.

International student—A student who is not a citizen or resident of the U.S. who intends to attend or is attending a college, university or other postsecondary educational institution.

Internship—Part-time job during the academic year or the summer months in which a student receives supervised practical training in a field.

IRS—Internal Revenue Service. U.S. government's tax assessment and collection agency.

LAWLOANS—A private loan for law students and law school graduates studying for the bar exam that is available from Sallie Mae.

Lender—A financial institution, agency or school that provides the money to make a loan to a borrower.

Leveraging Educational Assistance Partnership Program (LEAP)—Also known as the LEAP Program. Program was formerly known as the State Student Incentive Grant (SSIG) Program. This program, through matching formula grants to states, provides grant aid to students with substantial financial need to help them pay for their postsecondary education costs. The Secretary of Education is authorized to accept annual applications from the 50 states, the District of Columbia, the Commonwealth of Puerto Rico, American Samoa, Guam, the Commonwealth of the Northern Mariana Islands and the Virgin Islands for distribution of the LEAP funds.

Lifetime Learning Tax Credit—A tax credit of up to $2,000 per family, for postsecondary education courses. Only one credit may be claimed per tax year. To claim this credit, the individual (or in the case of a dependent child, the parents) must file a tax credit and owe taxes for that tax year.

Loan—A type of financial aid that is available to students and their parents. Student loan programs have varying interest rates and repayment provisions. An education loan must be repaid.

Loan counseling—Students with federal educational loans are required to receive counseling before they receive their first loan disbursement and before they graduate or withdraw, during which the borrower's rights and responsibilities and loan terms and conditions are reviewed with the student. These sessions may be conducted online, by video, in person with the FAA or FAO or in group meeting. See entrance and exit counseling.

Loan proceeds—The money the borrower receives from a loan (or the amount borrowed minus fees).

Master Promissory Note (MPN)—The promissory note a student signs when taking out a Stafford Loan. The Master Promissory Note covers both the Subsidized and Unsubsidized Stafford loans the student may receive for the same enrollment period. If the student is attending a four-year or graduate school, the Master Promissory Note also covers Subsidized and Unsubsidized Stafford loans the student may receive for future enrollment periods. Also known as MPN.

MBA LOANS—A private loan for graduate-level business administration students that is available from Sallie Mae.

MEDEX—A private loan that helps recent medical school graduates cover the costs of residency. This loan is available through Sallie Mae.

MEDLOANS—A private loan for allopathic medical students that is available through Sallie Mae.

Merit-based—A means of determining eligibility for certain types of financial aid using merit, such as a specific accomplishment or talent, as the determining factor, rather than financial need.

Multiple data entry processor—Company that processes FAFSAs submitted by students. Also known as MDE.

National Service Trust—A U.S. national community service program. If you participate in this program before attending school, the funds may be used to pay your educational expenses. If you participate after graduating, the funds may be used to repay your federal student loans. Eligible types of community service include education, human services, the environment and public safety.

National Student Loan Clearinghouse—Acts as a central repository for the collection of postsecondary enrollment status and related information. Its primary responsibility is to assist postsecondary institutions to meet their reporting responsibilities to student loan industry participants and the federal government.

Need—The difference between the Cost of Attendance and the Expected Family Contribution (EFC) is the student's financial need.

Need analysis—Technique used to determine a student's need for financial assistance for college expenses. The analysis determines the family's ability to contribute to costs compared to the student's cost of attendance.

Need-based—A means of determining eligibility for certain types of financial aid using financial need as the determining factor.

Net income—This is income after taxes, deductions and allowances have been subtracted.

NMSQT—National Merit Scholastic Qualifying Test. The National Merit Scholastic Qualifying Test is given during the junior year of high school in the form of the Preliminary Scholastic Assessment Test (PSAT). Sometimes abbreviated as PSAT/NMSQT.

Origination—The process whereby the lender, or a servicing agent on behalf of the lender, handles the initial application processing and disbursement of loan proceeds.

Origination fee—Fee, payable by the borrower and deducted from the principal of a loan prior to disbursement to the borrower. For federally-backed loans, the origination fee is paid to the federal government to offset the cost of the interest subsidy to borrowers. For private loan programs, the origination fee is generally paid to the originator to cover the cost of administering and insuring the program.

Overaward—The amount of loan proceeds that, when added to other student financial assistance, exceeds the borrower's educational need.

Parent Loans for Undergraduate Students—Federally-insured loans for parents of dependent students. Also known as PLUS loans.

Parent's contribution—Amount parents can be expected to contribute each year to the cost of their student's education as determined by the Federal Methodology. Also known as PC.

Pell Grant Program—The largest federal grant program. Eligibility and award amounts are determined by the college based on established federal guidelines.

Period of enrollment—The period for which aid is made as determined by the school. A period of enrollment coincides with an academic term such as the academic year, semester, trimester or quarter, and starts on the day classes begin.

Perkins Loan Program—Federally-insured loans funded by the federal government and awarded by the school. The loans feature a low interest rate and are repayable over an extended period.

PIN—Personal identification number. A number entered into computer and/or telephone systems to authenticate the user. PINs are frequently used to identify those who are taking online entrance and exit counseling.

PLUS—Parent Loans for Undergraduate Students. Federally-insured loans for parents of dependent students.

Postsecondary—This term means "after high school" and refers to all programs for high school graduates, including programs at two and four-year colleges, and vocational and technical schools.

Prepaid tuition plan—A college savings plan that is guaranteed to rise in value at the same rate as college tuition. For example, if a family purchases shares that are worth half a year's tuition at a state college, they will always be worth half a year's tuition, even 10 years later when tuition rates may have doubled.

Prepayment—Payment received for a borrower account for more than the amount due.

Prime rate—The prime interest rate is the rate charged by commercial financial institutions for short-term loans to corporations or individuals whose credit standing is so high that little risk to the lender is involved in making the loan. This rate fluctuates based on economic conditions and may be different among financial institutions. The prime rate serves as a basis for the interest rates charged for other, higher-risk loans.

Principal—Amount borrowed, which may increase as a result of interest capitalization, and the amount on which interest is calculated. Also known as principal balance.

Private loans—Private loans provide supplemental funding when other financial aid does not cover costs. These loans (not sponsored by government agencies) are offered by banks or other financial institutions and schools to parents and students.

Professional judgment—The financial aid administrator's ability to make changes to a student's financial aid package based on extenuating circumstances.

PROFILE (CSS/Financial Aid PROFILE)—A customized financial aid application form required at certain colleges, which collects additional financial information to determine eligibility for institutional aid.

Promissory note—Contract between a borrower and a lender that includes all the terms and conditions under which the borrower promises to repay the loan.

Proprietary school—Postsecondary schools that are private and are legally permitted to make a profit. Most proprietary schools offer technical and vocational courses.

PSAT—The Preliminary Scholastic Assessment Test, which helps prepare students for the SAT and, if taken during junior year, is part of the qualifying criteria for the National Merit Scholarship Program. A student usually takes this test as a high school sophomore or early in the junior year. Sometimes abbreviated as PSAT/NMSQT.

Reinsurance—The agreement between the guaranty agency and ED for the guarantor to receive reimbursement from ED for its losses on default claims.

Renewal application—A FAFSA application that is used for subsequent-year applications after the initial FAFSA has been filed.

Repayment—The time during which a borrower actively pays back an education loan.

Reserve Officers Training Corps—Programs that combine military education with baccalaureate degree study, often with financial support and required commitment to future service in the Armed Services. Scholarship recipients participate in summer training while in college and meet a service commitment after college. Also known as ROTC.

SallieMae.com—A comprehensive online resource to take the stress and the guesswork out of planning and paying for college. It walks you through the entire "go-to-college" process—from early planning and estimating to applying for federal and private loans.

SAT or SAT Reasoning Test—Used to measure a student's ability in math, critical reading and writing. SATs are administered during the junior and senior years in high school.

SAT Subject Tests or Subject Tests—Offered in many areas of study including English, mathematics, many sciences, history and foreign languages. Some colleges require students to take one or more SAT tests when they apply for admission.

Satisfactory Academic Progress (SAP)—To be eligible to receive federal student aid, a student must maintain satisfactory academic progress, based on the school's written standard, toward a degree or certificate. If the student is enrolled in a program that is longer than two years, the student must have a C average by the end of the second academic year of study or have an academic standing consistent with the school's graduation requirements and must continue to maintain satisfactory academic progress for the rest of the course of study. Also known as SAP.

Savings plan—A methodical approach to periodically putting money into an account with a financial institution with the goal of reaching a target amount that is to be used for a stated purpose. The account preferably is an interest-bearing account.

Scholarships—Funds used to pay for higher education that do not have to be repaid. Scholarships may be awarded based on any number of criteria, such as academics, achievements, hobbies, talents, affiliations with various groups or career aspirations. They usually do not provide funds for living expenses.

Secondary market—Institutions that buy student loans from the institutions that originate or own them.

Section 529 Plans—State tuition savings plans, named for the section of the IRS code authorizing their existence.

Self-help aid—Financial aid in the form of loans or student employment.

SEOG—Supplemental Educational Opportunity Grant Program; federal grant funds made available through some schools to a limited number of undergraduate students with financial need.

Serialization—Combining several loans into one account so that the borrower only pays one monthly bill. Original loan terms do not change with serialization.

Servicer—Organization that administers and collects loan payments. May be either the loan holder or an agent acting on behalf of the holder.

SSN—Social Security (account) Number. Unique nine-digit number assigned to individuals that identifies location of birth (or registration), becomes the key to contributing and receiving Social Security funds for retirement and is used by the IRS in associating income with an individual for the purpose of assessing taxes.

Stafford loans—Loans, both subsidized (need based) and unsubsidized (non-need based), guaranteed by the federal government and available to students to fund education.

Standard repayment—A repayment schedule reflecting equal monthly payments over a 10 to 15 year period.

Statement of Educational Purpose—A legal document in which the student agrees to use the financial aid for educational expenses only.

Student Aid Report (SAR)—A federal output document, containing financial and other information reported by the student on the FAFSA, sent to a student by the Federal application processor. The student's eligibility for aid is indicated by the Expected Family Contribution (EFC), which is printed on the document. Also known as SAR.

Subsidized Stafford loans—Subsidized Stafford loans are awarded to students who demonstrate financial need (i.e., need-based loans). Because the Department of Education subsidizes the interest, borrowers are not charged interest while they are enrolled in school at least half-time and during grace and deferment periods.

Tax credit—An amount subtracted from your federal income taxes dollar-for-dollar. A tax credit will save the taxpayer more than a deduction. Taxes must be owed for the given tax year and a tax return must be filed to receive any tax credit.

Term—A length of time in which to repay a loan. The term is usually agreed to by lender and borrower within the borrower's contract or promissory note. Also refers to language used in legal documents, such as the promissory note, that defines how a loan will be borrowed and repaid. Also refers to some postsecondary educational institutions' academic period.

TOEFL—Test of English as a Foreign Language.

Transcript—A list of all the courses that a student has taken at a particular high school or college with the grades that the student earned in each course. Transcripts are usually required for college applications.

Tuition—The amount of money colleges charge for classroom and other instruction, and use of some facilities such as libraries.

Undergraduate student—A degree-seeking student at a college or university who has not earned a first bachelor's degree.

Uniform Gifts to Minors Act (UGMA)—Legislation that introduced a tax effective manner of transferring property to minors without the complications of trusts or guardianship restrictions. In essence, this federal act allows an adult to place up to $12,000/year in a custodial account for a child without incurring a gift tax. The monies in a UGMA account can be invested into mutual funds, bank accounts or stocks. The adult controls the fund until the child reaches the age of majority. Also known as UGMA.

Uniform Transfer to Minors Act (UTMA)—This law offers you the same advantages as the Uniform Gifts to Minors Act, but allows the adult to control the custodial account for a longer period of time. The monies in a UTMA account can be invested into mutual funds, bank accounts or stocks and extends the definition of gifts to include real estate, paintings, royalties and patents. Also known as UTMA.

Unsubsidized Stafford loans—Unsubsidized Stafford loans are available to students regardless of financial need (i.e., non-need based). Borrowers are responsible for the interest that accrues during any period.

U.S. Department of Education—Government agency that administers several federal student financial aid programs, including the Federal Pell Grant, the Federal Work Study Program, the Federal Perkins Loan, the FFELP and the FDLP. Also known as ED.

U.S. Department of Health and Human Services (DHHS, HHS)—Government agency that administers several federal health education loan programs, including the HEAL, HPSL and NSL loan programs.

Variable interest—With a variable interest loan, the interest rate changes periodically. For example, the interest rate might be pegged to the cost of U.S. Treasury Bills (e.g., T-Bill rate plus 1.7 percent) and be updated monthly, quarterly, semi-annually or annually.

Verification—A process used to make sure that the information students report on their FAFSA is accurate. Verification prevents ineligible students from receiving aid by reporting false information and ensures that eligible students receive all of the aid for which they are qualified.

Verification worksheet—A form sent by the college to students who are selected for verification by the Department of Education's Central Processing System.

Veteran—For federal financial aid purposes, such as determining dependency status, a veteran is a former member of the U.S. Armed Forces who served on active duty and was discharged other than dishonorably.

W-2—A form listing an employee's wages and taxes withheld. Employers are required by the IRS to issue a W-2 for each employee before February 2.

Index